Contents

How to Use This Book xiii

A

'About 1
AcisIn 2
AcisOut 3
Ai_Box, *etc.* .... ■ 4
Align 7
AmeConvert .... ■ 8
'Aperture 9
'AppLoad 10
Arc 11
Area 13
Array 14
Arx 16

AutoCAD SQL Eextension

AseAdmin 17
AseExport 20
AseLinks 21
AseRows 22
AseSelect 24
AseSqlEd 26

AttDef 28
'AttDisp 30
AttEdit 31
AttExt 33
   Quick Start: Extracting Attributes from the Drawing   34
'AttRedef 36
Audit 37
'AV 38

B

'Base 39
BHatch 40
'Blipmode 43
Block 44
Boundary 46
Box 48
Break 50

C̄

'Cal 51
Chamfer 53
Change 55
ChProp 57
Circle 58
'Color *or* 'Colour 60
   Color Numbers, Names, and Abbreviations **60**

Compile 61
Cone 62
Config 64
Copy 66
Cylinder 68

D̄

DbList 70
DdAttDef 71
DdAttE 73
DdAttExt 74
DdChProp 75
'DdColor 77
DdEdit 78
'DdEModes 79
'DdGrips 82
DDim 84
DdInsert 89
'DdLModes 90
'DdLtype 92
DdModify 93
'DdOsnap 104
'DdPtype 105
DdRename 106
'DdRModes 107
'DdSelect 110
DdUcs 113
DdUcsP 115
'DdUnits 116
DdView 118
DdVpoint 120
'Delay 122

DIM Commands

Dim 123
Dim1 125
DimAligned 126
DimAngular 127
DimBaseline 128

DimCenter 129
DimContinue 130
DimDiameter 131
DimEdit 132
DimLinear 133
DimOrdinate 134
DimOverride 135
DimRadius 136
DimStyle 137
DimTEdit 138

'Dist 140
Divide 141
DlgColor 142
'DlxHelp 144
Donut *or* Doughnut 147
'Dragmode 148
DText 149
DView 151
DxbIn 153
DxfIn 154
DxfOut 155

E

Edge 156
EdgeSurf 157
'Elev 159
Ellipse 160
End 162
Erase 163
Explode 164
Extend 166
Extrude 168

F

'Files 170
'Fill 172
Fillet 174
'Filter 176

G

'GifIn 178
'GraphScr 180
'Grid 181
Group 183

H

Hatch 185
   Hatch Pattern Library **186**
HatchEdit 189
'Help *or* '? 191
Hide 193
HpMPlot 195
   Quick Start: *Using HpMPlot* **196**

I

'Id 199
Insert 200
Interfere 202
Intersect 204
'Isoplane 205

L

'Layer 206
Leader 207
Lengthen 208
Light 210
   Definitions: *Lighting Terms* **214**
'Limits 215
Line 217
'Linetype 218
   Linetype Library **219**
   Quick Start: *Creating a Custom Linetype* **221**
List 222
Load 223
   Quick Start: *Using Shapes in Your Drawing* **223**
LogFileOff 224
LogFileOn 225
'LtScale 226

M

MakePreview 227
MassProp 229
   Definitions: *Mass Property Terms* **230**
MatLib 232
Measure 234
Menu 235
MInsert 237
Mirror 239
Mirror3d 240
MlEdit 241
MLine 243

MlStyle 245
Move 249
MSlide 250
MSpace 251
MText 252
'MtProp 254
Multiple 255
MView 256
MvSetup 258
    Quick Start: *Adding a Border and Views* **260**

N̄

New... 261

Ō

Offset 263
Oops... 264
Open 265
'Ortho 267
'OSnap 268
    Object Snap Modes **270**

P̄

'Pan 271
'PcxIn 273
PEdit 275
PFace 280
Plan 281
PLine 282
Plot 284
Point 290
Polygon 291
Preferences 293
PsDrag.. 294
PsFill... 295
    PostScript Fill Library **295**
PsIn 298
PsOut 300
PSpace 301
    Quick Start: *Enabling Paper Space* **302**
Purge 303

Q̄

QSave 304
QText 305
Quit 307

R

Ray 308
RConfig 309
   Quick Start: Setting Up Render for the First Time 310
Recover 311
Rectang 312
Redefine 313
Redo 314
'Redraw 315
'RedrawAll 317
Regen 318
RegenAll 319
'RegenAuto 320
Region 321
Reinit 323
Rename 324
Render 325
   Quick Start: Your First Rendering 327
'RenderUnload 328
RendScr 329
Replay 330
'Resume 332
Revolve 333
RevSurf 335
   Definitions: Revolved Surfacing Terms 336
RMat 337
   Definitions: Rendering Material Terms 339
Rotate 341
Rotate3D 342
RPref 343
'RScript 345
RuleSurf 346

S

Save 348
SaveAs 349
SaveAsR12 350
SaveImg 353
Scale 355
Scene 356
'Script 358
   Quick Start: Writing a Script File 358
Section 360
Select 362
'SetVar 363
Shade 364
Shape 366

Shell 367
  Quick Start: Adding a Command to Acad.Pgp **367**
ShowMat 369
Sketch 370
  Sketch Button Definitions **371**
Slice... 372
'Snap 373
Solid 374
'Spell 375
Sphere 377
Spline 378
SplinEdit 379
Stats 381
  Definitions: Rendering Statistics Terms **381**
'Status.. 382
  Definitions: Drawing Status Terms **383**
StlOut 384
  Definitions: Stereolithography Terms **385**
Stretch 386
'Style 388
  PostScript, Shx, and TrueType Fonts **389**
Subtract.. 393

T̄

Tablet 394
  Tablet Drawing **395**
  Definitions: Tablet Configuration Terms **396**
TabSurf... 397
Text 399
  Justification Modes **400**
'TextScr... 401
'TiffIn 402
'Time 403
Tolerance 404
  Definitions: Tolerance Dimensioning Terms **406**
Torus 407
Trace 408
'TreeStat 409
  Definitions: Tree-Node Statistics Terms **410**
Trim 411

Ū

U... 413
Ucs 414
  Definitions: User Coordinate System Terms **415**
Ucsicon 416

Undefine 417
Undo.. 418
Union 419
'Units 420

V

'View 422
ViewRes 423
VlConv 424
VpLayer 425
VPoint 426
ViewPorts *or* VPorts 427
VSlide 429

W

WBlock 430
Wedge 431
'WhatsNew 432

X

XBind 433
XLine 434
'Xplode 435
Xref 436
XrefClip 437

Z

'Zoom 438

3

3D 440
3dArray 442
3dFace 443
3dMesh 444
3dPoly 445
3dsIn 446
3dsOut 448

Appendices

A: System Variables 451
   Dimension Variables 455
B: Obsolete Commands 469

Topical Index 471

How to Use This Book

The *Illustrated AutoCAD Quick Reference, 3rd Ed.,* presents concise facts about all commands found in AutoCAD Release 13 for DOS. The clear format of this reference book demonstrates each command starting on its own page, plus these exclusive features:

- The 30 commands that are undocumented or underdocumented by Autodesk in the Release 13 manuals.

- Ten "Quick Start" mini-tutorials that help you get started quicker.

- Over 100 definitions of acronyms and hard-to-understand terms.

- More than 600 context-sensitive tips.

- All system variables, including those not listed by the **SetVar** command, in Appendix A.

- Obsolete commands and features that no longer work in Release 13, in Appendix B.

Each command includes the following information:

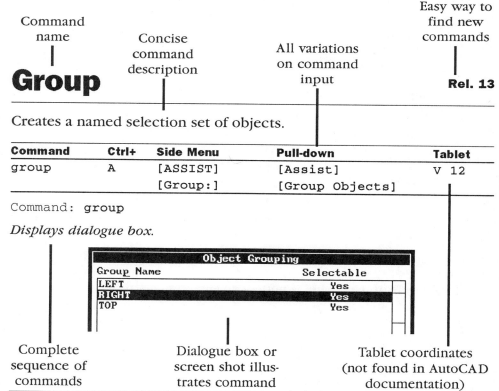

	Command	Ctrl+	Side Menu	Pull-down	Tablet
	group	A	[ASSIST]	[Assist]	V 12
			[Group:]	[Group Objects]	

Command: **group**

Displays dialogue box.

Complete sequence of commands — Dialogue box or screen shot illustrates command — Tablet coordinates (not found in AutoCAD documentation)

COMMAND NAME & INPUT OPTIONS

The name of the command is in mixed upper and lower case, such as **AseSqlEd**, to help understand the construction of the command name, which tend to be condensed.

All alternative methods of command input are listed for each command:

- Alternate command name spelling, such as **Donut** and **Doughnut**.
- ' (the apostrophe prefix) indicates transparent commands, such as **'BlipMode**. The list of transparent commands in this book is more accurate than found in the Release 13 documentation.
- Aliases, such as **L** for the **Line** command.
- Side Menu picks, such as **[DRAW 1] [Line:]** for the **Line** command.
- Pull-down menu picks, such as **[Construct] [Region]** for the **Region** command.
- Table menu coordinates, such as **N 1** for the **Hide** command.
- Control-key combinations, such as **[Ctrl]+E** for the **Isoplane** toggle.
- Function keys, such as **[F7]** for the **Grid** toggle.

The brief command description includes the following notes:

- Explanation of condensed command names; for example, the **VpLayer** command name is short for ViewPort LAYER.
- "External" commands are defined by an AutoLISP, ADS, or ARx routine, rather than being part of the AutoCAD core. These commands do not operate when AutoCAD cannot access the external routines. For example, the **DdModify** command is an external command defined by the DdModify.Lsp AutoLISP routine.
- Renamed commands had a different name in an earlier release of AutoCAD; for example, the **Box** command used to be known as the **SolBox** command.
- "Undocumented" commands that Autodesk did not document in the Release 13 printed manuals or on-line documentation. For example, the **DlxHelp** command is not documented by Autodesk.

VERSION & RELEASE NUMBERS

The version or release number indicates when the command first appeared in AutoCAD, such as **Ver. 1.4** or **Rel. 13**. This is useful when working with older versions of AutoCAD. See Appendix B for the list of commands removed from AutoCAD up to and including Release 13.

RELATED COMMANDS & VARIABLES

Following the **Command Options** section, each command includes one or more of the following, where applicable:

- Related AutoCAD commands
- Related AutoLISP programs
- Related Autodesk programs
- Related system variables
- Related dimension variables
- Related environment variables
- Related files
- Related blocks
- Input options

DEFINITIONS & TIPS

Many commands include one or more tips that help you use the command more efficiently or warn you of the command's limitations. Twelve commands include a list of definitions of acronyms and jargon words.

OPERATING SYSTEM

This edition of the *Illustrated AutoCAD Quick Reference* is specific to the DOS version of AutoCAD Release 13. An edition of this book is also available for the Windows version, which has a different command structure and additional commands not found in the DOS version.

Ralph Grabowski
Abbotsford, British Columbia
February 25, 1995

Email: ralphg@haven.uniserve.com
or 72700,3205 via CompuServe

FOR MORE INFORMATION, CONTACT:

Delmar Publishers
3 Columbia Circle, Box 15015
Albany, New York 12212-5015

International Thomson Publishing Europe
Berkshire House 168-173
High Holborn
London, WC1V 7AA
England

Thomas Nelson Australia
102 Dodds Street
South Melbourne, 3205
Victoria
Australia

Nelson Canada
1120 Birchmont Road
Scarborough, Ontario
M1K 5G4
Canada

International Thomson Editores
Campos Eliseos 385, Piso 7
Col Polanco
11560 Mexico D F Mexico

International Thomson Publishing, GmbH
Konigswinterer Strasse 418
D-53227 Bonn
Germany

International Thomson Publishing Asia
221 Henderson Road
#05-10 Henderson Building
Singapore 0315

International Thomson Publishing – Japan
Hirakawacho Kyowa Building, 3F
2-2-1 Hirakawacho
Chiyoda-ku, Tokyo 102
Japan

'About

Displays the AutoCAD version and serial number, along with the contents of the Acad.Msg file.

Command	Alias	Side Menu	Pull-down	Tablet
'about	. . .	[HELP]	[Help]	. . .
		[About:]	[About AutoCAD]	

Command: **about**

Displays dialogue box:

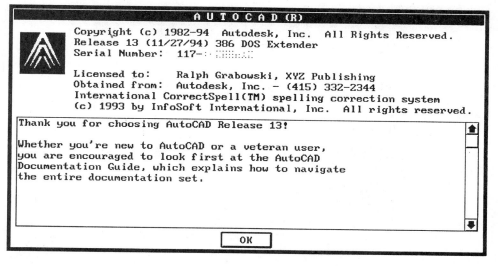

```
                        A U T O C A D  (R)
        Copyright (c) 1982-94  Autodesk, Inc.  All Rights Reserved.
        Release 13 (11/27/94) 386 DOS Extender
        Serial Number:  117-:·:::::::::

        Licensed to:    Ralph Grabowski, XYZ Publishing
        Obtained from:  Autodesk, Inc. - (415) 332-2344
        International CorrectSpell(TM) spelling correction system
        (c) 1993 by InfoSoft International, Inc.  All rights reserved.
┌─────────────────────────────────────────────────────────────────────┐
│Thank you for choosing AutoCAD Release 13!                          ▲ │
│                                                                      │
│Whether you're new to AutoCAD or a veteran user,                      │
│you are encouraged to look first at the AutoCAD                       │
│Documentation Guide, which explains how to navigate                   │
│the entire documentation set.                                         │
│                                                                      │
│                                                                    ▼ │
└─────────────────────────────────────────────────────────────────────┘
                          ┌─────────┐
                          │   OK    │
                          └─────────┘
```

COMMAND OPTIONS
None

RELATED AUTOCAD COMMANDS
- **Status**   Displays information about the drawing and environment.
- **Stats**   Displays information about the rendering environment.

RELATED SYSTEM VARIABLE
- **_PkSer**   Displays the AutoCAD software serial number.

RELATED FILE
- **Acad.Msg** The ASCII text file displayed by the **About** command.

TIPS
- Edit the \Acad13\Common\Support**Acad.Msg** file with a text editor to change the message displayed by the **About** command.

- "Serial" is an alias for the **_PkSer** system variable.

AcisIn

Imports an SAT file (*short for Save As Text, an ASCII-format ACIS file*) into the drawing, then creates 3D solids, 2D regions, and bodies.

Command	Alias	Side Menu	Pull-down	Tablet
acisin	. . .	[FILE]	[File]	. . .
		[IMPORT]	[Import]	
		[SATin:]	[SAT]	

Command: **acisin**

Displays dialogue box.

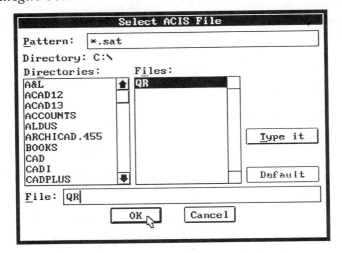

COMMAND OPTIONS
None

RELATED AUTOCAD COMMANDS
- **AcisOut** Exports ACIS objects – 3D solids, 2D regions, and bodies – to a SAT file.
- **AMEconvert** Converts AME v2.0 and v2.1 solid models and regions into ACIS solids.

RELATED SYSTEM VARIABLES
None

RELATED FILE
- ***.SAT** The ASCII format of ACIS model files.

AcisOut

Exports AutoCAD 3D solids, 2D regions, and bodies to a SAT file.

Command	Alias	Side Menu	Pull-down	Tablet
acisout	...	[FILE]	[File]	...
		[EXPORT]	[Export]	
		[ACISout:]	[SAT]	

Command: **acisout**
Select objects: **[pick]**

COMMAND OPTIONS
None

RELATED AUTOCAD COMMANDS
- **AcisIn** Imports a SAT file and creates 3D solids, 2D regions, and bodies.
- **StlOut** Exports ACIS solid model in STL format.
- **3dsOut** Exports ACIS solid models as 3D faces.

RELATED FILE
- ***.SAT** The ASCII format of ACIS model files. Sample output:

```
105 31 1 0
body $1 $2 $-1 $-1 #
f_body-lwd-attrib $-1 $3 $-1 $0 #
lump $4 $-1 $5 $0 #
ref_vt-lwd-attrib $-1 $-1 $1 $0 $6 $7 #
...
color-adesk-attrib $-1 $29 $-1 $23 256 #
vertex $-1 $23 $30 #
intcurve-curve $-1 0 { surfintcur nubs 3 periodic 41
...
2 18.996755648173917 2
19.187154530129618 3
8.2317032253755595  6.7400931724018447  0
8.2317032253755595  6.7400931724018447  -0.06346629398523311
8.2294598728158608  6.7508848507648285  -0.12180055063975684
...

} #
epar-lwd-attrib $-1 $-1 $26 $23 #
point $-1 8.2317032253755595 6.7400931724018447 0 #
```

TIP
- **AcisOut** does not export objects that are not 3D solids, 2D regions, or bodies.

Ai_Box, *etc.*

Draws nine basic 3D surface objects from polygon meshes: box, cone, dish, dome, mesh, pyramid, torus, and wedge (*an external command in 3d.Lsp*).

Command	Alias	Side Menu	Pull-down	Tablet
ai_box	...	[DRAW 2] [SURFACES] [Box:]	[Draw] [Surfaces] [3D Objects]	...
ai_cone	...	[DRAW 2] [SURFACES] [Cone:]	[Draw] [Surfaces] [3D Objects]	...
ai_dish	...	[DRAW 2] [SURFACES] [Dish:]	[Draw] [Surfaces] [3D Objects]	...
ai_dome	...	[DRAW 2] [SURFACES] [Dome:]	[Draw] [Surfaces] [3D Objects]	...
ai_mesh	...	[DRAW 2] [SURFACES] [Mesh:]	[Draw] [Surfaces] [3D Mesh]	...
ai_pyramid	...	[DRAW 2] [SURFACES] [Pyramid:]	[Draw] [Surfaces] [3D Objects]	...
ai_torus	...	[DRAW 2] [SURFACES] [Torus:]	[Draw] [Surfaces] [3D Objects]	...
ai_wedge	...	[DRAW 2] [SURFACES] [Wedge:]	[Draw] [Surfaces] [3D Objects]	...

```
Command: ai_box
Corner of box:
Length:
Cube/<Width:

Command: ai_cone
Base center point:
Diameter/<radius> of base:
Diameter/<radius> of top:
Height:
Number of segments <16>:
```

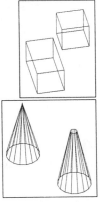

```
Command: ai_dish
Center of dish:
Diameter/<radius>:
Number of longitudinal segments <16>:
Number of latitudinal segments <16>:
```

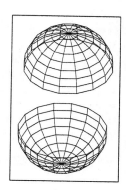

```
Command: ai_dome
Center of dome:
Diameter/<radius>:
Number of longitudinal segments <16>:
Number of latitudinal segments <16>:
```

```
Command: ai_mesh
First corner:
Second corner:
Third corner:
Fourth corner:
Mesh M size:
Mesh N size:
```

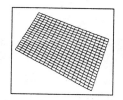

```
Command: ai_pyramid
First base point:
Second base point:
Third base point:
Tetrahedron/<Fourth base point>:
Ridge/Top/<Apex point>:
```

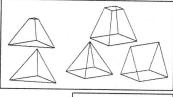

```
Command: ai_sphere
Diameter/<radius>:
Number of longitudinal segments <16>:
Number of latitudinal segments <16>:
```

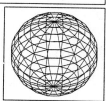

```
Command: ai_torus
Center of torus:
Diameter/<radius> of torus:
Diamter/<radius> of tube:
Segments around tube circumference <16>:
Segments around torus circumference <16>:
```

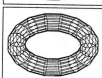

```
Command: ai_wedge
Corner of wedge:
Length:
Width:
Height:
Rotation angle about Z axis:
```

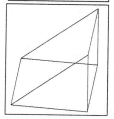

RELATED AUTOCAD COMMANDS

- **3D**   Displays a dialogue box with all nine 3D surface objects.
- **Box**   Draws a 3D solid box.
- **Cone**   Draws a 3D solid cone.
- **Cylinder** Draws a 3D solid cylinder.
- **Sphere** Draws a 3D solid sphere.
- **Torus**   Draws a 3D solid torus.
- **Wedge**   Draws a 3D solid wedge.

RELATED SYSTEM VARIABLES

- **SurfU**   Surface mesh density in the m-direction.
- **SurfV**   Surface mesh density in the n-direction.

TIPS

- You cannot perform Boolean operations (intersect, subtract, and union) on 3D surface objects.

- You cannot convert 3D surface objects into 3D solid objects.

- You can convert 3D solid objects into 3D surface objects by exporting with the **3dsIn** command, then importing with the **3dsOut** command.

- By default, 3D solid models look sparse; increase the mesh densityfrom 4 to 16 with the **IsoLines** system variable.

- Varients of objects drawn by the **Ai_** commands:
    - **Box**   Draws rectangular box or cube.
    - **Cone**   Draws pointy cone or truncated cone.
    - **Pyramid** Draws pyramid and truncated pyramid, tetrahedron and truncated tetrahedron, and roof shape.
    - **Torus**   Draws donut or football.

- Mesh m- and n-sizes are limited to values between 2 and 256.

Align

Moves, transforms, and rotates objects in three dimensions (*an external command in Geom3d.Exp*).

Command	Alias	Side Menu	Pull-down	Tablet
align	...	[MODIFY]	[Modify]	Y 19
		[Align:]	[Align]	

```
Command: align
Select objects: [pick]
Select objects: [Enter]
1st source point: [pick]
1st destination point: [pick]
2nd source point: [pick]
2nd destination point: [pick]
3rd source point: [pick]
3rd destination point: [pick]
```

COMMAND OPTIONS
None

RELATED AUTOCAD COMMANDS
- **Move**   Performs a move in two dimensions.
- **Mirror3d** Mirrors objects in three dimensions.
- **Rotate3d** Rotates objects in three dimensions.

RELATED SYSTEM VARIABLES
None

TIPS
- Enter the first pair of points to define the move distance:
```
1st source point: [pick]
1st destination point: [pick]
2nd source point: [Enter]
```

- Enter two pairs of points to define a 2D (or 3D) transformation and rotation:
```
1st source point: [pick]
1st destination point: [pick]
2nd source point: [pick]
2nd destination point: [pick]
3rd source point: [Enter]
<2d> or 3d transformation:
```

- The third pair defines the 3D transformation.

AmeConvert

Converts solid models and regions created by AME v2.0 and v2.1 (from Release 12) into ACIS solids models.

Command	Alias	Side Menu	Pull-down	Tablet
ameconvert	...	[DRAW 2]	[Draw]	...
		[SOLIDS]	[Solids]	
		[AMEconv:]	[AME Convert]	

```
Command: ameconvert
Select objects: [pick]
Processing 1 of 17 Boolean operations. | / - \
```

COMMAND OPTIONS
None

RELATED AUTOCAD COMMAND
■ **AcisIn**   Imports ACIS models from an SAT file.

RELATED SYSTEM VARIABLES
None

TIPS
■ After conversion, the AME model remains in the drawing in the same location as the ACIS model. Erase, if necessary.

■ AME holes may become blind holes in ACIS.

■ AME fillets and chamfers may be placed higher or lower in ACIS.

■ Once the **AmeConvert** command converts a Release 12 PADL drawing into Release 13 ACIS model, it cannot be converted back to PADL format.

■ Old AME models are stored in Release 13 as an anonymous block reference.

'Aperture

Sets the size in pixels of the object snap target height (the box cursor).

Command	Alias	Side Menu	Pull-down	Tablet
'aperture	...	...	...	...

```
Command: aperture
Object snap target height (1-50 pixels) <10>:
```

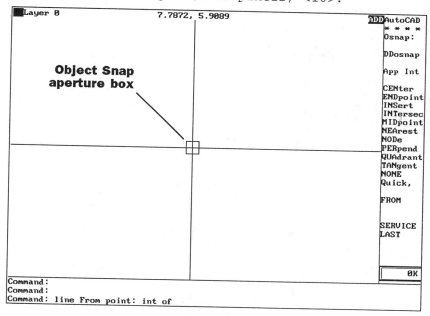

Object Snap aperture box

RELATED AUTOCAD COMMANDS
- **DdOSnap** Sets the aperture size interactively.
- **DdSelect** Sets the size of the object selection pickbox.
- **OSnap** Sets the object snap modes.

RELATED SYSTEM VARIABLES
- **Aperture** Contains the current target height:
  - **1** Minimum size.
  - **10** Default size.
  - **50** Maximum size.

'AppLoad

Creates a list of AutoLISP, ADS, and ARx applications to load (*an external file in Acadapp.Exp; short for APPlication LOADer*).

Command	Alias	Side Menu	Pull-down	Tablet
'appload	. . .	. . .	[Tools]	V 25
			[Applications]	

Command: **appload**
Display dialogue box:

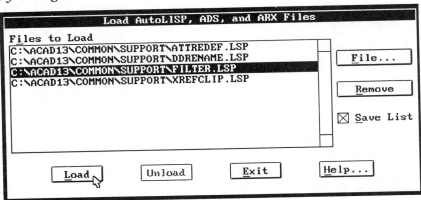

COMMAND OPTIONS

File	Displays file dialogue box to select LSP (AutoLISP), EXP (ADS), and ARx files.
Remove	Removes selected filenames from the list.
Save List	Saves the list to file AppLoad.Dfs.
Load	Loads all or selected files into AutoCAD.
Unload	Unloads all or selected files out of AutoCAD.
Exit	Exits the dialogue box.

RELATED AUTOCAD COMMAND
- **Arx**   Lists ARx programs currently loaded in AutoCAD.

RELATED AUTOLISP FUNCTIONS
- **(load)**   Loads an AutoLISP program.
- **(xload)**   Loads an ADS program.
- **(autoload)** Predefines commands to load AutoLISP program.
- **(autoxload)** Predefines commands to load ADS program.

RELATED FILES
- **AppLoad.Dfs**   Contains list of programs to load.
- ***.Lsp,*.Exp,*.Arx** AutoLISP, ADS, and ARx programs loaded by **AppLoad**.

Arc

Draws a 2D arc of less than 360 degrees by eleven different methods.

Command	Alias	Side Menu	Pull-down	Tablet
arc	a	[DRAW 1]	[Draw]	M 9
		[Arc:]	[Arc >]	

```
Command: arc
Center/<Start point>: [pick]
Center/End/<Second point>: [pick]
End point: [pick]
```

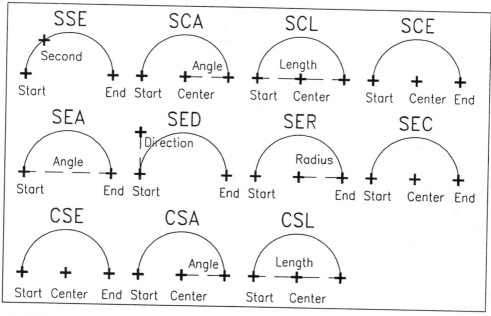

COMMAND OPTIONS

SSE arc:

<Start point> Indicates the start point of a 3-point arc (*see figure above*):

   <Second point> Indicates a second point anywhere along the arc.

   End point Indicates the endpoint of the arc.

SCA, SCL, and SCE arcs:

<Start point> Indicates the start point of a two-point arc:

   Center Indicates the center point of the arc:

     Angle Indicates the arc's included angle.

     Length of chord

         Indicates the length of the arc's chord.

     <End point> Indicates the endpoint of the arc.

SEC, SEA, SED, and SER arcs:

<Start point> Indicates the start point of a two-point arc:

  End   Indicates the endpoint of the arc:

    <Center point>

               Indicates the arc's center point.

    Angle   Indicates the arc's included angle.

    Direction   Indicates the tangent direction from the arc's start point.

    Radius   Indicates the arc's radius.

CSE, CSA, and CSL arcs:

Center   Indicates the center point of a two-point arc:

  Start point   Indicates the arc's start point:

    <End point> Indicates the arc's endpoint.

    Angle   Indicates the arc's included angle.

    Length of chord

               Indicates the length of the arc's chord.

[Enter]   Continues arc from endpoint of last-drawn line or arc.

RELATED AUTOCAD COMMANDS

- **Circle**   Draws an arc of 360 degrees.
- **Ellipse** Draws elliptical arcs.
- **Polyline** Draws connected polyline arcs.
- **ViewRes** Controls the roundness of arcs.

RELATED SYSTEM VARIABLE

- **LastAngle** Saves the included angle of the last-drawn arc (read-only).

TIPS

- To precisely start an arc from the endpoint of the last line or arc, press **[Enter]** at the "Enter/<Start point>" prompt.

- You can only drag the arc with the cursor during the last-entered option.

- Specifying an x,y,z-coordinate as the starting point of the arc draws the arc at the z-elevation.

- In some cases, it may be easier to draw a circle and use the **Break** and **Trim** commands to convert the circle into an arc.

Area

Calculates the area and perimeter of areas, closed objects, and polylines.

Command	Alias	Side Menu	Pull-down	Tablet
area	...	[ASSIST]	[Assist]	R 1
		[INQUIRY]	[Inquiry]	
		[Area:]	[Area]	

```
Command: area
<First point>/Object/Add/Subtract: [pick]
Next point: [pick]
Next point: [Enter]
Area = 1.8398, Perimeter = 6.5245
```

COMMAND OPTIONS

<First point> Indicates the first point to begin measurement.
Object   Indicates the entity to be measured.
Add   Switches to add-area mode.
Subtract   Switches to subtract-area mode.
[Enter]   Indicates the end of the area outline.

RELATED AUTOCAD COMMANDS

- **DbList** Lists all information of the entire drawing.
- **List**   Lists all information of the selected entity.

RELATED SYSTEM VARIABLES

- **Area**   Contains the most recently calculated area.
- **Perimeter** Contains the most recently calculated perimeter.

TIPS

- AutoCAD automatically "closes the polygon" before measuring the area.

- You can specify 2D x,y-coordinates or 3D x,y,z-coordinates.

- The **Object** option returns the following information:
  - **Circle, ellipse**   Area and circumference.
  - **Planar closed spline**   Area and circumference.
  - **Closed polyline, polygon** Area and perimeter.
  - **Open objects**   Area and length.
  - **Region**   Area summed for all objects in region.
  - **Solid**   Surface area.

- The area of a wide polyline is measured along its centerline; closed polylines must have only one closed area.

Array

Creates a 2D rectangular or polar array of objects.

Command	Alias	Side Menu	Pull-down	Tablet
array	...	[CONSTRCT]	[Construct]	W 21
		[Array:]	[Array]	

Rectangular array:

```
Command: array
Select objects: [pick]
Select objects: [Enter]
Rectangular or Polar array (R/P): r
Number of rows (—) <1>:
Number of columns (| | |) <1>:
Unit cell or distance between rows (—):
Distance between columns (| | |):
```

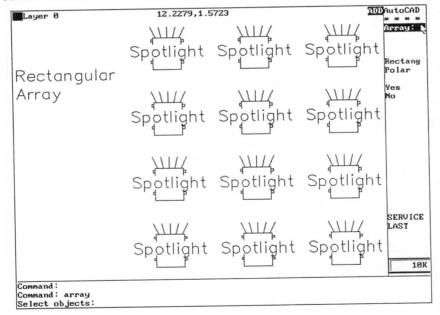

Polar array:

```
Command: array
Select objects: [pick]
Select objects: [Enter]
Rectangular or Polar array (R/P): p
Center point of array: [pick]
Number of items:
```

```
Angle to fill (+=ccw, -=cw) <360>:
Rotate objects as they are copied? <Y>
```

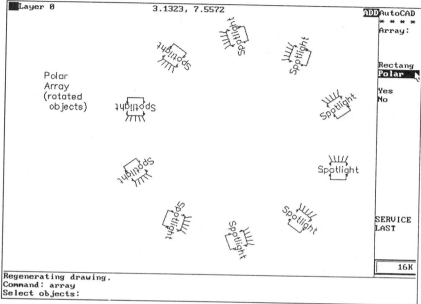

COMMAND OPTIONS

R	Creates a rectangular array of the selected object.
P	Creates a polar array of the selected object.

RELATED AUTOCAD COMMANDS

- **3dArray** Creates rectangular or polar array in 3D space.
- **Copy** Creates one or more copies of the selected object.
- **MInsert** Creates a rectangular block array of blocks.

RELATED SYSTEM VARIABLE

- **SnapAng** Determines the angle of rectangular arrays.

TIPS

- To array at an angle, use the **Rotation** option of the **Snap** command.

- Rectangular array draws up in the positive x-direction, and draws right in the positive y-direction; to draw the array in the opposite directions, specify negative row and column distances.

- Polar arrays are drawn in the counter-clockwise direction; to draw the array in the opposite direction, specify a negative angle.

- Use the **Divide** or **Measure** commands to create an array along a path.

Arx

Displays information regarding currently-loaded ARx programs.

Command	Alias	Side Menu	Pull-down	Tablet
arx	. . .	. . .	. . .	. . .

```
Command: arx
Load/Popcmds/Unload/?/<eXit>: ?
What to List:  CLasses/<Commands>/Objects/Programs/Services:
```

COMMAND OPTIONS

Load   Explicitly loads an ARx application.

Popcmds   Specifies the name of the first subdirectory where AutoCAD
               looks for commands contained in ARx programs.

Unload   Explicitly unloads an ARx application to recover memory.

?   Lists further options:

  CLasses   Lists the class hierarchy for ARx objects.

  Commands Lists the commands registered by ARx programs.

  Objects   Lists the names of objects entered into the "system registry."

  Programs   Lists the names of loaded ARx programs.

  Services   Lists the names of services entered into the ARx "service
                 dictionary."

RELATED AUTOCAD COMMAND

- **AppLoad** Loads AutoLISP, ADS, and ARx programs.

RELATED AUTOLISP FUNCTIONS

- **(arx)**   Lists currently loaded ARx programs.
- **(arxload)**   Loads an ARx application.
- **(autorxload)**Predefines commands that load the ARx program.
- **(arxunload)** Unloads an ARx application.
- **(load)**   Loads an AutoLISP program.
- **(xload)**   Loads an ADS program.
- **(ads)**   Lists the ADS programs currently loaded.

RELATED FILE

- ***.Arx,*.Dll** ARx program files.

AseAdmin

Administers links between the drawing and an external database
(*short for Autocad Sql Extension ADMINistration; formerly the*
AseSetDBMS, AseSetDB, AseSetTable, AseEraseTable,
AseCloseTable, AseCloseDB, AseEraseDB, AseEraseDBMS,
AseEraseAll, AsePost, and AseReloadDA commands; an exernal
command in Ase.Arx).

Command	Alias	Side Menu	Pull-down	Tablet
aseadmin	...	[TOOLS]	[Tools]	...
		[EXT DBMS]	[External Database]	
		[Admin:]	[Administration]	

Command: aseadmin

Displays dialogue box:

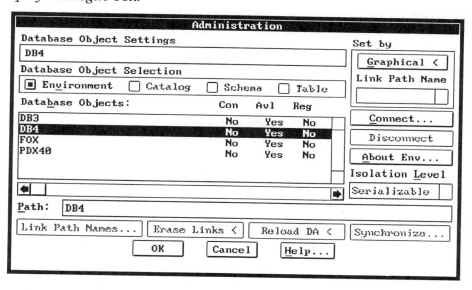

COMMAND OPTIONS

Database Object Selection:

Environment	Displays list of environments.
Catalog	Displays list of catalogs after connection with DBMS driver.
Schema	Displays list of schemas; not supported by all databases.
Table	Displays list of tables in current schema.

Database Objects:

Yes	Available.
No	Not available.
?	Not detected by AutoCAD.

Path　　　　Name of database object or logical path name.
Set By　　　Sets database object by:
　Graphical　Select object in drawing.
　Link Path Name
　　　　　　　Database object hierarchy with key column definitions.
Connect　　Loads database driver and connects it with AutoCAD; displays
　　　　　　　dialogue box:

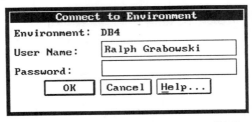

Disconnect Disconnects database driver from AutoCAD.
About Env Displays information about the ASE environment via dialogue
　　　　　　　box:

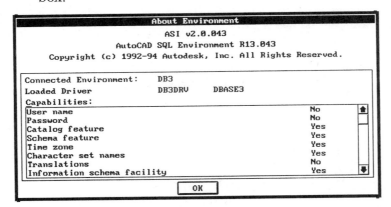

Isolation Level
　Serializable　Concurrent SQL transactions have same result as sequential
　　　　　　　　transactions.
　Uncommitted Does not lock records in use.
　Committed　Locks out in-use records.
　Repeatable　Does not lock out selection sets being changed.
Erase Links Removes all links with selected database objects.
Reload DA Updates Displayable Attributes; deleted rows show ****.
Synchronize Resynchronizes link info between drawing and database.
Link Path Names
　　　　　　　Displays **Link Path Names** dialogue box.

Key Selection:

On	Makes the selected column a key column.
Off	Turns off key column status.

Link Path:

New	Specifies a new link path.
Existing	The current link path.
Erase	Erases links to current database object.
Erase All	Erases all link paths and links to database objects.
Rename	Changes the link path.

RELATED FILES

- **Asi.Ini** ASI initialization file.
- **Asi*.Exp** ASI SQL drivers for DOS database programs:
- **Asi*.Xmx** Database driver message files.
- ***.Dbf** Sample database files in \Acad13\Common\Sample\Dbf.
- **AseSmp.Dwg**

  Sample ASE drawing file in \Acad13\Common\Sample.
- ***.Xmx** International languge message files in \Acad13\Dos\Ase\Lang.
- ***.H, *.Lib** ASI programming support files in \Acad13\Dos\Ase\Sample.

TIP

- The **Undo** command does not work reliably with ASE commands.

AseExport

Export link information to an external database file (*an external command in Ase.Arx*).

Command	Alias	Side Menu	Pull-down	Tablet
aseexport	...	[TOOLS]	[Tools]	...
		[EXT DBMS]	[External Database]	
		[Export:]	[Export Links]	

```
Command: aseexport
All/Environment/Catalog/Schema/<Table>/Lpn: [Enter]
Sdf/Cdf/<Native>/sKip:
Name of file:
```

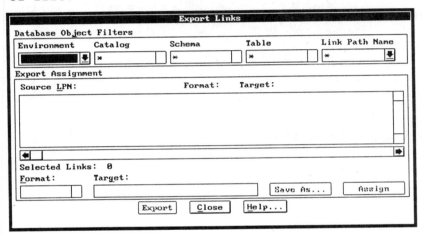

COMMAND OPTIONS

All	Exports all link information.
Environment	Exports environment-related link information.
Catalog	Exports a catalog with links to selected objects.
Schema	Exports a schema with links to selected objects.
<Table>	Exports a table with links to selected objects.
Lpn	Exports links for a single table registration (*LPN is short for Link Path Name*).
Sdf	Space-delimited file, 1 line per link, space-padded to 16 characters.
Cdf	Comma-delimited file, one line per link.
<Native>	Native database file format, one file per source LPN and one record per link.
sKip	Exits the command.

TIP

■ Enter * to export all link information.

AseLinks

Lists, edits, and displays link information between drawing and database (*formerly the AseEditLink, AseViewLink, and AseDelLink commands; an external command in Ase.Arx*).

Command	Alias	Side Menu	Pull-down	Tablet
aselinks	. . .	[TOOLS]	[Tools]	. . .
		[EXT DBMS]	[External Database]	
		[Links"]	[Links]	

```
Command: aselinks
All/Environment/Catalog/Schema/Table/Lpn/Object/<eXit>: A
Browse/Next/Prior/First/Del/delAll/Update/Rows/<eXit>: R
Cursor-state/Textual/Keys/<eXit>: C
Scrollable/Updatable/<Read-only>: K
Enter value for key-column-name-n: {enter value]
Browse/Next/Prior/First/Last/<eXit>:
```

COMMAND OPTIONS

All Selects all links and displays the following options:
  Browse Displays all links.
  Next Displays next link.
  Prior Displays prior link.
  First Displays first link.
  Last Displays last link.
  Del Deletes current link.
  delAll Deletes all links to the selected object.
  Update Updates key values to the current link.
  Rows Edits the current link; if a read-only cursor cannot be opened, displays the following options:
    Textual Selects a row or rows matching an SQL search condition.
    Keys Selects a row that matches the key values.
  Cursor-state Displays the following options:
    Scrollable Makes a row the current row.
    Updateable Rows can be edited but not scrolled.
    <Read-only>Rows cannot be edited or deleted.
EnvironmentSelects all links within the current environment.
Catalog Selects all links in the current catalogue.
Schema Selects all links in the current schema.
Table Selects all links in the current table.
Lpn Selects all links in the current link path name.
Object Filters our nested links in blocks and xrefs.
<eXit> Exits the command.

RELATED AUTOCAD COMMANDS

All ASE commands.

AseRows

Creates links and selection sets; displays and edits table data *(formerly the AseAddRow, AseDelRow, AseEditRow, AseQEdit, AseQView, AseViewRow, AseMakeDA, AseMakeLink, AseQLink, and AseMakeDA commands; an external command in Ase.Arx).*

Command	Alias	Side Menu	Pull-down	Tablet
aserows	...	[TOOLS]	[Tools]	...
		[EXT DBMS]	[External Database]	
		[ROWS:]	[Rows]	

```
Command: aserows
Settings/Insert/Cursor-state/Textual/Keys/<eXit>/Select
object: [pick]
Browse/Next/Prior/First/Last/Select/Unselect/Edit/Insert/Del/
Mlink/MDA/linKs/<eXit>: M
Enter a column name or ? for list:
Justify/Style/<Start point>:
```

*When system variable **CmdDia** is turned on (= 1), the **AseRows** command displays the following dialogue box:*

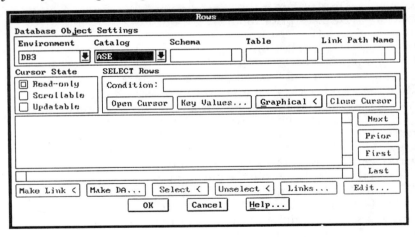

COMMAND OPTIONS

Settings   Displays the following options:

Environment Sets up an environment or selects a different one.

Catalog   Changes the catalogue.

Schema   Changes the current schema.

Table   Changes the current table.

Lpn   Sets the current link path name.

Insert	Inserts a new row in the current table.
Cursor-state	Displays the following options:
Scrollable	Makes a row the current row.
Updateable	Rows can be edited but not scrolled.
<Read-only>	Rows cannot be edited or deleted.
Textual	Selects a row or rows from a table.
Keys	Selects a new row that matches key values.
Select object	After you select an object, displays the following options:
Browse	Displays all links.
Next	Displays next link.
Prior	Displays prior link.
First	Displays first link.
Last	Displays last link.
Select	Highlights linked objects and adds them to selection set.
Unselect	Removes objects from selection set.
Edit	Changes the current row.
Insert	Inserts row into table.
Del	Deletes current link.
Mlink	Makes link between row and selected object.
MDA	Makes displayable attribute.
linKs	Displays link information.
<eXit>	Exits the command.

RELATED AUTOCAD COMMANDS

All ASE commands

TIPS

■ Press [Enter] to the 'Enter text condition:' prompt to select all rows in the table.

■ A read-only cursor is nonscrollable.

AseSelect

Creates a selection set from rows linked to graphic and text selection sets *(an external command in Ase.Arx)*.

Command	Alias	Side Menu	Pull-down	Tablet
aseselect	...	[TOOLS]	[Tools]	...
		[EXT DBMS]	[External Database]	
		[Select:]	[Select Objects]	

Command: **aseselect**
Graphical/Textual/<eXit>: **T**
All/Environment/Catalog/Schema/<Table>/Lpn: **L**
Union/Intersect/subtractA/SubtractB/<eXit>:

When system variable ***CmdDia*** *is turned on (= 1), the AseSelect command displays the following dialogue box:*

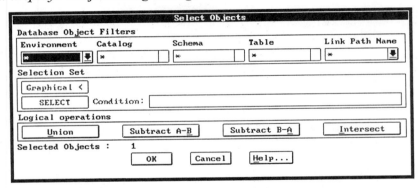

COMMAND OPTIONS

Graphical   Select objects from screen.
Textual   Makes SQL selection; displays the following options:
    All   Selects all objects linked to rows matching SQL condition.
Environment Selects all objects within the current environment.
    Catalog   Selects all objects in the current catalogue.
    Schema   Selects all objects in the current schema.
    <Table>   Selects all objects in the current table.
    Lpn   Selects all objects in the current link path name.
Union   Selection set contains all linked objects meeting criteria and selected graphic objects.
Intersect   Selection set contains objects in both sets.
subtractA   Subtracts first selection set from second set.
SubtractB   Subtracts second selection set from first set.
<eXit>   Exits the command.

RELATED AUTOCAD COMMANDS

All ASE commands

TIPS

- By default, all external database objects can be selected.

- Enter * (asterisk) to select all.

- Type an **SQL WHERE** sentence at the 'Enter text condition:' prompt.

- An **SQL WHERE** sentence operates on a single table at a time.

AseSqlEd

Executes SQL statements (*short for SQL EDitor; an external command in Ase.Arx*).

Command	Alias	Side Menu	Pull-down	Tablet
asesqled	...	[TOOLS]	[Tools]	...
		[EXT DBMS]	[External Database]	
		[SQLedit:]	[SQL Editor]	

Command: **asesqled**
Settings/Options/Isolation/Autocommit/File/<SQL>/Native/Commit/Rollback/eXit: **I**
Uncommitted/Committed/Repeatable/<Serializable>:

*When system variable **CmdDia** is turned on (= 1, the default), the AseSqlEd command displays the following dialogue box:*

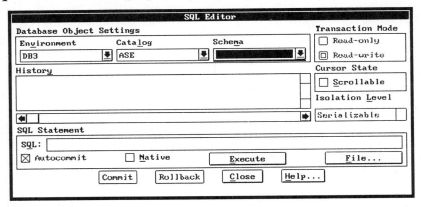

COMMAND OPTIONS:

Settings   Changes database object settings:
  Environment Sets up an environment or selects a different one.
  Catalog   Changes the catalogue.
  Schema   Changes the current schema.
Options   Transaction mode and cursor type:
  Scrollable Makes a row the current row.
  read-Write Rows can be edited and deleted.
  Read-only Rows cannot be edited or deleted.
Isolation   Select level of SQL isolation:
  Uncommitted Other users can access any record.
  Committed Other users can access completed records.
  Repeatable Other users can access the current selection set.
  <Serializable> Concurrent transactions have same result as consecutive ones.

Autocommit Automatic, multiple changes to the database.
File   Run SQL statements from a file in batch mode.
<SQL>   Executes an SQL statement at the **SQL>** prompt.
Native   Allows use of non-SQL database commands.
Commit   Saves changes made to database.
Rollback   Cancels changes made to database.
eXit   Exits the command.

RELATED AUTOCAD COMMANDS
All ASE commands

RELATED FILE
■ ***.Txt**   File containing SQL statements to be executed in batch mode.

TIPS
■ Database column values (except column names) are case-sensitive.

■ Search string character values are enclosed by ' ' (single quotes).

■ Use a pair of single quotes (") to create an apostrophe.

■ Use the following metacharacters when entering column data at the Command prompt:
   ■ A period (.) represents a null.
   ■ A pair of periods (..) represents a single period.
   ■ Pressing **[Enter]** leaves column data unchanged.

■ The SQL batch file can use the following metacharacters:
   ■ **;**   Semi-colon prefix indicates a comment line.
   ■ **$**   Dollar prefix indicates a comment echoed to the command line.
   ■ **&**   Ampersand suffix continues SQL command on the next line.

The documented AseUnload command dos not exist in Release 13.

AttDef

Defines attribute modes and prompts (*short for ATTribute DEFinition*).

Command	Alias	Side Menu	Pull-down	Tablet
attdef	. . .	. . .	. . .	. . .

```
Command: attdef
Attribute modes — Invisible:N  Constant:N  Verify:N  Preset:N
Enter (ICVP) to change, RETURN when done: [Enter]
Attribute tag:
Attribute prompt:
Default attribute value:
Justify/Style/<Start point>: [pick]
```

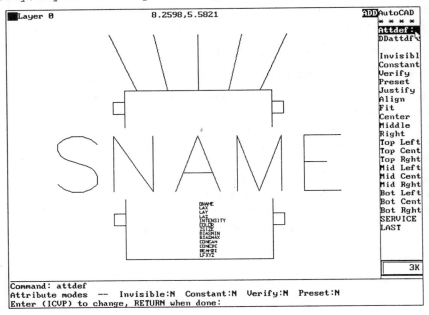

COMMAND OPTIONS

Attribute mode Selects the modes for the attribute:

I	Toggles visibility of attribute text in drawing (*short for Invisible*).
C	Toggles fixed or variable value of attribute (*short for Constant*).
V	Toggles confirmation prompt during input (*short for Verify*).
P	Toggles automatic insertion of default values (*short for Preset*).

Justify   Selects the justification mode for the attribute text.
Style   Selects the text style for the attribute text.
<Start point> Indicates the start point of the attribute text.

RELATED AUTOCAD COMMANDS

- **AttDisp**   Controls the visibility of attributes.
- **AttEdit**   Edits the values of attributes.
- **AttExt**   Extracts attributes to disk.
- **AttRedef** Redefines an attribute or block.
- **Block**   Binds attributes to objects.
- **DdAttDef** Defines attributes via a dialogue box.
- **DdAttE**   Extracts the values of attributes via a dialogue box.
- **DdEdit**   Edits the values of attributes via a dialogue box.
- **Insert**   Inserts a block and prompts for attribute values.

RELATED SYSTEM VARIABLES

- **AFlags**   Contains the value of modes in bit form:
  - 0 No attribute mode selected.
  - 1 Invisible.
  - 2 Constant.
  - 4 Verify.
  - 8 Preset.
- **AttDia**   Toggles use of dialogue box during **Insert** command:
  - 0 Uses command-line prompts.
  - 1 Uses dialogue box.
- **AttReq**   Toggles use of defaults or user prompts during **Insert** command:
  - 0 Assume default values of all attributes.
  - 1 Prompts for attributes.

TIPS

- Constant attributes cannot be edited.

- Attribute tags cannot be null (have no value); attribute values may be null.

- When you press **[Enter]** at the 'Starting point:' prompt, **AttDef** automatically places the next attribute below the previous one.

'AttDisp

Controls the display of all attributes in the drawing (*short for ATTribute DISPlay*).

Command	Alias	Side Menu	Pull-down	Tablet
'attdisp	...	[OPTIONS]	[Options]	...
		[DISPLAY]	[Display]	
		[AttDisp:]	[Attribute Display]	

Command: **attdisp**
Normal/ON/OFF <Normal>:

COMMAND OPTIONS

Normal   Displays attributes according to **Attdef** setting.
ON   Displays all attributes, regardless of **AttDef** setting.
OFF   Displays no attribute, regardless of **AttDef** setting.

RELATED AUTOCAD COMMAND

■ **AttDef**   Defines new attributes, including their default visibility.

RELATED SYSTEM VARIABLE

■ **AttMode** Contains current setting of **AttDisp**:
        0 Off.
        1 Normal.
        2 On.

TIPS

■ If **RegenAuto** is off, use the **Regen** command after **AttDisp** to see changes to attributes.

■ If you define invisible attributes, **AttDisp** lets you turn them on.

AttEdit

Edits attributes in a drawing (*short for ATTribute EDIT*).

Command	Alias	Side Menu	Pull-down	Tablet
attedit	. . .	. . .	[Modify]	. . .
		. . .	[Attribute]	
			[Edit Globally]	

```
Command: attedit
Edit attributes one at a time? <Y> [Enter]
Block name specification <*>:
Attribute tag specification <*>:
Attribute value specification <*>:
Select Attributes: [pick]
1 attributes selected.
Value/Position/Height/Angle/Style/Layer/Color/Next <N>:
```

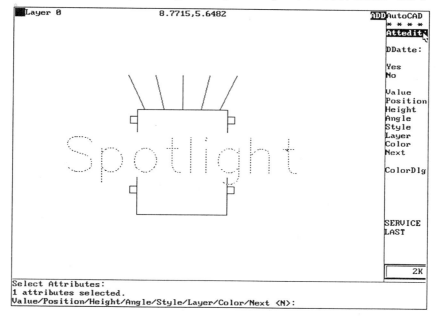

COMMAND OPTIONS

Value	Changes or replaces the value of the attribute:
Change	Changes the attribute value.
Replace	Replaces attribute with a new value.
Position	Moves the text insertion point of the attribute.
Height	Changes the attribute text height.
Angle	Changes the attribute text angle.

Style	Changes the text style of the attribute text.
Layer	Moves the attribute to a different layer.
Color	Changes the color of the attribute text.
Next	Edits the next attribute.

RELATED AUTOCAD COMMANDS

- **AttDef**   Defines an attribute's original value and parameter.
- **AttDisp**   Toggles an attributes visibility.
- **AttEdit**   Edits the values of attributes.
- **AttRedef**   Redefines attributes and blocks.
- **DdAttDef** Define attributes via a dialogue box.
- **DdAttE**   Edits the values of attributes.
- **DdEdit**   Edits the values of an attribute.
- **Explode**   Reduces an attribute to its tag.

TIPS

- Constant attributes cannot be edited with **AttEdit**.

- You can only edit attributes parallel to the current UCS.

- To edit null attribute values, use **AttEdit**'s global edit option and enter \
(backslash) at the 'Attribute value specification:' prompt.

- The wildcard characters ? and * are interpreted literally at the 'String to
change:' and 'New String:' prompts.

AttExt

Extracts attribute data from the drawing to a file on disk (*short for ATTribute EXTract*).

Command	Alias	Side Menu	Pull-down	Tablet
attext	. . .	. . .	. . .	. . .

Command: **attext**
CDF, SDF or DXF Attribute extract (or Objects)? <C>:

*Displays the **Select Template File** and **Create Extract File** dialogue boxes.*

COMMAND OPTIONS

CDF   Outputs attributes in comma-delimited format.
SDF   Outputs attributes in space-delimited format.
DXF   Outputs attributes in DXF format.
Objects Selects attributes to extract.

RELATED AUTOCAD COMMANDS

■ **AttDef**   Defines attributes.
■ **DdAttExt** Defines attribute extraction via a dialogue box.

RELATED FILES

■ ***.Txt**   Required extension for the template file.
■ ***.Txt**   Extension for CDF and SDF extraction files.
■ ***.Dxx**   Extension for DXF extraction files.

TIPS

■ To output the attributes to the printer, specify:
   ■ **CON**   Extracted attributes appear on the text screen.
   ■ **PRN** or **LPT1** Extracted attributes print on parallel port 1.
   ■ **LPT2** or **LPT3** Extracted attributes print to parallel port 2 or 3.

■ Before you can specify the SDF or CDF option, you must create the template file.

■ CDF files use the following conventions:
   ■ Specified field widths are the maximum width.
   ■ Positive number fields have a leading blank.
   ■ Character fields are enclosed in ' ' (single quote marks).
   ■ Trailing blanks are deleted.
   ■ Null strings are '' (two single quote marks).
   ■ Use spaces; do not use tabs.
   ■ Use the C:DELIM and C:QUOTE records to change the field and string

QUICK START: Extracting Attributes from the Drawing

How to extract attribute data from a drawing:

1. CREATE A TEMPLATE FILE

If you want the attribute data extracted in CDF or SDF format, you must first create a template file (the DXF format does not use a template file). The **AttExt** (and **DdAttExt**) commands use the *template file* to (1) determine which attributes to extract; and (2) how to format of the extracted data. The template file uses the following format codes:

- **Type**   Describes the type of attribute data (*C or N, for short*) :
  - **C**   Alpha-numeric characters.
  - **N**   Numbers only.

- **Width**   Describes the field width from 001 to 999 characters wide, padded with leading zeros (*www, for short*).

- **Precision** Describes the number of decimal places from 001 to 999 (*ie, .1 to .00000...001*), padded with leading zeros (*ddd, for short*).

The complete set of format codes recognized by AutoCAD:

Field Name	Type, Width, Precision	Description
BL:NAME	Cwww000	Name of block
BL:NUMBER	Nwww000	Number of occurances
CHAR_ATTRIBUTE_TAG	Cwww000	Character attribute tag
NUMERIC_ATTR_TAG	Nwwwddd	Numeric attribute tag
BL:LAYER	Cwww000	Block's layer name
BL:ORIENT	Nwwwddd	Block rotation angle
BL:LEVEL	Nwww000	Block's nesting level
BL:X	Nwwwddd	Block insertion x-coordinate
BL:Y	Nwwwddd	Block insertion y-coordinate
BL:Z	Nwwwddd	Block insertion z-coordinate
BL:XSCALE	Nwwwddd	Block's x-scale factor
BL:YSCALE	Nwwwddd	Block's y-scale factor
BL:ZSCALE	Nwwwddd	Block's z-scale factor
BL:XEXTRUDE	Nwwwddd	Block's x-extrusion
BL:YEXTRUDE	Nwwwddd	Block's y-extrusion
BL:ZEXTRUDE	Nwwwddd	Block's z-extrusion
BL:HANDLE	Cwwwddd	Block's handle hex-number.

Shell out of AutoCAD and create the template file with a text editor. Here is an example:

Example Field	Example Template	Example Description
BL:NAME	C008000	*8-character block name*
BL:NUMER	N004000	*Number of occurances*
VENDOR	C016000	*Vendor attribute (16 chars)*
MODELNO	N012000	*Model # attr (12 digits)*

Save the file as ASCII text with the .TXT extension and return to AutoCAD.

2. SELECT OUTPUT FORMAT

Use either the **AttExt** or **DdAttExt** command to extract attribute data. Decide on the output format:

- **CDF** Comma-delimited format (the default), best for importing into a spreadsheet; sample output:

  `'Desk',55,'Steelcase',2248599597`

- **DXF** Drawing interchange fomat, similar to an objects-only DXF file.
- **SDF** Space-delimited format, best for importing into a database program; sample output:

  `Desk      55            Steelcase   2248599597`

3. SELECT OBJECTS

Either select the blocks you want to extract attributes from, or select all objects in the drawing. AutoCAD ignores all non-block objects and blocks with no attributes.

4. SPECIFY TEMPLATE FILE

Enter the name of the template file you created earlier.

5. (Optional) SPECIFY OUTPUT FILENAME

If you do not specify an output filename, AutoCAD uses the drawing's name, appending a .TXT to CDF and SDF files, or .DXX to DXF files. Otherwise, specify any name except the template file's name.

6. CLICK [OK]

Click the **OK** button and AutoCAD places extracted attribute data into the output file. AutoCAD will stop if it finds any errors in the format of the template file, or if the selection set contains no attributes.

'AttRedef

Rel. 13

Redfines blocks and attributes (*short for ATTribute REDEFinition; an external command in AttRedef.Lsp*).

Command	Alias	Side Menu	Pull-down	Tablet
'attredef	...	...	[Modify]	...
			[Attribute]	
			[Redefine]	

```
Command: redefine
Name of Block you wish to redefine:
Select objects for new Block...
Select objects: [pick]
Select objects: [Enter]
Insertion base point of new block: [pick]
```

RELATED AUTOCAD COMMANDS
- **AttDef**   Defines an attribute's original value and parameter.
- **AttDisp** Toggles an attribute's visibility.
- **AttEdit** Edits the values of attributes.
- **DdAttDef** Defines attributes via a dialogue box.
- **DdAttE**   Edits the values of attributes.
- **DdEdit**   Edits the value of one attribute.
- **Explode** Reduces an attribute to its tag.

TIPS
- Existing attributes retain their values.

- Existing attributes not included in the new block are erased.

- New attributes added to an existing block take on default values.

Audit

Examines a drawing file for structural errors.

Command	Alias	Side Menu	Pull-down	Tablet
audit	...	[FILE]	[File]	...
		[MANAGE]	[Management]	
		[Audit:]	[Audit]	

Command: **audit**
Fix any errors detected? <N> **y**

Sample output:
0 Blocks audited
Pass 1 132 objects audited
Pass 2 132 objects audited
Total errors found 0 fixed 0

COMMAND OPTIONS

<N>   Reports errors found; does not fix errors.
Y   Reports and fixes errors found in drawing file.

RELATED AUTOCAD COMMANDS

- **Save**   Saves a recovered drawing to disk.
- **Recover**   Recovers a damaged drawing file.

RELATED SYSTEM VARIABLE

- **Auditctl**   Controls the creation of the ADT audit log file:
    - **0** No log file written.
    - **1** ADT audit log file is written in drawing's directory.

RELATED FILE

- ***.ADT**   The audit log file; reports the progress of the auditing process.

TIPS

- The **Audit** command is a diagnostic tool for validating and repairing the contents of a DWG file.

- Objects with errors are placed in the previous selection set. Use an edit command, such as **Copy**, to view the objects.

- If **Audit** cannot fix a drawing file, use the **Recover** command.

Displays the bird's-eye view window; provides real-time pan and zoom (*short for Aerial View; an undocumented command*).

Command	Alias	Side Menu	Pull-down	Tablet
av	. . .	. . .	. . .	. . .

Command: **av**
Displays AV window:

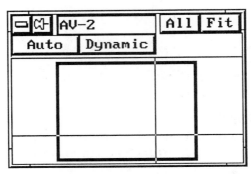

COMMAND OPTIONS

All	Equivalent to the **Zoom Vmax** command.
Fit	Equivalent to the **Zoom Extents** command.
Auto	Toggles button:
Auto	Automatically zooms and pans.
DZoom	Simulate the Zoom Dynamic command.
Zoom-only	Performs zoom only; no pans.
Pan-only	Performs pan only; no zooms.
Dynamic	Toggle between dynamic (real-time zoom and pan) and static (zoom or pan occurs after new view is selected).
Bar	Dismisses the Aerial View window.
Pushpin	Keeps Aerial View window on-screen.

RELATED AUTOCAD COMMANDS

- **Config**   Configures some parameters of the Aerial View window.
- **DlxHelp**   Provides help on additional Aerial View commands.
- **Pan**   Moves the drawing view.
- **View**   Creates and displays named views.
- **Zoom**   Makes the view larger or smaller.

TIP

- The **AV** command does not work in perspective mode (created by the **DView** command) nor in paper space, with the curious error message "Non-zoomable viewport."

'Base

Changes the 2D or 3D insertion point of a drawing, located at (0,0,0) by default.

Command	Alias	Side Menu	Pull-down	Tablet
'base	. . .	. . .	. . .	. . .

```
Command: base
Base point <0.0000,0.0000,0.0000>:
```

COMMAND OPTIONS
None

RELATED AUTOCAD COMMANDS
- **Block**   Allows you to specify the insertion point of a new block.
- **Insert**   Inserts another drawing into the current drawing.
- **Xref**   References another drawing.

RELATED SYSTEM VARIABLE
- **InsBase**   Contains the current setting of the drawing insertion point.

BHatch

Automatically applies an associative hatch pattern within a boundary (*short for Boundary HATCH*).

Command	Alias	Side Menu	Pull-down	Tablet
bhatch	...	[CONSTRCT]	[Draw]	W 16
		[Bhatch:]	[Hatch]	
			[Hatch]	

Command: **bhatch**
Displays dialogue box:

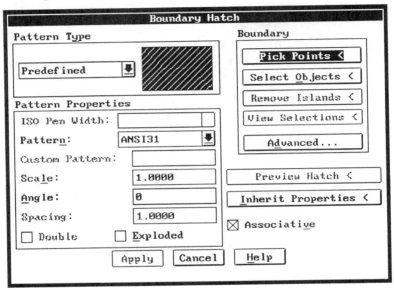

COMMAND OPTIONS

Pattern Type Selects type of hatch pattern.

Pattern Properties:

ISO Pen Width	When an ISO hatch pattern is selected, scales pattern according to pen width.
Pattern	Name of hatch pattern (defined in Acad.Pat).
Custom Pattern	Specify name of a user-defined pattern.
Scale	Hatch pattern scale (default: 1.0).
Angle	Hatch pattern angle (default: 0 degrees).
Spacing	Spacing between lines of a user-defined hatch pattern.
Double	Toggles double hatching.
Exploded	Places hatch pattern as lines, rather than as a block.

Preview Hatch   Previews the hatch pattern before it is applied.
Inherit Properties Selects the hatch pattern parameters from an existing hatch pattern.
Default Properties Changes pattern parameters back to default values.
Associative   Toggles between associative and non-associative pattern.
Boundary:
  Pick Points   Picks points that define the hatch pattern boundary.
  Select Objects   Selects objects to be hatched.
  Remove Islands   Removes islands from the hatch pattern selection set.
  View Selections   Views hatch pattern selection set.
  Advanced...   Displays the **Advanced Options** dialogue box:

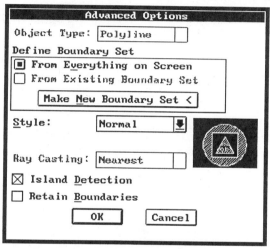

Object Type Boundary is made from a polyline or as a region.
Define Boundary Set:
  From Everything on Screen   All objects visible in current view.
  From Existing Boundary Set   Current boundary selection set.
  Make New Boundary Set   Dialogue boxes disappear to allow you to select the boundary.
Style   Sets hatching style:
     Normal Alternate areas are hatched.
     Outer   Only the outermost areas are hatched.
     Ignore   Everything within boundary is hatched.
Ray Casting Determines how AutoCAD searches for the hatch boundary:
     Nearest From pick point to nearest object.
     +X   From pick point in +x direction.
     -X   From pick point in -x direction.
     +Y   From pick point in +y direction.
     -Y   From pick point in -y direction.

Island Detection Toggles whether islands are detected.
Retain Boundaries Toggles whether the boundary is retained after hatch is placed.

RELATED AUTOCAD COMMANDS
- **Boundary** Automatically traces a polyline around a closed boundary.
- **Explode** Reduces a group of hatch patterns.
- **Hatch** Creates a non-associative hatch within a manually-selected perimeter.
- **PsFill** Fills a closed polyline with a PostScript pattern.

RELATED SYSTEM VARIABLES
- **DelObj** Toggles whether boundary is erased after hatch is placed.
- **HpAng** Current hatch pattern angle.
- **HpBound** Hatch boundary made from:
  - 0 Polyline.
  - 1 Region (*default*)
- **HpDouble** Single or double hatching:.
  - 0 Single (*default*).
  - 1 Double.
- **HpName** Current hatch pattern name (*up to 31 characters long*):
  - "" No current hatch pattern name.
  - "." Eliminates current name.
- **HpScale** Current hatch pattern scale factor.
- **HpSpace** Current hatch pattern spacing factor.
- **PickStyle** Controls hatch selection:
  - 0 Groups and associative hatches not selected.
  - 1 Groups selected.
  - 2 Associative hatches selected.
  - 3 Both selected.
- **SnapBase** Starting coordinates of hatch pattern.

RELATED FILE
- **Acad.Pat** Hatch pattern definition file.

TIPS
- The **BHatch** command first generates a boundary polyline, then hatches the inside area. Use the **Boundary** command to obtain just the boundary polyline.

- **BHatch** stores hatching parameters in the pattern's extended entity data; use the **List** command to display parameters stored in extended entity data.

- See the **Hatch** command for a list of hatch patterns supplied with AutoCAD.

'Blipmode

Turns off and on the display of pick point markers, known as "blips."

Command	Alias	Side Menu	Pull-down	Tablet
blipmode	. . .	. . .	. . .	. . .

Command: **blipmode**
ON/OFF <On>: off

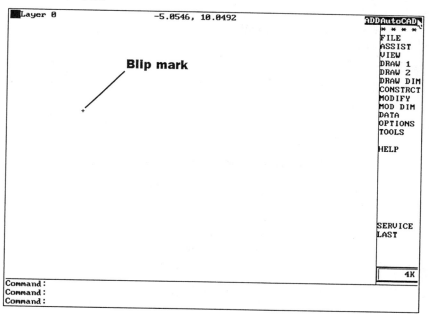

COMMAND OPTIONS

ON	Turns on display of pick point markers.
OFF	Turns off display of pick point markers.

RELATED AUTOCAD COMMANDS

- **DdRModes** Allows blipmode toggling via a dialogue box.
- **Redraw** Cleans blips off the screen.

RELATED SYSTEM VARIABLE

- **Blipmode** Contains the current setting of blipmode.

Block

Defines a group of objects as a single named object; creates symbols.

Command	Alias	Side Menu	Pull-down	Tablet
block	...	...	[Construct] [Block]	W 9

```
Command: block
Block name (or ?):
Insertion base point: [pick]
Select objects:
```

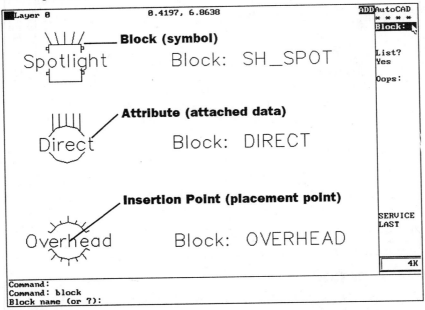

COMMAND OPTION

?   Lists the blocks stored in the drawing.

RELATED AUTOCAD COMMANDS

- **Explode**   Reduces a block into its original objects.
- **Insert**   Adds a block or another drawing to the current drawing.
- **Oops**   Returns objects to the screen after creating the block.
- **WBlock**   Writes a block to a file on disk as a drawing.
- **XRef**   Displays another drawing in the current drawing.

RELATED FILE

- ***.DWG**   All drawing files are insertable as blocks.

TIPS

■ A block name has up to 31 alpha-numeric characters, including $, -, and _ . However, blocks stored on disk are limited to eight characters.

■ Release 13 has five types of blocks:
- **User Blocks**   Blocks you create.
- **Nested Blocks**   A block within a block.
- **Unnamed Blocks**   Blocks created by AutoCAD commands, such as hatches created by the **Hatch** command.
- **ExternalReferences**   Externally referenced drawings.
- **Dependent Blocks**   Blocks in an externally referenced drawing.

■ Use the INSertion object snap to select the block's insertion point.

■ A block created on a layer other than layer 0 is always inserted on that other layer; a block created on layer 0 is inserted on the current layer.

Boundary

Creates a boundary as a polyline or 2D region (*formerly the BPoly command*).

Command	Alias	Side Menu	Pull-down	Tablet
boundary	...	[CONSTRCT]	[Construct]	...
		[Boundar:]	]Boundary]	

Command: **-boundary**
Advanced options/<Internal point>: **A**
Boundary set/Island detection/Object type/<eXit>: **O**
Region/Polyline: **R**
Boolean subtract inner islands?

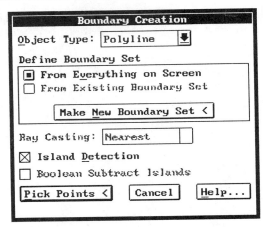

COMMAND OPTIONS

Object Type Boundary is made from a polyline or as a region.
Define Boundary Set:
   From Everything on Screen
         All objects visible in current view.
   From Existing Boundary Set
         Current boundary selection set.
   Make New Boundary Set
         Dialogue boxes disappear to allow you to select the boundary.
Ray Casting Determines how AutoCAD searches for the hatch boundary:
   Nearest   From pick point to nearest object.
   +X   From pick point in +x direction.
   -X   From pick point in -x direction.
   +Y   From pick point in +y direction.
   -Y   From pick point in -y direction.

Island Detection
> Toggles whether islands are detected.

Boolean Subtract Island
> Deletes islands from the boundary.

RELATED AUTOCAD COMMANDS

- **Polyline** Draws a polyline.
- **PEdit** Edits a polyline.
- **Region** Creates a 2D region from a collection of objects.

RELATED SYSTEM VARIABLE

- **HpBound** Object used to create boundary:
  > **0** Draw as polyline.
  > **1** Draw as region (*Default*)

TIPS

- Use the **Boundary** command together with the **Offset** command to help create poching.

- Use the - (*dash*) prefix to force the **Boundary** command to display its prompt at the Command prompt.

- Although the **Boundary Creation** dialogue box looks identical to the **BHatch** command's **Advanced Options** dialogue box, be aware that there are differences between the two dialogue boxes.

Box

Draws a 3D box as an ACIS solid model (*an external command in Acis.Dll; formerly the SolBox command*).

Command	Alias	Side Menu	Pull-down	Tablet
box	. . .	[DRAW 2]	[Draw]	M 7
		[SOLIDS]	[Solids]	
		[Box:]	[Box]	

```
Command: box
Center/<Corner of box> <0,0,0>: [pick]
Cube/Length/<other corner>: [pick]
Height:
```

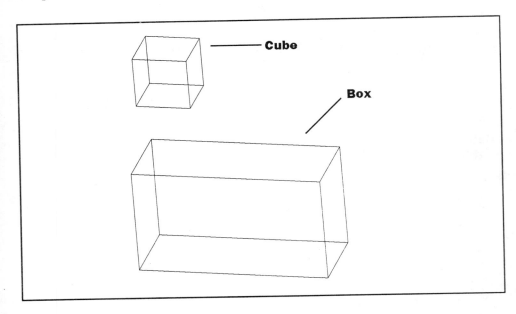

COMMAND OPTIONS

Center   Draws the box about a center point.

<Corner of box>:
        Specifies one corner for the base of box.

Cube   Draws a cube box, where all sides are the same length.

Length   Specifies the x, y, z-lengths.

Height   Specifies the height of the box.

RELATED AUTOCAD COMMANDS

- **Ai_Box** Draws a 3D wireframe box.
- **Cone** Draws a 3D solid cone.
- **Cylinder** Draws a 3D solid tube.
- **Sphere** Draws a 3D solid ball.
- **Torus** Draws a 3D solid donut.
- **Wedge** Draws a 3D solid wedge.

RELATED SYSTEM VARIABLES

- **DispSilh** Toggles display of 3D objects as a silhouette after hidden-line removal and shading.
- **IsoLines** Number of isolines on solid surfaces:
    - **0** Minimum (*No isolines*).
    - **4** Default.
    - **16** A reasonable value.
    - **2,047** Maximum value.

TIPS

■ To bring an ACIS solid model into Release 12, don't use the **SaveAsR12** command, since solid models are decomposed to polylines and circles. Instead, use the **3dsOut** command, which converts ACIS solid models into 3D faces.

■ Once the **AmeConvert** command converts a Release 12 AME drawing into Release 13 ACIS model, it cannot be converted back to Release 12's format.

Break

Removes a portion of a line, trace, 2D polyline, arc, or circle.

Command	Alias	Side Menu	Pull-down	Tablet
break	. . .	. . .	[Modify]	X 13
			[Break]	
				X 14

```
Command: break
Select object: [pick]
Enter second point (or F for first point): f
Enter first point: [pick]
Enter second point: [pick]
```

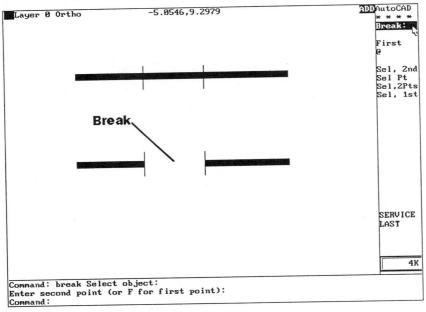

COMMAND OPTIONS

F   Specifies the first break point.

@   Uses the first break point coordinates for the second break point.

RELATED AUTOCAD COMMANDS

■ **Change** Changes the length lines.

■ **PEdit** Removes and relocates vertices of polylines.

■ **Trim**   Shortens the lengths of lines.

'Cal

Algebraic and vector geometry calculator used at the command lline
(*an external command in GeomCal.Exp*).

Command	Button	Side Menu	Pull-down	Tablet
'cal	[#2]	[TOOLS]	[Assist]	P 3
	[Calculator]	[GeomCal:]	[Calculator]	

Command: **cal**
>>Expression:

COMMAND OPTIONS

( )	Grouping of expressions.
[ ]	Vector expressions.
+	Addition.
-	Subtraction.
*	Multiplication.
/	Division.
^	Exponentiation.
&	Vector product of vectors.

sin	Sine.
cos	Cosine.
tang	Tangent.
asin	Arc sine.
acos	Arc cosine.
atan	Arc tangent.
ln	Natural logarithm.
log	Logarithm.
exp	Natural exponent.
exp10	Exponent.
sqr	Square.
sqrt	Square root.
abs	Absolute value.
round	Round off.
trunc	Truncate.

cvunit	Converts units using Acad.Unt unit definition file.
w2u	WCS to UCS conversion.
u2w	UCS to WCS conversion.

r2d	Radians-to-degrees conversion.
d2r	Degrees-to-radians conversion.
pi	The value PI.

xyof	x- and y-coordinates of a point.
xzof	x- and z-coordinates of a point.

yzof	y- and z-coordinates of a point.
xof	x-coordinate of a point.
yof	y-coordinate of a point.
zof	z-coordinate of a point.
rxof	Real x-coordinate of a point .
ryof	Real y-coordinate of a point.
rzof	Real z-coordinate of a point.
cur	x,y,z-coordinates of picked point.
rad	Radius of object
pld	Point on line, distance from.
plt	Point on line, using parameter t.
rot	Rotate point though angle about origin.
ill	Intersection of two lines.
ilp	Intersection of line and plane.
dist	Distance between two points.
dpl	Distance between point and line.
dpp	Distance between point and plane.
ang	Angle between lines.
nor	Unit vector normal.

RELATED AUTOCAD COMMANDS
- *All*

RELATED SYSTEM VARIABLES
- **UserI1 — UserI5**   User-definable integer variables.
- **UserR1 — UserR5**   User-definable real variables.

RELATED FILE
- **Acad.Unt**   Unit conversion file, found in Acad13\Common \Support.

TIPS
- Since 'Cal is a transparent command, it can be used to perform a calculation in the middle of another command.

- **Cal** understands the following prefixes:
    - *   Scalar product of vectors.
    - &   Vector product of vectors

- And the following suffixes:
    - r   Radian (*Default: degrees*)
    - g   Grad
    - '   Feet (*Default: unitless distance.*)
    - "   Inches

Chamfer

Bevels the intersection of two lines, all vertices of a 2D polyline, or the faces of 3D solid models.

Command	Alias	Side Menu	Pull-down	Tablet
chamfer	...	[CONSTRCT]	[Construct]	X 21
		[Chamfer:]	[Chamfer]	

```
Command: chamfer
Polyline/Distances/Angle/Trim/Method<Select first line>: D
Enter first chamfer distance:
Enter second chamfer distance:
Polyline/Distances/Angle/Trim/Method<Select first line>: [pick]
Select second line: [pick]
```

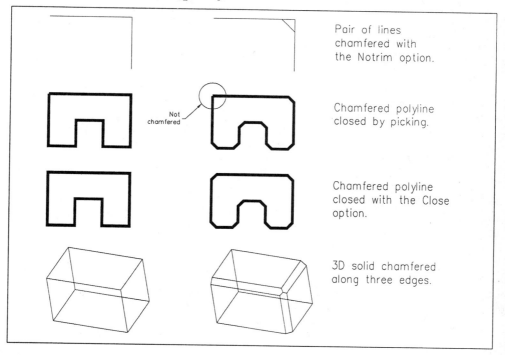

Pair of lines chamfered with the Notrim option.

Not chamfered

Chamfered polyline closed by picking.

Chamfered polyline closed with the Close option.

3D solid chamfered along three edges.

COMMAND OPTIONS

Polyline   Chamfers all vertices of a polyline.
Distances Specifies the chamfer distances.
Angle   Specifies the chamfer by a distance and an angle (*new to R13*).
Trim   Toggles whether lines are trimmed after chamfer (*new to R13*).
Method   Toggles distance or angle mode (*new to Release 13*).

RELATED AUTOCAD COMMAND

■ **Fillet**   Rounds the intersection with a radius.

RELATED SYSTEM VARIABLES

■ **ChamferA** First chamfer distance.
■ **ChamferB** Second chamfer distance.
■ **ChamferC** Length of chamfer (*new to Release 13*).
■ **ChamferD** Chamfer angle (*new to Release 13*).
■ **ChamMode** Toggles chamfer measurement (*new to Release 13*):
        0 Chamfer by two distances.
        1 Chamfer by distance and angle.
■ **TrimMode** Toggles whether lines/edges are trimmed after chamfering (*new to Release 13*).

Change

Ver. 1.0

Modifies the color, elevation, layer, linetype, linetype scale, and thickness of any object, and certain properties of lines, circles, blocks, text, and attributes.

Command	Alias	Side Menu	Pull-down	Tablet
change	...	[MODIFY]	...	...
		[Change:]		

```
Command: change
Select objects: [pick]
Select objects: [Enter]
Properties/<Change point>: p
Change what property (Color/Elev/LAyer/LType/ltScale/
Thickness)?
```

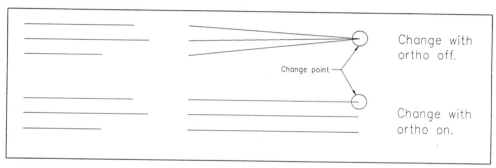

COMMAND OPTIONS

‹Change point› Picks an object to change:

    ‹pick line› Indicates the new length of line.

    ‹pick circle› Indicates the new radius of circle.

    ‹pick block› Indicates the new insertion point or rotation angle of a block.

    ‹pick text› Indicates the new location of text.

    ‹pick block› Indicates an attribute's new text insertion point, text style, new height, rotation angle, text, tag, prompt, or default value.

[Enter] Changes the insertion point, style, height, rotation angle, and string of text (*works only if text is selected*).

Properties Changes properties of the object, as follows:

    Color Changes the color of the object.

    Elev Changes the elevation of the object.

    LAyer Moves the object to a different layer.

    LType Changes the linetype of the object.

ltScale   Changes the scale of the linetype.
Thickness Changes the thickness of any object, except blocks.

RELATED AUTOCAD COMMANDS

- **AttReDef** Changes a block or attributes.
- **ChProp** Contains the properties portion of the **Change** command.
- **Color**   Changes the current color setting.
- **Colour** Changes the current color setting.
- **DdChProp** Dialogue box for changing object properties.
- **Elev**   Changes the working elevation and thickness.
- **Modify** Changes most aspects of all objects.

RELATED SYSTEM VARIABLES

- **CeColor** The current color setting.
- **CeLType** The current linetype setting.
- **CircleRad** The current circle radius.
- **CLayer**   The name of the current layer.
- **Elevation** The current elevation setting.
- **LtScale** The current linetype scale.
- **TextSize** The current height of text.
- **TextStyle** The current text style.
- **Thickness** The current thickness setting.

TIPS

- The **Change** command cannot change the size of donuts, the radius or length of arcs, the length of polylines, or the justification of text.

- Use the **Change** command to change the endpoints of a group of lines to a common vertex.

- Turn ortho mode on to extend or trim a group of lines, without needing a cutting edge (as do the **Extend** and **Trim** commands).

ChProp

Modifies the color, layer, linetype, linetype scale, and thickness of most objects.

Command	Alias	Side Menu	Pull-down	Tablet
chprop	. . .	. . .	. . .	. . .

```
Command: chprop
Select objects: [pick]
Select objects: [Enter]
Change what property (Color/LAyer/LType/ltScale/Thickness) ?
```

COMMAND OPTIONS

Color	Changes the color of the object.
LAyer	Moves the object to a different layer.
LType	Changes the linetype of the object.
ltScale	Changes the linetype scale (*new to Release 13*).
Thickness	Changes the thickness of any object except blocks.

RELATED AUTOCAD COMMANDS

- **Change** — Changes lines, circles, blocks, text, and attributes.
- **Color** — Changes the current color setting.
- **Colour** — Changes the current color setting.
- **DdChProp** — Dialogue box version of the **ChProp** command.
- **Elev** — Changes the working elevation.
- **LtScale** — Sets the linetype scale.
- **Modify** — Changes most aspects of all objects.

RELATED SYSTEM VARIABLES

- **CeColor** — The current color setting.
- **CeLtype** — The current linetype name.
- **CLayer** — The name of the current layer.
- **LtScale** — The current linetype scale.
- **Thickness** — The current thickness setting.

TIP

- Use the **Change** command to change the elevation of an object.

Circle

Draws 2D circles by five different methods.

Command	Alias	Side Menu	Pull-down	Tablet
circle	...	[DRAW 1]	[Draw]	M 10
		[Circle:]	[Circle]	

```
Command: circle
3P/2P/TTR/<Center point>: [pick]
Diameter/<Radius>: [pick]
```

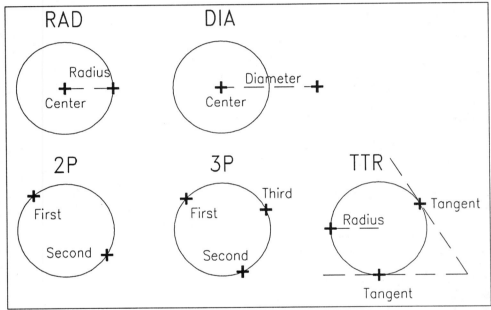

COMMAND OPTIONS

<Center point>   Indicates the circle's center point:
  <Radius>   Indicates the circle's radius.
  Diameter   Indicates the circle's diameter.

3P   Draws a three-point circle:
  First point: Indicates first point on circle.
  Second point: Indicates second point on circle.
  Third point: Indicates third point on circle.

2P   Draws a two-point circle:
  First point on diameter:
        Indicates first point on circle.
  Second point on diameter:
        Indicates second point on circle.

TTR   Draws a circle tangent to two lines:
   Enter Tangent spec:
                Indicates first point of tangency; and
   Enter second Tangent spec:
                Indicates second point of tangency; and
   Radius: Indicates first point of radius; and
   Second point: Indicates second point of radius.

RELATED AUTOCAD COMMANDS
- **Arc**   Draws an arc.
- **Donut**   Draws a solid-filled circle or donut.
- **Ellipse** Draws an elliptical circle or arc.
- **Sphere**   Draws a 3D solid ball.
- **ViewRes** Controls the visual roundness of circles.

RELATED SYSTEM VARIABLE
- **CircleRad**   The current circle radius.

TIPS
- Sometimes it is easier to create an arc by drawing a circle, then using the **Break** or **Trim** commands to convert the circle into an arc

- Giving a circle thickness turns it into a cylinder.

'Color *or* 'Colour

Ver. 2.5

Sets the new working color.

Command	Alias	Side Menu	Pull-down	Tablet
'color	...	...	...	...
'colour				

```
Command: color
New object color <BYLAYER>:
```

COMMAND OPTIONS

BYLAYER   Sets working color to color of current layer.
BYBLOCK   Sets working color of inserted blocks.
Color Number Sets working color using number (1 to 255), color name, or abbreviation:

Color name	Number	Abbreviation
Red	1	R
Yellow	2	Y
Green	3	G
Cyan	4	C
Blue	5	B
Magenta	6	M
White	7	W

RELATED AUTOCAD COMMANDS

- **Change** Changes the color of objects.
- **ChProp** Changes the color of objects.
- **DdEModes** Sets new working color via a dialogue box.
- **DdChProp** Changes the color of objects via a dialogue box.

RELATED SYSTEM VARIABLES

- **CeColor** The current object color setting:
  - 1 (*red*) Minimum value.
  - 7 (*white*) Default value.
  - 255 Maximum value.

TIPS

- 'BYLAYER' means that objects take on the color assigned to that layer.

- 'BYBLOCK' means that objects take on the color in effect at the time the block is inserted.

- White objects display as black when the background color is white.

Compile

Compiles SHP shape, SHP font, and PFB PostScript font definition files into SHX format.

Command	Alias	Side Menu	Pull-down	Tablet
compile	...	[TOOLS]	[Tools]	...
		[Compile:]	[Compile]	

Command: **compile**

COMMAND OPTIONS
None

RELATED AUTOCAD COMMANDS
- **Load**   Loads a compiled SHX shape file into the current drawing.
- **Style**   Loads SHP, SHX, TTF, PFA, and PFB font files into the current drawing.

RELATED SYSTEM VARIABLE
- **ShpName** Contains the current SHP filename.

TIPS
- As of Release 12, the **Style** command converts SHP and PFB font files on-the-fly; it is only necessary to use the **Compile** command to obtain an SHX font file.

- The **Compile** command lets you convert any of the 10,000 PostScript fonts into AutoCAD's SHX format.

- TrueType fonts cannot be compiled.

Cone

Draws a 3D ACIS cone with a circular or elliptical base *(formerly the SolCone command; an external command in Acis.Dll).*

Command	Alias	Side Menu	Pull-down	Tablet
cone	. . .	[DRAW 2]	[Draw]	J 7
		[SOLIDS]	[Solids]	
		[Cone:]	[Cone]	

```
Command: cone
Elliptical/<center point> <0,0,0>: E
<Axis endpoint>/Center: C
Center of ellipse <0,0,0>: [pick]
Axis endpoint: [pick]
Other axis endpoint: [pick]
Apex/<Height>: A
Apex: [pick]
```

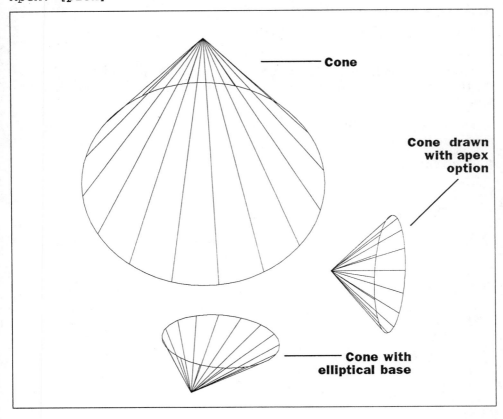

Cone

Cone drawn
with apex
option

Cone with
elliptical base

COMMAND OPTIONS

<Center point> Center of the cone's base.
Elliptical Draw cone with an elliptical base.
Apex Determines height and orientation.

RELATED AUTOCAD COMMANDS

- **Ai_Cone** Draws a 3D wireframe cone.
- **Box** Draws a 3D solid box.
- **Cylinder** Draws a 3D solid tube.
- **Sphere** Draws a 3D solid ball.
- **Torus** Draws a 3D solid donut.
- **Wedge** Draws a 3D solid wedge.

RELATED SYSTEM VARIABLES

- **DispSilh** Toggles display of 3D objects as silhousette after hidden-line removal and shading.
- **IsoLines** Number of isolines on solid surfaces:

  0 Minimum (*no isolines*).
  4 Default.
  16 A reasonable value.
  2,047 Maximum value.

TIP

- To draw a cone at an angle, use the Apex option.

Config

Reconfigures AutoCAD for the graphics board, digitizer, plotter, and operating parameters (*short for CONFIGuration*).

Command	Alias	Side Menu	Pull-down	Tablet
config	...	[OPTIONS]	[Options]	...
		[Config:]	[Configure]	

Command: **config**

COMMAND OPTIONS

<0>	Exits **Config** back to the drawing screen.
1	Shows the current configuration of AutoCAD.
2	Allows detailed configuration.
3	Configures video display.
4	Configures digitizer.
5	Configures plotter.
6	Configures system console.
7	Configures operating parameters.

RELATED DOS COMMANDS

- **acad -r**   Start AutoCAD with the **-r** parameter to reconfigure.
- **Set**   Sets environment variables prior to starting AutoCAD for DOS.

RELATED AUTOCAD COMMANDS

- **DxlConfig** Configures the accelerated display driver.
- **RConfig** Configures **Render** with rendering graphics board and printer.
- **ReInit** Reinitializes peripherals.

RELATED ENVIRONMENT VARIABLES

- **AcadCfg**   Points to the subdirectory containing the **Acad.Cfg** configuration file.
- **Acad**   Points to the subdirectories AutoCAD should search for support files.
- **AcadAltMenu** Points to name of alternate tablet menus.
- **AcadDrv** Points to subdirectories containing device drivers.
- **AcadMaxMem** Maximum bytes of memory pager requests from DOS.
- **AcadPageDir** Points to subdirectory for paging file.
- **AcadMaxPage** Maximum bytes written to first pager file.
- **AcadPlCmd** Command to launch plot queue software.
- **AcadServer** Network license server (*default: Netinel*).
- **RenderCfg** Points to subdirectory containing the **Render** configuration file.
- **RdpAdi** Points to protected-mode ADI rendering display driver.
- **RhpAdi** Points to protected-mode ADI hardcopy rendering driver.

- **AveFaceDir** Points to subdirectory containing the temporary face file.
- **Ignore_Big_Screen**
  Allows pre-ADI v.42 display drivers to use Release 12 and 13's virtual screen.
- **Ignore_Dragg**
  Digitizer driver does not use mouse-button-down drag mode.

RELATED FILES

- **Acad.Cfg** Configuration file for AutoCAD.
- **Acad.Ini** Initialization file for AutoCAD.
- **Asi.Ini** Initialization file for ASE module.
- **Render.Cfg** Configuration file for Render module.
- **DI53100.Cfg** Configuration file for accelerated display driver.

RELATED SYSTEM VARIABLES

- **DctCust** Name of user spelling dictionary.
- **DctMain** Name of current spelling dictionary.
- **Platform** Reports the AutoCAD hardware platform version: "386 DOS Extender" for the DOS version.

TIPS

- Options 6 reports: "The 386 DOS Extender system console has no configurable options."

- When AutoCAD appears to be unable to display the graphics screen, you may have to reconfigure:
  - Start AutoCAD from the operating system with **acad -r**
  - Erase the **Acad.Cfg** file, then start AutoCAD.
  - Change AutoCAD's display from the Null driver.

- Option 2, 'Allow detailed configuration,' is now incorporated in the other options.

Copy

Creates one or more copies of an object.

Command	Alias	Side Menu	Pull-down	Tablet
copy	cp	[EDIT]	[Modify]	X 15
		[COPY:]	[Copy]	

```
Command: copy
Select objects: [pick]
Select objects: [Enter]
<Base point or displacement>/Multiple: [pick]
Second point of displacement: [pick]
```

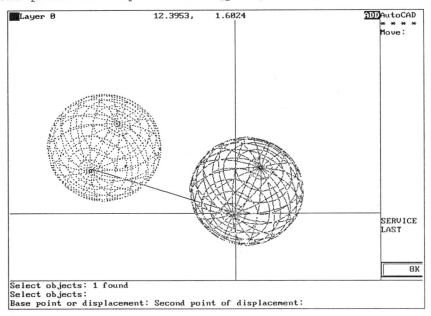

```
Select objects: 1 found
Select objects:
Base point or displacement: Second point of displacement:
```

COMMAND OPTIONS

<Base point or displacement>
> Indicates the starting point, or the distance to move.

Second point of displacement
> Indicates the point to move.

Multiple   Allows an object to be copied more than once.

[Esc]   Cancels multiple object copying.

RELATED AUTOCAD COMMANDS

■ **Array**   Draws a rectangular or polar array of objects.
■ **MInsert**   Places an array of blocks.

- **Move**   Moves an object to a new location.
- **Offset**   Draws parallel lines, polylines, circles and arcs.

TIPS

- Use the **M** (multiple) option to quickly place several copies of the original object.

- Inserting a block multiple times is more effecient than placing multiple copies.

- Turn ortho mode on to copy objects in a precise horizontal and vertical direction.

- Turn snap mode on to copy objects in precise increments.

- Use object snap modes to precisely copy objects from one geometric feature to another.

- To copy an object by a known distance, enter 0,0 as the 'Base point.' Then, enter the known distance as the 'Second point'

- **Copy** works in 2D (supply coordinate pairs) and 3D (supply coordinate triplets). In 2D, the current elevation is used as the z-coordinate.

Cylinder

Draws a 3D ACIS cylinder with a circular or elliptical cross section *(formerly the SolCyl command; an external command in Acis.Dll).*

Command	Alias	Side Menu	Pull-down	Tablet
cylinder	...	[DRAW 2]	[Draw]	L 7
		[SOLIDS]	[Solids]	
		[Cylindr:]	[Cylinder]	

```
Command: cylinder
Elliptical/<center point> <0,0,0>: [pick]
Diameter/<Radius>: [pick]
Center of other end/<Height>: [pick]
```

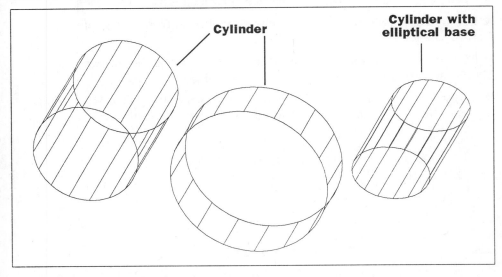

Cylinder

Cylinder with elliptical base

RELATED AUTOCAD COMMANDS

- **Ai_Cyl**   Draws a 3D wireframe cylinder.
- **Box**   Draws a 3D solid box.
- **Cone**   Draws a 3D solid cone.
- **Extrude**   Creates a cylinder with an arbitrary cross-section and sloped walls.
- **Sphere**   Draws a 3D solid ball.
- **Torus**   Draws a 3D solid donut.
- **Wedge**   Draws a 3D solid wedge.

RELATED SYSTEM VARIABLES

- **DispSilh** Toggles display of 3D objects as silhouette after hidden-line removal and shading.
- **IsoLines** Number of isolines on solid surfaces:

0	Minimum (*no isolines*).
4	Default.
16	A reasonable value.
2,047	Maximum value.

TIP

- The **Ellipse** option draws a cylinder with an elliptical cross-section.

DbList

Lists information on all objects in the drawing (*short for Data Base LISTing*).

Command	Alias	Side Menu	Pull-down	Tablet
dblist	...	...	...	...

Command: **dblist**
Example listing:

```
          LINE        Layer: 1
                      Space: Model space
       from point, X=    3.7840   Y=    4.7169   Z=    0.0000
         to point, X=    4.1440   Y=    4.7169   Z=    0.0000
   Length =    0.3600,   Angle in X-Y Plane =        0
  Delta X =    0.3600, Delta Y = 0.0000, Delta Z = 0.0000


           ARC         Layer: 2
                       Space: Model space
      center point, X=    2.1000   Y=    7.0000   Z=    0.0000
      radius      1.2000
       start angle       0
         end angle      180
```

COMMAND OPTIONS

[Enter]	Continues display after pause.
[Esc]	Cancels database listing.

RELATED AUTOCAD COMMANDS

- **Area**   Lists the area and perimeter of objects.
- **Dist**   Lists the 3D distance and angle between two points.
- **Id**   Lists the 3D coordinates of a point.
- **List**   Lists information about selected objects in the drawing.

RELATED SYSTEM VARIABLES

- *None*

DdAttDef

Rel. 12

Define an attribute definition via a dialogue box (*short for Dynamic Dialogue ATTribute DEFinition; an external file in Ddattdef.Lsp*).

Command	Alias	Side Menu	Pull-down	Tablet
ddattdef	...	[CONSTRCT]	[Construct]	W 7
		[DDatDef:]	[Attribute]	

Command: **ddattdef**
Displays dialogue box:

```
                    Attribute Definition
 Mode                Attribute
  [ ] Invisible       Tag:    [                    ]
  [ ] Constant        Prompt: [                    ]
  [ ] Verify          Value:  [                    ]
  [ ] Preset
 Insertion Point     Text Options
  [ Pick Point < ]    Justification: [ Left        |v]
  X: [0.0000]         Text Style:    [ STANDARD    |v]
  Y: [0.0000]         [ Height < ]   [0.2000]
  Z: [0.0000]         [ Rotation < ] [0]
  [ ] Align below previous attribute
           [ OK ]  [ Cancel ]  [ Help... ]
```

COMMAND OPTIONS

Mode	Sets the attribute text modes:
Invisible	Makes the attribute text invisible.
Constant	Uses constant values for the attributes.
Verify	Verifies the text after input.
Preset	Presets the variable attribute text.
Attribute	Sets the attribute text:
Tag	Identifies the attribute.
Prompt	Prompts the user for input.
Value	Default value for the attribute.
Insertion point	Specifies the attributes insertion point:
Pick point	Picks insertion point with cursor.
X	X-coordinate insertion point.
Y	Y-coordinate insertion point.
Z	Z-coordinate insertion point.

Text options Specifies the attribute text options:
  Justification Sets the justification.
  Text style Selects a style.
  Height   Specifies the height.
  Rotation Sets the rotation angle.
Align   Automatically places the text below the previous attribute.

RELATED AUTOCAD COMMAND
- **AttDef**   Defines attribute definitions from the command line.

RELATED SYSTEM VARIABLES
- **AFlags**   Attribute mode:
      0 No mode specified.
      1 Invisible.
      2 Constant.
      4 Verify.
      8 Preset.
- **AttMode** Attribute display modes:
      0 Off.
      1 Normal.
      2 On.
- **AttReq**   Toggles prompt for attributes:
      0 Assumes default values.
      1 Enables dialogue box or prompts for attributes.

DdAttE

Edits attribute data via a dialogue box (*short for Dynamic Dialogue ATTribute Editor*).

Command	Alias	Side Menu	Pull-down	Tablet
ddatte	...	[MODIFY]	[Modify]	X 7
		[AttEd:]	[Attribute]	
			[Edit]	

```
Command: ddatte
Select block: [pick]
```

Displays dialogue box.

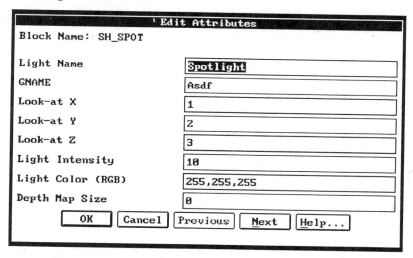

COMMAND OPTIONS
None

RELATED AUTOCAD COMMANDS
- **AttEdit**   Global attribute editor.
- **AttReDef** Changes the definition of attributes.
- **DdEdit**   Edits attribute definitions.

RELATED SYSTEM VARIABLE
- **AttDia**   Toggles use of **DdAttE** during **Insert** command.

TIP
- The **DdEdit** command edits attribute definitions.

DdAttExt

Extracts attribute information to a file (*short for Dynamic Dialogue ATTribute EXTraction; an external command in Ddattext.Lsp*).

Command	Alias	Side Menu	Pull-down	Tablet
ddattext	...	[FILE]	[File]	...
		[EXPORT]	[Export]	
		[DDattEx:]	[Attributes]	

Command: **ddattext**

Displays dialogue box.

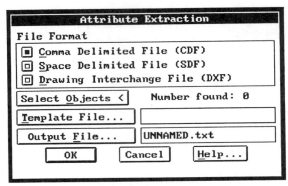

COMMAND OPTIONS
Comma delimited
> Creates a CDF text file, where commas separate fields.

Space delimited
> Creates a SDF text file, where spaces separate fields.

Drawing interchange
> Creates an ASCII DXF file.

Select Objects
> Returns to the graphics screen to select attributes for export.

Template file
> Specifies the name of the TXT template file for CDF and SDF files.

Output File Specifies the name of the attribute output file (TXT for CDF and SDF formats; DXX for DXF format).

RELATED AUTOCAD COMMAND
■ **AttExt** Attribute extraction via command line interface.

DdChProp

Modifies the color, layer, linetype, linetype scale, and thickness of most objects via a dialogue box (*short for Dynamic Dialogue CHange PROPerties; an external command in DdChProp.Lsp*).

Command	Alias	Side Menu	Pull-down	Tablet
ddchprop	...	[MODIFY]	...	...
		[Ddchpro:]		

Command: **ddchprop**
Select objects: **[pick]**
Displays dialogue box:

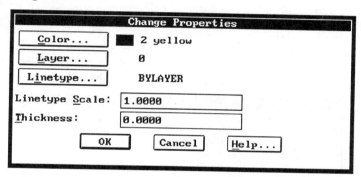

COMMAND OPTIONS

Color   Change the color of the selected objects by dialogue box:

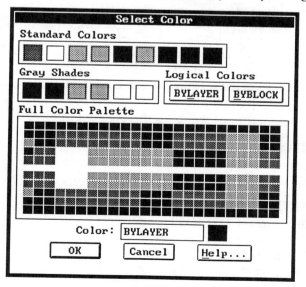

Layer name Moves the selected objects to a different layer by dialogue box:

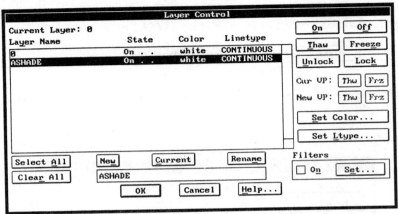

LIinetype Changes the linetype of the selected objects via a dialogue box:

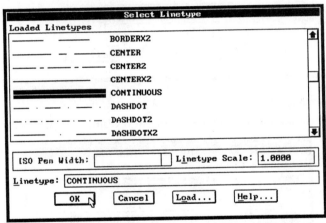

LinetypeScale Changes the linetype scale of the selected objects.
Thickness Changes the thickness of the selected objects.

RELATED AUTOCAD COMMANDS
- **ChProp** Changes properties via command line.
- **Change** Allows changes to lines, circles, blocks, text, and attributes.

RELATED SYSTEM VARIABLES
- **CeColor** The current object color setting.
- **CeLtype** The current object linetype setting.
- **CLayer** The name of the current layer.
- **Thickness** The current thickness setting.

'DdColor

Set the current working color by dialogue box (*an external command in DdColor.Lsp*).

Command	Alias	Side Menu	Pull-down	Tablet
'ddcolor	...	[DATA]	[Data]	...
		[Color:]	[Color]	
		[ColorDlg]		

Command: **ddcolor**

Displays the dialogue box:

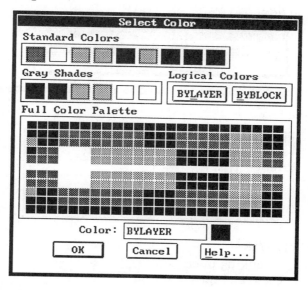

COMMAND OPTION
Color   Enters color number, BYBLOCK, or BYLAYER.

RELATED AUTOCAD COMMANDS
- **Color**   Changes the color from the Command: prompt.
- **DdChProp** Changes the color of selected objects.

RELATED SYSTEM VARIABLE
- **CeColor**   Contains the number for the current working color.

DdEdit

Edits a single line of text or a single attribute using a dialogue box; launches the text editor for editing multiline text (*short for Dynamic Dialogue EDITor*).

Command	Alias	Side Menu	Pull-down	Tablet
ddedit	...	[MODIFY]	[Modify]	U 5
		[Ddedit:]	[Edit Text]	

Command: **ddedit**
<Select a TEXT or ATTDEF object>/Undo: **[pick text]**

Displays dialogue box.

<Select a TEXT or ATTDEF object>/Undo: **[pick attribute definition]**

Displays dialogue box.

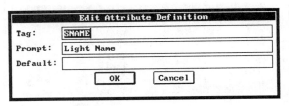

COMMAND OPTIONS

U   Undoes editing operation.
[Esc]   Cancels to end the command.

RELATED AUTOCAD COMMANDS

■ **DdAttE**   Edits all text attributes connected with a block.
■ **Change**   Edits some text attributes.

RELATED SYSTEM VARIABLE

■ **MTextEd** Name of the text editor used for editing multi-line text.

TIPS

■ The **DdEdit** command automatically repeats; press [Esc] to cancel the command.

■ Use the **DdAttE** command to edit all attribute values in a block.

'DdEModes

Sets the working parameters (*short for Dynamic Dialogue Object MODES*).

Command	Alias	Side Menu	Pull-down	Tablet
'ddemodes	. . .	[DATA]	[Data]	Y 9
		[DDemode:]	[Object Creation]	

Command: **ddemodes**

Displays dialogue box.

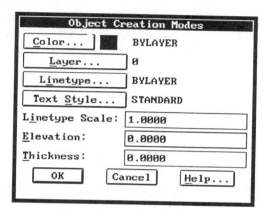

COMMAND OPTIONS

Elevation   Sets the new working elevation.
Thickness   Sets the new working thickness.
Layer   Sets the new working layer; displays dialogue box:

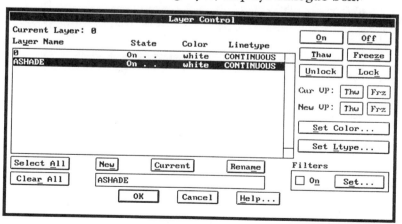

Color   Sets the new working color; displays dialogue box:

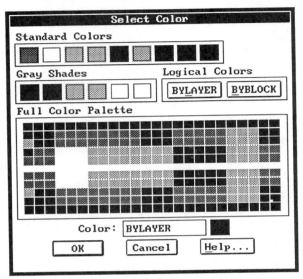

Linetype   Sets the new working linetype; displays dialogue box:

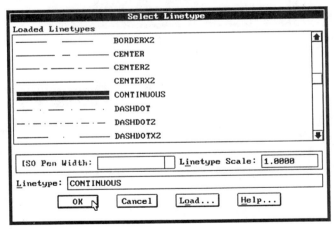

Text Style   Sets the new working textstyle; displays dialogue box:

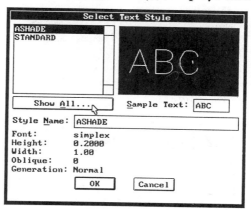

RELATED AUTOCAD COMMANDS

- **Change**   Changes the color, layer, linetype, text elevation and thickness.
- **ChProp**   Changes the color, layer, linetype and thickness.
- **Color**   Sets a new working color.
- **Colour**   Sets a new working colour.
- **DdAttE**   Edits attribute values
- **DdChProp**   Changes the color, layer, linetype, linettype scale, and thickness.
- **DdEdit**   Changes text or attribute definition.
- **Elevation** Sets a new working elevation.
- **Layer**   Sets a new working layer.
- **Linetype** Sets a new working linetype.
- **Style**   Sets a new text style.

RELATED SYSTEM VARIABLES

- **CeColor**   The current object color.
- **CeLtype**   The current object linetype.
- **CLayer**   The current layer name.
- **Elevation** The current elevation setting.
- **TextStyle** The current text style setting.
- **Thickness** The current thickness setting.

'DdGrips

Turns object grips on and off; defines the size and color of grips (*an external command in DdGrips.lsp*).

Command	Alias	Side Menu	Pull-down	Tablet
'ddgrips	...	[OPTIONS]	[Options]	...
		[DDgrips:]	[Grips]	

Command: **ddgrips**

Displays dialogue box.

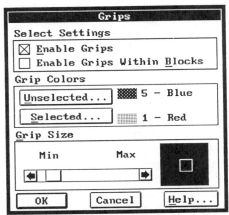

COMMAND OPTIONS

Enable grips Toggles the display of object grips.

Enable grips within Blocks

              Displays grips on objects within blocks.

Grip size   Change the size of the grip box.

Unselected Defines the color of unselected grips; displays dialogue box.

Selected   Defines the color of selected grips; displays dialogue box.

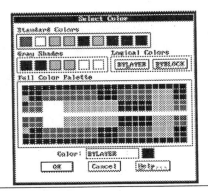

RELATED AUTOCAD COMMAND

■ **Select**   Creates a selection set of objects.

RELATED SYSTEM VARIABLES

■ **Grips**   Toggles use of grips:
      0   Disables grips.
      1   Enables grips (*Default*).

■ **GripBlock** Toggles display of grips inside blocks:
      0   Displays grip only in block insertion point (*Default*).
      1   Displays grips on objects inside block.

■ **GripColor** Color of unselected grips (*Default=5, blue*).

■ **GripHot** Color of selected grips (*Default=1, red*).

■ **GripSize** Size of grip, in pixels:
      1   Minimum size.
      3   Default size.
    255 Maximum size.

DDim

Sets dimension styles and variables via a dialogue box (*short for Dialogue DIMension*).

Command	Alias	Side Menu	Pull-down	Tablet
ddim	...	[DATA]	[Data]	V 5-6
		[DDim:]	[Dimension Style]	

Command: **ddim**

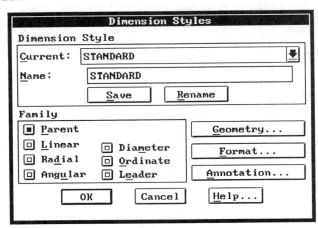

COMMAND OPTIONS

Dimension Style

Creates and selects a dimension style:

Current	Selects a dimstyle name.
Name	Creates a new named dimstyle.
Save	Saves the dimstyle.
Rename	Rename the dimstyle.

Geometry Specifies the dimension geometry variables:
- Dimension, extension, and center lines.
- Center marks.
- Arrowhead style.
- Overall scale.

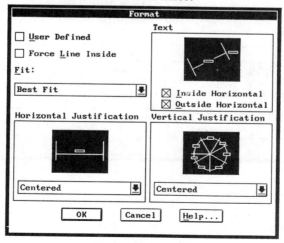

Format Specify the dimension format variables:
Location of dimension text.
Arrowheads.
Leader and dimension lines.

Annotation Specifies the dimension annotation variables:
- Controls the look of dimension text.
- Primary and alternate units.
- Tolerance suffix.

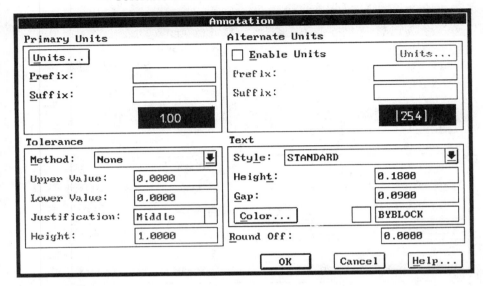

Primary Units Specifies the display of the primary dimensioning units.

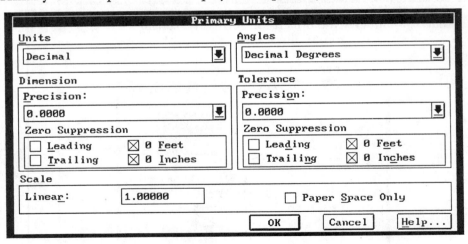

Alternate Units   Specifies the display of the alternate dimensioning units.

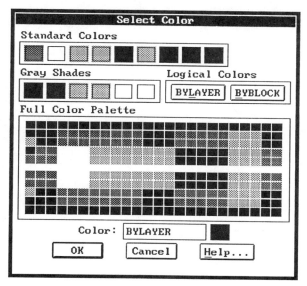

Color   Specifies the text color.

RELATED AUTOCAD COMMANDS

- **DimStyle** Changes dimension variables at the Command prompt.
- *All commands beginning with **Dim**.*

RELATED SYSTEM VARIABLES

■ **DimStyle** Contains the name of the current dimension style.

■ *All dimensioning variables.*

TIPS

■ An overridden dimstyle has a + (plus) prefix to the dimstyle name, as in '+STANDARD'.

■ You cannot rename the default dimstyle named 'Standard'.

■ The current dimstyle name is stored in system variable **DimStyle**.

■ You can access dimstyles stored in externally-referenced drawings via the **XBind** command.

■ Use the **DimStyle** command to change dimension styles at the Command: prompt.

DdInsert

Insert blocks via dialogue box (*short for Dialogue Dynamic INSERT;*
an external command in DdInsert.Lsp).

Command	Alias	Side Menu	Pull-down	Tablet
ddinsert	...	[DRAW 2]	[Draw]	W 10
		[DDinsert]	[Insert]	
			[Block]	

Command: **ddinsert**

Displays dialogue box.

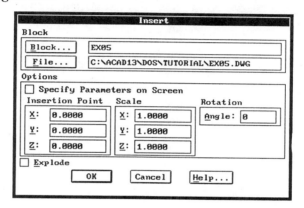

COMMAND OPTIONS

Block   Selects the block name from a second dialogue box.
File   Selects the drawing name from a second dialogue box.
Specify parameters on screen
     Uses the cursor to position the block.
Insertion point Specifies the block's insertion point coordinates.
Scale   Specifies the block's scale.
Rotation   Specifies the block's angle of rotation.
Explode   Inserts the block as individual objects.

RELATED AUTOCAD COMMANDS

- **Block**   Create a block from a group of objects.
- **Explode** Explodes a block after insertion.
- **Insert**   Inserts a block via the command line.
- **MInsert** Inserts an array as a block.

RELATED SYSTEM VARIABLE

- **InsName** Default name for most-recently inserted block.

'DdLModes

Controls the layer settings in the drawing via a dialogue box (*short for Dynamic Dialogue Layer MODES*).

Command	Alias	Side Menu	Pull-down	Tablet
'ddlmodes	...	[DATA]	[Data]	L 4-5
		[DDlmode:]	[Layers]	

Command: **ddlmodes**

Displays dialogue box.

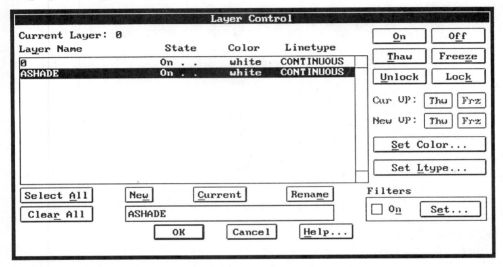

COMMAND OPTIONS

Clear all	Clears all selected layers.
Current	Sets the working (current) layer name.
Freeze	Freezes the selected layers.
Lock	Locks the selected layers.
New	Creates a new layer name.
Off	Turns off the selected layers.
On	Turns on the selected layers.
Rename	Renames a layer.
Select All	Selects all layers.
Set Color	Sets a new color for the selected layers.
Set Ltype	Sets a new linetype for the selected layers.
Thaw	Thaws the selected frozen layers.
Unlock	Unlocks the selected locked layers.

Set filters   Creates a filter set via dialogue box:

```
┌────────────────────────────────────────────┐
│             Set Layer Filters              │
│  On/Off :           ┌──────────────┬───┐   │
│                     │ Both         │ ▼ │   │
│  Freeze/Thaw:       ┌──────────────┬───┐   │
│                     │ Both         │ ▼ │   │
│  Lock/Unlock:       ┌──────────────┬───┐   │
│                     │ Both         │ ▼ │   │
│  Current Vport:     ┌──────────────┬───┐   │
│                     │ Both         │ ▼ │   │
│  New Vports:        ┌──────────────┬───┐   │
│                     │ Both         │ ▼ │   │
│  Layer Names:       ┌──────────────────┐   │
│                     │ *                │   │
│  Colors:            ┌──────────────────┐   │
│                     │ *                │   │
│  Ltypes:            ┌──────────────────┐   │
│                     │ *                │   │
│         ┌──────────────────────────┐       │
│         │          Reset           │       │
│   ┌──────────┐ ┌──────────┐ ┌───────────┐ │
│   │    OK    │ │  Cancel  │ │  Help...  │ │
│   └──────────┘ └──────────┘ └───────────┘ │
└────────────────────────────────────────────┘
```

RELATED AUTOCAD COMMANDS

- **Layer**   Controls the current layer setting.
- **Rename**   Renames a layer.
- **VpLayer** Controls the layer settings in paper space.

RELATED SYSTEM VARIABLE

- **CLayer**   The current layer setting.

TIPS

■When a layer has been turned off, AutoCAD no longer displays nor plots objects on that layer.

■ When a layer is frozen, AutoCAD no longer takes its objects into account during a regeneration; in addition, AutoCAD no longer displays nor plots objects on that layer.

■ Freezing a layer is more efficient than turning the layer off.

■ When a layer is locked, its objects are displayed and you can draw on the layer but you cannot edit the layer's objects.

■ Locking layers is useful for redlining; you can make additions and notes but not change the drawing.

'DdLtype

Loads linetype definitions, sets the working linetype, and scale.

Command	Alias	Side Menu	Pull-down	Tablet
'ddltype	. . .	[DATA]	[Data]	Y 8
		[DDltype:]	[Linetype]	

Command: **ddltype**
Displays dialogue box:

COMMAND OPTIONS
ISO Pen Width   Pen width for ISO linetypes *(measured in millimeters)*.
Linetype Scale Working linetype scale.
Linetype   Name of working linetype pattern.

RELATED AUTOCAD COMMANDS
■ **Linetype** Loads and sets the working linetype at the Command prompt.
■ **LtScale**   Sets the linetype scale.

RELATED SYSTEM VARIABLES
■ **CeLtype** The name of the current linetype.
■ **LtScale** The scale of the current linetype.

RELATED FILES
■ **Acad.Lin** Definitions of all linetypes used by AutoCAD.
■ **TypeShp.Lin** Text shapes for linetypes.

DdModify

Views and edits properties of all objects via a dialogue box (*an external command in DdModify.Lsp*).

Command	Alias	Side Menu	Pull-down	Tablet
ddmodify	. . .	. . .	[Modify]	V 9-10
		. . .	[Object...]	

Command: **ddmodify**
Select object to list: **[pick object]**
A different dialogue box appears for type of object, as shown below.

COMMAND OPTIONS

Color   Changes the object's color via a dialogue box.
Layer name Moves the object to a different layer.
Linetype   Changes the object's linetype via a dialogue box.
Linetype Scale
                Changes the object's linetype scale (*new in Release 13*).
Thickness   Changes the object's thickness.

[pick arc]   Displays the **Modify Arc** dialogue box.
Displays dialogue box.

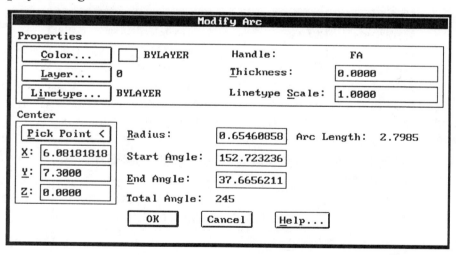

[pick hatch] Displays the **Modify Associative Hatch** dialogue box
Displays dialogue box.

```
┌─────────────────────────────────────────────────────────────┐
│                  Modify Associative Hatch                     │
│ Properties                                                    │
│  ┌──────────────┐                                             │
│  │   Color...   │  ██ BYLAYER    Handle:         E6           │
│  ├──────────────┤                                             │
│  │   Layer...   │  0             Thickness:    [0.0000]       │
│  ├──────────────┤                                             │
│  │  Linetype... │  BYLAYER       Linetype Scale: [1.0000]     │
│  └──────────────┘                                             │
│  Block Name: *X0 - Associative Hatch                          │
│       [   OK   ]  [ Cancel ]  [ Hatch Edit... ]  [ Help... ]  │
└─────────────────────────────────────────────────────────────┘
```

[pick attribute] Displays the **Modify Attribute Definition** dialogue box
Displays dialogue box.

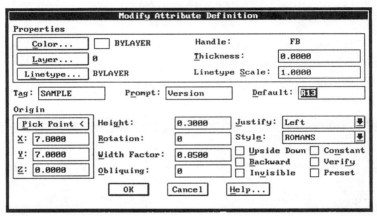

[pick block] Displays the **Modify Block Insertion** dialogue box
Displays dialogue box.

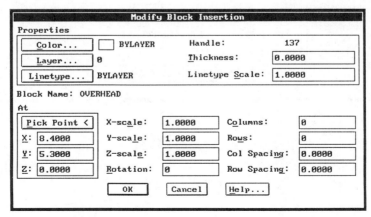

[pick body] Displays the **Modify Body** dialogue box
Displays dialogue box.

```
╔══════════════════ Modify Body ══════════════════╗
║  Properties                                      ║
║   ┌─────────────┐  ┌──┐                           ║
║   │  Color...   │  │  │ BYLAYER   Handle:    F6   ║
║   ├─────────────┤  └──┘                           ║
║   │  Layer...   │  0          Thickness:  [0.0000]║
║   ├─────────────┤                                 ║
║   │  Linetype...│  BYLAYER    Linetype Scale:[1.0000]║
║   └─────────────┘                                 ║
║                                                   ║
║         ┌────────┐  ┌────────┐  ┌────────┐        ║
║         │   OK   │  │ Cancel │  │ Help...│        ║
║         └────────┘  └────────┘  └────────┘        ║
╚══════════════════════════════════════════════════╝
```

[pick circle] Displays the **Modify Circle** dialogue box
Displays dialogue box.

```
╔══════════════════ Modify Circle ══════════════════╗
║  Properties                                        ║
║   ┌─────────────┐  ┌──┐                             ║
║   │  Color...   │  │  │ BYLAYER   Handle:    105    ║
║   ├─────────────┤  └──┘                             ║
║   │  Layer...   │  0          Thickness:  [0.0000]  ║
║   ├─────────────┤                                   ║
║   │  Linetype...│  BYLAYER    Linetype Scale:[1.0000]║
║   └─────────────┘                                   ║
║  Center                                            ║
║   ┌─────────────┐                                   ║
║   │ Pick Point <│   Radius:       [0.5000]          ║
║   └─────────────┘   Diameter:      1.0000           ║
║   X: [0.7000]       Circumference: 3.1416           ║
║   Y: [5.3000]       Area:          0.7854           ║
║   Z: [0.0000]                                       ║
║         ┌────────┐  ┌────────┐  ┌────────┐          ║
║         │   OK   │  │ Cancel │  │ Help...│          ║
║         └────────┘  └────────┘  └────────┘          ║
╚════════════════════════════════════════════════════╝
```

[pick dimension] Displays the **Modify Dimension Object** dialogue box
Displays dialogue box.

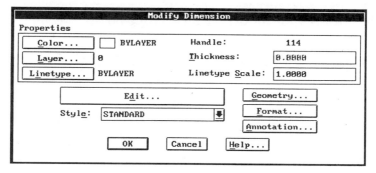

[pick ellipse] Displays the **Modify Ellipse** dialogue box
Displays dialogue box.

```
┌─────────────────────── Modify Ellipse ───────────────────────┐
│ Properties                                                    │
│  ┌──────────────┐  ┌─┐ BYLAYER    Handle:        116          │
│  │   Color...   │  └─┘                                        │
│  ├──────────────┤  Θ           Thickness:   ┌──────────┐      │
│  │   Layer...   │              Thickness:   │ 0.0000   │      │
│  ├──────────────┤                           └──────────┘      │
│  │  Linetype... │  BYLAYER     Linetype Scale: ┌─────────┐    │
│  └──────────────┘                              │ 1.0000  │    │
│                                                └─────────┘    │
│  ┌─ Center ──────┐  Major Radius: ┌────────┐  ┌Major Axis Vector┐
│  │ ┌───────────┐ │                │ 0.7000 │  │ X:   0.7000     │
│  │ │Pick Point<│ │  Minor Radius: ┌──────────┐│                 │
│  │ └───────────┘ │                │0.31622776││ Y:   0.0000     │
│  │ X: │5.9000│   │  Radius Ratio: 0.4518      │                 │
│  │ Y: │5.2000│   │  Start Angle:  ┌────┐      │ Z:   0.0000     │
│  │ Z: │0.0000│   │                │ Θ  │      │                 │
│  │               │  End Angle:    │360 │      │ Area:  0.6954   │
│  └───────────────┘                └────┘                         │
│            ┌────OK────┐  ┌─Cancel─┐  ┌─Help...─┐                │
│            └──────────┘  └────────┘  └─────────┘                │
└───────────────────────────────────────────────────────────────┘
```

[pick leader]   Displays the **Modify Leader** dialogue box
Displays dialogue box.

```
┌─────────────────────── Modify Leader ────────────────────────┐
│ Properties                                                    │
│  ┌──────────────┐  ┌─┐ BYLAYER    Handle:        145          │
│  │   Color...   │  └─┘                                        │
│  ├──────────────┤  Θ           Thickness:   ┌──────────┐      │
│  │   Layer...   │                           │ 0.0000   │      │
│  ├──────────────┤                           └──────────┘      │
│  │  Linetype... │  BYLAYER     Linetype Scale: ┌─────────┐    │
│  └──────────────┘                              │ 1.0000  │    │
│                                                └─────────┘    │
│  ┌──────────────────────┐     ┌──────────┐  ┌Type─────────┐  │
│  │       Edit...        │     │Geometry..│  │ ■ Straight  │  │
│  └──────────────────────┘     ├──────────┤  │ □ Spline    │  │
│  Style: │STANDARD     ▼│      │ Format.. │  │             │  │
│                               ├──────────┤  │ ⊠ Arrow     │  │
│                               │Annotation│  └─────────────┘  │
│            ┌────OK────┐  ┌─Cancel─┐  ┌─Help...─┐             │
│            └──────────┘  └────────┘  └─────────┘             │
└───────────────────────────────────────────────────────────────┘
```

[pick line]   Displays the **Modify Line** dialogue box
Displays dialogue box.

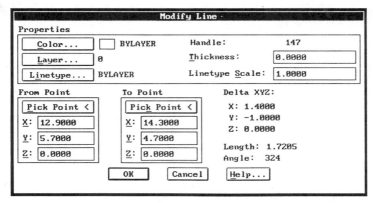

[pick multiline]   Displays the **Modify MLine** dialogue box
Displays dialogue box.

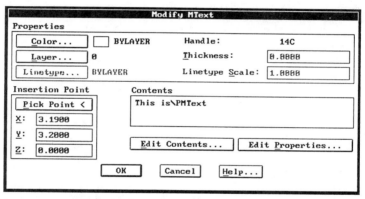

[pick multi-line text] Displays the **Modify MText**dialogue box
Displays dialogue box.

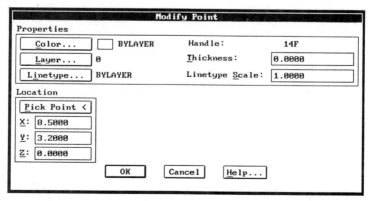

[pick point] Displays the **Modify Point** dialogue box
Displays dialogue box.

[pick polyline] Displays the **Modify Polyline** dialogue box
Displays dialogue box.

```
╔═══════════════════════ Modify Polyline ═══════════════════════╗
  Properties
    ┌─────────────┐  ┌─┐                Handle:        150
    │  Color...   │  │ │ BYLAYER        Thickness:   ┌────────┐
    └─────────────┘  └─┘                             │ 0.0000 │
    ┌─────────────┐                                  └────────┘
    │  Layer...   │ 0                  Linetype Scale:┌────────┐
    └─────────────┘                                  │ 1.0000 │
    ┌─────────────┐                                  └────────┘
    │  Linetype...│ BYLAYER
    └─────────────┘
  Polyline Type: 2D polyline
  Vertex Listing    Fit/Smooth      Mesh              Polyline
  ┌──────────────┐  ┌─────────────┐ ┌─────────────┐  ┌──────────────┐
  │Vertex:1 │Next││ │ ■ None      │ │M: □ Closed  │  │ □ Closed     │
  │              │  │ □ Quadratic │ │N: □ Closed  │  │ □ LT Gen     │
  │X: 10.5000    │  │ □ Cubic     │ │U: ┌───┐     │  └──────────────┘
  │Y: 3.7000     │  │ □ Bezier    │ │   └───┘     │
  │Z: 0.0000     │  │ □ Curve Fit │ │U: ┌───┐     │
  └──────────────┘  └─────────────┘ └───└───┘─────┘
                ┌──────┐  ┌────────┐  ┌────────┐
                │  OK  │  │ Cancel │  │ Help...│
                └──────┘  └────────┘  └────────┘
╚═══════════════════════════════════════════════════════════════╝
```

[pick ray] Displays the **Modify Ray** dialogue box
Displays dialogue box.

```
╔═══════════════════════ Modify Ray ════════════════════════════╗
  Properties
    ┌─────────────┐  ┌─┐                Handle:        156
    │  Color...   │  │ │ BYLAYER        Thickness:   ┌────────┐
    └─────────────┘  └─┘                             │ 0.0000 │
    ┌─────────────┐                                  └────────┘
    │  Layer...   │ 0                  Linetype Scale:┌────────┐
    └─────────────┘                                  │ 1.0000 │
    ┌─────────────┐                                  └────────┘
    │  Linetype...│ BYLAYER
    └─────────────┘
  Start Point       Second Point      Direction Vector
  ┌──────────────┐  ┌──────────────┐
  │ Pick Point < │  │ Pick Point < │   X: 0.8000
  └──────────────┘  └──────────────┘   Y: -0.6000
  X: │ 12.9000 │    X: │ 13.7000 │     Z: 0.0000
  Y: │ 3.7000  │    Y: │ 3.1000  │
  Z: │ 0.0000  │    Z: │ 0.0000  │
                ┌──────┐  ┌────────┐  ┌────────┐
                │  OK  │  │ Cancel │  │ Help...│
                └──────┘  └────────┘  └────────┘
╚═══════════════════════════════════════════════════════════════╝
```

[pick region] Displays the **Modify Region** dialogue box
Displays dialogue box.

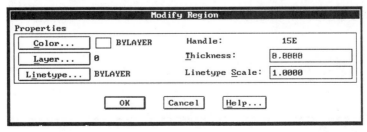

```
╔═══════════════════════ Modify Region ═════════════════════════╗
  Properties
    ┌─────────────┐  ┌─┐                Handle:        15E
    │  Color...   │  │ │ BYLAYER        Thickness:   ┌────────┐
    └─────────────┘  └─┘                             │ 0.0000 │
    ┌─────────────┐                                  └────────┘
    │  Layer...   │ 0                  Linetype Scale:┌────────┐
    └─────────────┘                                  │ 1.0000 │
    ┌─────────────┐                                  └────────┘
    │  Linetype...│ BYLAYER
    └─────────────┘
                ┌──────┐  ┌────────┐  ┌────────┐
                │  OK  │  │ Cancel │  │ Help...│
                └──────┘  └────────┘  └────────┘
╚═══════════════════════════════════════════════════════════════╝
```

[pick shape] Displays the **Modify Shape** dialogue box.
Displays dialogue box.

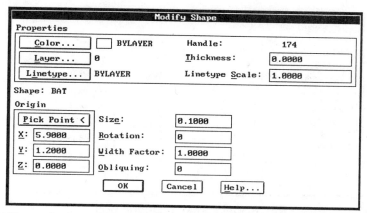

[pick solid]   Displays the **Modify Solid** dialogue box.
Displays dialogue box.

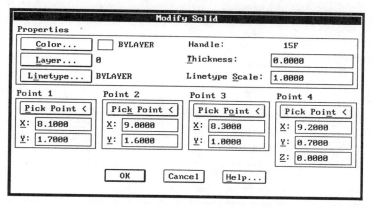

[pick spline]   Displays the **Modify Spline** dialogue box.
Displays dialogue box.

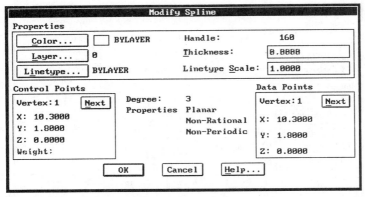

[pick text]   Displays the **Modify Text** dialogue box.
Displays dialogue box.

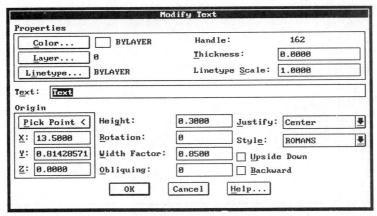

[pick tolerance]   Displays the **Modify Tolerance** dialogue box.
Displays dialogue box.

[pick trace]　　Displays the **Modify Trace** dialogue box.
Displays dialogue box.

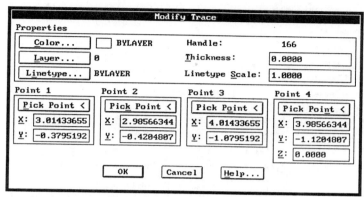

[pick viewport] Displays the **Modify Viewport** dialogue box.
Displays dialogue box.

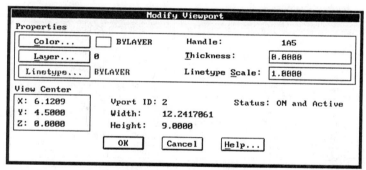

[pick xline] Displays the **Modify Xline** dialogue box.
Displays dialogue box.

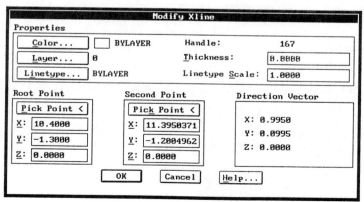

[pick xref]Displays the **Modify External Reference** dialogue box.
Displays dialogue box.

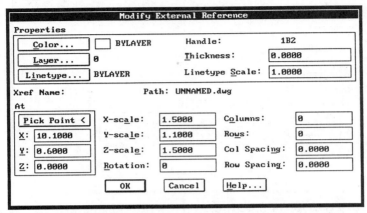

[pick 3D face]   Displays the **Modify 3DFace** dialogue box.
Displays dialogue box.

[pick 3D solid]   Displays the **Modify 3DSolid** dialogue box.
Displays dialogue box.

RELATED AUTOCAD COMMANDS

- **Change**   Changes most properties of objects.
- **ChProp**   Changes some properties of objects.
- **DdChProp** Edits properties via dialogue box.
- **DdEdit**   Edits text via dialogue box.
- **PEdit**   Edits polylines and meshes.

RELATED SYSTEM VARIABLES

- *Many system variables*

'DdOsnap

Sets object snap modes and aperture size via dialogue box (*short for Dynamic Dialogue Object SNAP; an external command in DdOsnap.Lsp*).

Command	Button	Side Menu	Pull-down	Tablet
'ddosnap	[#2]	[* * * *]	[Options] [Running Object Snap]	T12-U 13

Command: **ddosnap**

Displays dialogue box.

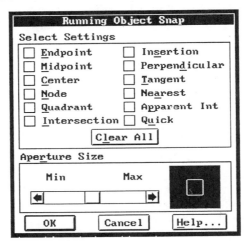

COMMAND OPTIONS
Select settings Selects the object snaps.
Aperture size Changes the size of the aperture.

RELATED AUTOCAD COMMANDS
- **OSnap** Setss object snap modes via the command line.
- **<middle button>**
  Displays list of object snap modes.

RELATED SYSTEM VARIABLES
- **Aperture** Size of the object snap aperture.
- **OsMode** The current object snap modes.

'DdPtype

Sets the type and size of points via a dialogue box (*short for Dynamic Dialogue Point TYPE; an external command in DdPtype.Lsp*).

Command	Alias	Side Menu	Pull-down	Tablet
'ddptype	. . .	[OPTIONS]	[Options]	. . .
		[DISPLAY]	[Display]	
		[DDptype:]	[Point Style]	

Command: **ddptype**

Displays dialogue box.

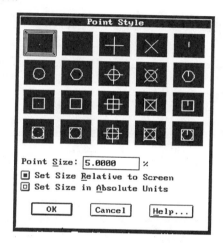

COMMAND OPTIONS
Point size   Sets size in percent or pixels.
Set size Relative to screen
        Sets size in percent.
Set size in Absolute units
        Sets size in pixels.

RELATED AUTOCAD COMMAND
■ **Point**   Draws points.

RELATED SYSTEM VARIABLES
■ **PdMode** Determines the look of a point.
■ **PdSize**   Contains the size of the point.

DdRename

Changes the names of blocks, dimension styles, layers, linetypes, text styles, UCS, views and viewports via a dialogue box (*an external command in DdRename.Lsp*).

Command	Alias	Side Menu	Pull-down	Tablet
ddrename	...	[DATA]	[Data]	...
		[Rename:]	[Rename]	

Command: **ddrename**

Displays dialogue box.

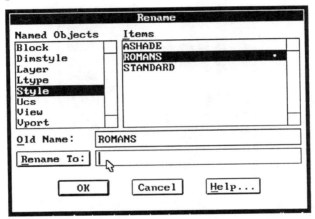

COMMAND OPTIONS

Old name   Specifies the name (or group of names) to change.
Rename to   Indicates the new name.

RELATED AUTOCAD COMMANDS

■ **DdModify**   Changes names (and all other attributes) of objects.
■ **Rename**   Changes the names of objects via the command line.

TIPS

■ You cannot rename layer '0', dimstyle 'Standard', anonymous blocks, groups, and linetype 'Continuous.'

■ To rename a group of similarl names, use * (the wildcard for "all") and ? (the wildcard for a single character).

■ Names can be up to 31 characters in length, including the $, - and _ characters.

'DdRModes

Controls the current settings of snap, snap angle, grid, axes, ortho, blip marks, and isometric modes (*short for Dynamic Dialogue dRawing MODES*).

Command	Alias	Side Menu	Pull-down	Tablet
'ddrmodes	...	[OPTIONS]	[Options]	Y 10
		[DDrmode:]	[Drawing Aids]	

Command: **ddrmodes**

Displays dialogue box.

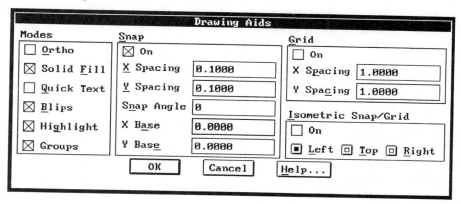

COMMAND OPTIONS

Ortho	Turns orthographic mode on and off.
Solid Fill	Turns solid fill on and off.
Quick Text	Turns quick text on and off.
Blips	Turns blipmarks on and off.
Highlight	Turns object highlighting on and off.
Groups	Turns automatic group selection on and off.
Snap	Turn snap mode on and off:
Snap X spacing	
	Sets x-spacing for snap.
Snap Y spacing	
	Sets y-spacing for snap.
Snap angle	Sets angle for snap and grid.
X Base	Sets snap, grid hatch x-basepoint.
Y base	Sets snap, grid hatch y-basepoint.
Grid	Turns grid marks on and off:
X spacing	Sets grid x-spacing.
Y spacing	Sets grid y-spacing.

Isometric   Turns isometric mode on and off:
  Left   Switches to left isometric plane.
  Top   Switches to top isometric plane.
  Right   Switches to right isometric plane.

RELATED AUTOCAD COMMANDS

- **Blipmode** Toggles visibility of blip markers.
- **Fill** Toggles fill mode.
- **Grid** Sets the grid spacing and toggles visibility.
- **Highlight** Toggles highlight mode.
- **Isoplane** Selects the working isometric plane.
- **Ortho** Toggles orthographic mode.
- **QText** Toggles quick text mode.
- **Snap** Sets the snap spacing and isometric mode.

RELATED SYSTEM VARIABLES

- **BlipMode** Current blip marker visibility:
    0 Off.
    1 On
- **FillMode** Current fill mode:
    0 Off.
    1 On.
- **GridMode** Current grid visibility:
    0 Off.
    1 On.
- **GridUnit** Current grid spacing.
- **Highlight** Current highlight mode:
    0 Off.
    1 On.
- **OrthoMode** Current orthographic mode setting:
    0 Off.
    1 On.
- **QTextMode** Current quick text mode setting:
    0 Off.
    1 On.
- **PickStyle** Controls group selection:
    0 Groups and associative hatches not selected.
    1 Groups selected.
    2 Associative hatches selected.
    3 Both selected.
- **SnapAng** Current snap and grid rotation angle.
- **SnapBase** Base point of snap and grid rotation angle.

- **SnapIsoPair**
  Current isoplane:
  0 Left.
  1 Top.
  2 Right.
- **SnapMode** Current snap mode setting:
  0 Off.
  1 On.
- **SnapStyl** Snap style setting:
  0 Standard.
  1 Isometric.
- **SnapUnit** Current snap spacing.

TIPS

- **DdRModes** is an alternative to the **SetVar** command for checking the status of the above 14 system variables.

- Use the function key **F7** (or control key **[Ctrl]+G**) to turn the grid on and off during a command.

- Use the function key **F8** (or control key **[Ctrl]+O**) to change ortho mode during a command.

- Use the function key **F9** (or control key **[Ctrl]+B**) to change snap mode during a command.

- Use the control key **[Ctrl]+A** to change the status of groups.

'DdSelect

Defines the type of object selection mode and pickbox size via a dialogue box (*an external command in DdSelect.Lsp*).

Command	Alias	Side Menu	Pull-down	Tablet
'ddselect	. . .	[OPTIONS]	[Options]	. . .
		[Dselec:]	[Selection]	

Command: **ddselect**

Displays dialogue box.

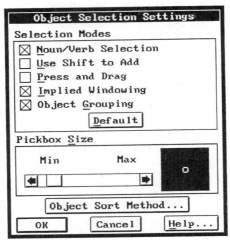

COMMAND OPTIONS

Selection modes

Specify the style of object selection mode:

Noun/verb Select objects first, then enter the command.

Use shift to add

The **[Shift]** key adds objects to selection set.

Press and drag

Create windowed selection set by pressing mouse key and dragging window, rather than specifying two points.

Implied windowing

Automatically creates a windowed selection box.

Default selection mode

Resets modes to turn Noun/verb and Implied windowing on.

Pickbox size Interactively change the size of the pickbox.

110 ■ The Illustrated AutoCAD Quick Reference

Object sort method

Displays a second dialogue box to specify the commands that sort objects by drawing database order:

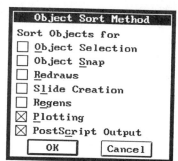

Object Selection

Objects are added to the selection in database order.

Object Snap Object snap modes find objects in database order.
Redraws Redraws objects in database order.
Slide Creation **MSlide** command draws objects in database order.
Regens Regenerates objects in database order.
Plotting **Plot** command processes objects in database order.
PostScript Output

PsOut command processes objects in database order.

RELATED AUTOCAD COMMAND

Select Creates a selection set before executing an editing commands.

RELATED SYSTEM VARIABLES

■ **PickAdd** Determines effect of [Shift] key on creating selection set:
    0   [Shift] key adds to selection set.
    1   [Shift] key removes from selection set (*Default*).
■ **PickAuto** Determines automatic windowing:
    0   Disabled.
    1   Enabled (*Default*).
■ **PickBox** Specifies the size of the pickbox.
■ **PickDrag** Method of creating selection window:
    0   Click at both corners (*Default*).
    1   Click one corner, drag to second corner.
■ **PickFirst** Method of object selection:
    0   Enter command first.
    1   Select objects first (*Default*).

■ **SortEnts** Objects are displayed in database order during:
>   0 Off.
>   1 Object selection.
>   2 Object snap.
>   4 Redraw.
>   8 Slide generation.
>   16 Regeneration.
>   32 Plots.
>   64 PostScript output.

TIPS

■ These commands work with noun-verb selection: **Array, Block, Change, ChProp, Copy, DdChProp, DView, Erase, Explode, Hatch, List, Mirror, Move, Rotate, Scale, Stretch**, and **WBlock**.

■ A larger pickbox makes it easier to select objects, but also makes it easier to inadvertently select objects.

■ Use **Object Sort Method** if the drawing requires that object be processed in the order they appear in the drawing, such as for NC applications.

■ **Plotting** and **PostScript Output** are turned on, by default; setting more sort methods increases processing time.

DdUcs

Creates and controls UCS planes via a dialogue box (*short for Dynamic Dialogue User Coordinate System*).

Command	Alias	Side Menu	Pull-down	Tablet
dducs	. . .	[VIEW]	[View]	J 5
		[DDucs:]	[Named UCS]	

Command: **dducs**

Displays dialogue box.

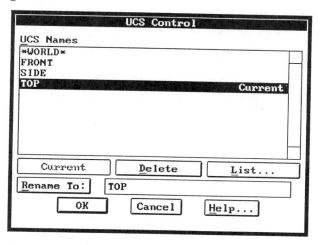

COMMAND OPTIONS

Current	Makes the selected name the current UCS.
Delete	Deletes a named UCS.
Rename to	Renames a UCS.
List	Lists information about the selected UCS in a dialogue box:

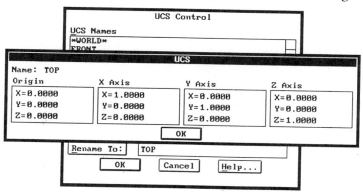

RELATED AUTOCAD COMMANDS
- **DdUcsP**   Selects a predefined UCS from a dialogue box.
- **Ucs**   Creates and save user-defined coordinate systems.

RELATED SYSTEM VARIABLES
- **UcsFollow** New UCS is displayed in plan view.
- **UcsName** Current name of UCS.
- **UcsOrg**   WCS origin of the current UCS.
- **UcsXdir**   X-direction of the current UCS.
- **UcsYdir**   Y-direction of the current UCS.
- **ViewMode** Current clipped viewing mode.
- **WorldUcs** UCS=WCS toggle.
- **WorldView** UCS or WCS for **Dview** and **Vpoint** commands.

DdUcsP

Selects one of seven predefined user coordinate systems (*short for Dynamic Dialogue UCS Preset; an external command in DdUcsP.Lsp*).

Command	Alias	Side Menu	Pull-down	Tablet
dducsp	...	[View]	[View]	K 5
		[DDucsp:]	[Preset UCS]	

Command: **dducsp**

Displays dialogue box.

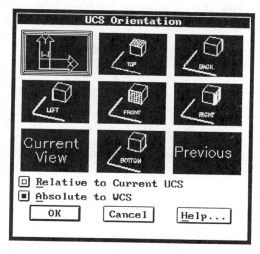

COMMAND OPTIONS
None

RELATED AUTOCAD COMMANDS
- **DdUcs** Creates and selects named UCS.
- **Ucs** Sets the current UCS via the command line.

RELATED SYSTEM VARIABLES
- **UcsFollow** New UCS is displayed in plan view.
- **UcsName** Current name of UCS.
- **UcsOrg** WCS origin of the current UCS.
- **UcsXdir** X-direction of the current UCS.
- **UcsYdir** Y-direction of the current UCS.
- **ViewMode** Current clipped viewing mode.
- **WorldUcs** UCS = WCS toggle.
- **WorldView** UCS or WCS for **DView** and **VPoint** commands.

'DdUnits

Selects the display of units and angles via a dialogue box (*an external command in DdUnits.Lsp*).

Command	Alias	Side Menu	Pull-down	Tablet
'ddunits	...	[DATA]	[Data]	Y 7
		[Units:]	[Units]	

Command: **ddunits**

Displays dialogue box.

COMMAND OPTION

Direction   Displays a second dialogue box to specify the direction of 0 degrees:

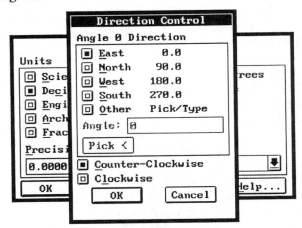

RELATED AUTOCAD COMMANDS

- **MvSetup** Sets up the drawing with border, title, and units.
- **Units**   Sets units and angles via the command line

RELATED SYSTEM VARIABLES

- **AngBase** Direction of zero degrees relative to the current UCS.
- **AngDir** Direction of angle measurement:
  - **0** Clockwise
  - **1** Counterclockwise (*Default*).
- **AUnits** Style of angle units:
  - **0** Decimal degrees (*Default*).
  - **1** Degree-minutes-seconds.
  - **2** Grads.
  - **3** Radians.
  - **4** Surveyor's units.
- **AuPrec** Decimal places of angle units.
- **LUnits** Style of linear units:
  - **0** Scientific
  - **1** Decimal (*Default*).
  - **2** Engineering.
  - **3** Architectural.
  - **4** Fractional.
- **LuPrec** Decimal places of linear units.
- **ModeMacro** Customizes the status line via the Diesel language.
- **UnitMode** Displays input units:
  - **0** As set by **DdUnits** or **Units** command (*Default*).
  - **1** As input by the user.

TIPS

- Distance formats:
  - Decimal: 0.0000 (*Default*)
  - Architectural: 0'-0/64" (*Feet and fractional inches*)
  - Engineering: 0'-0.0000" (*Feet and decimal inches*)
  - Fractional: 0 0/64 (*Unitless fractional*)
  - Scientific: 0.0000E+01

- Angular formats:
  - Decimal: 0.0000 (*Default*)
  - Deg-Min-Sec: 0d0'0.0000" (*Degrees, minutes, decimal seconds*)
  - Radian: 0.0000r
  - Grad: 0.0000g
  - SurveyorUnits: N0d'0.0000"E

DdView

Select named views via dialogue box (*external command in DdView.Lsp*).

Command	Alias	Side Menu	Pull-down	Tablet
ddview	. . .	[VIEW]	[View]	J 2
		[DDview:]	[Named Views]	

Command: **ddview**

Displays dialogue box.

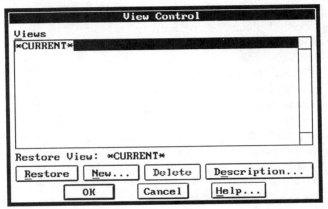

COMMAND OPTIONS

Views   Lists the currently defined views.
Restore   Restores a named view.
Delete   Deletes a named view.
Description Lists the parameters of the selected view.
New   Displays a second dialogue box to define a new view:

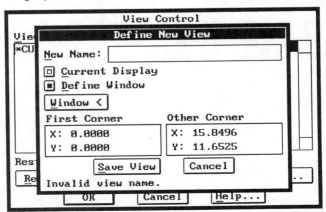

RELATED AUTOCAD COMMAND

■ **View**   Defines and displays named views via the command line.

RELATED SYSTEM VARIABLES

■ **ViewCtr**   Coordinates of the view's centerpoint.
■ **ViewDir**   View direction relative to UCS
■ **ViewMode** View mode:
> 0 Normal view.
> 1 Perspective view.
> 2 Front clipping.
> 4 Back clipping.
> 8 UCS-follow on.
> 16 Front clip not at eye.

■ **ViewSize** View height.
■ **ViewTwist** Twist angle of current view.

DdVpoint

Changes the viewpoint of drawings via a dialogue box (*short for Dynamic Dialogue ViewPOINT; an external command in DdVpoint.Lsp*).

Command	Alias	Side Menu	Pull-down	Tablet
ddvpoint	...	[VIEW]	[View]	J 1
		[Vpoint:]	[3D Viewpoint]	
		[DDvpoint]	[Rotate]	

Command: **ddvpoint**

Displays dialogue box.

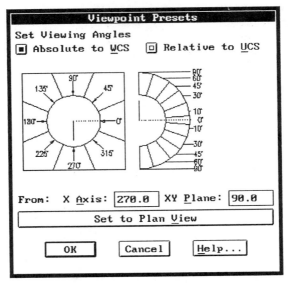

COMMAND OPTIONS

Set viewing angles
        Selects view in:
  Absolute to Wcs WCS.
  Relative to Ucs UCS.
From   Measures viewpoint from:
  X Axis   X-axis.
  Xy Plane   X,y-plane
Set to Plan View
        Changes view to plan view.

RELATED AUTOCAD COMMANDS

- **DView**   Interactively changes the viewpoint.
- **VPoint**   Adjusts the viewpoint from the command line.

RELATED SYSTEM VARIABLES

- **VpointX** X-coordinate of current 3D view.
- **VpointY** Y-coordinate of current 3D view.
- **VpointZ** Z-coordinate of current 3D view.
- **WorldView** Determines whether viewpoint coordinates are in WCS or UCS.

TIP

- After changing the viewpoint, AutoCAD performs an automatic **Zoom** extents.

'Delay

Delays the next script command, in milliseconds.

Command	Alias	Side Menu	Pull-down	Tablet
'delay	. . .	. . .	. . .	. . .

Command: **delay**
Delay time in milliseconds:

COMMAND OPTIONS
None

RELATED AUTOCAD COMMAND
■ **Script**   Initiates a script.

TIPS
■ Use the **Delay** command to slow down the execution of a script file.

■ The maximum delay is 32,767, just over 32 seconds.

Dim

Changes the prompt from 'Command:' to 'Dim:' ; allows access to AutoCAD's old dimensioning commands (*short for DIMensions*).

Command	Alias	Side Menu	Pull-down	Tablet
dim	. . .	. . .	. . .	. . .

```
Command: dim
Dim:
```

COMMAND OPTIONS

Aliases for the dimension commands are shown in uppercase (version or release introduced in brackets):

ALigned	Draws linear dimension aligned with object (ver. 2.0).
ANgular	Draws angular dimension that measures an angle (ver. 2.0).
Baseline	Continues a dimension from a basepoint (ver. 1.2).
CEnter	Draws a centermark on circle and arc centers (ver. 2.0).
COntinue	Continues a dimension from the previous dimension's second extension line (ver. 1.2).
Diameter	Draws diameter dimension on circles, arcs, and polyarcs (ver. 2.0).
Exit	Returns to Command: prompt from Dim: prompt (ver. 1.2).
HOMetext	Returns associative dimension text to its original position (ver. 2.6).
HORizontal	Draws a horizontal dimension (ver. 1.2).
LEAder	Draws a leader (ver. 2.0).
Newtext	Edits text in associative dimensions (ver. 2.6).
OBlique	Changes angle of extension lines in associative dimensions (rel. 11).
ORdinate	Draws x- and y-ordinate dimensions (rel. 11).
OVerride	Overrides the current set of dimension variables (rel. 11).
RAdius	Draws radial dimension on circles, arcs, and polyline arcs (ver. 2.0).
REDraw	Redraws the current viewport (same as 'R; ver. 2.0).
REStore	Restores a dimension to the current dimstyle (rel. 11).
ROtated	Draws a linear dimension at any angle (ver. 2.0).
SAve	Saves the current setting of dimension styles as a dimstyle (rel. 11).
STAtus	Lists the current settings of dimension variables (ver. 2.0).
STYle	Sets a text style for the dimension text (ver. 2.5).
TEdit	Changes location and orientation of text in associative dimensions (rel. 11).
TRotate	Changes the rotation of text in associative dimensions (rel. 11)
Undo	Undeso the last dimension action (ver. 2.0).
UPdate	Updates selected associative dimensions to the current dimvar settings (ver. 2.6).
VAriables	Lists values of variables associated with a dimstyle (not dimvars; rel. 11).
VErtical	Draws vertical linear dimensions (ver. 1.2).

RELATED AUTOCAD COMMANDS

- **Ddim**   Displays dialogue box for setting dimension variables.
- **Style**   Determines the text style of the dimensioning text.
- **Units**   Determines the angular and linear styles of dimensioning text.

RELATED DIM VARIABLES

- **DimAso** Determines whether dimensions are drawn associatively.
- **DimScale** Determines the dimension scale.

RELATED DIM BLOCK

- **Dot**   Dim uses a dot in place of the arrowhead.

TIPS

■ The dimension commands that operate at the Dim: prompt are included for compatibility with Release 12.

■ The old, Release 12-compatible dimension commands do not have the dimension features new to Release 13. For example, the old **Dim:Leader** command draws a leader with discrete objects (one or more connected lines, an arrowhead, and text); the new **Leader** command draws the leader using the new leader object and MText.

■ Only transparent commands and dimension commands work at the Dim: prompt. To use other commands, you must exit the Dim: prompt back to the Command prompt with the **Exit** comand.

■ Most dimensions consists of four basic components: dimension line, extension lines, arrowheads, and text, as shown below.

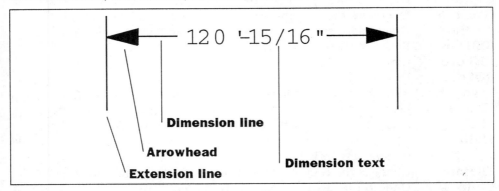

■ All the components of an *associative dimension* are treated as a single object; components of a non-associative dimension are treated as individual objects.

Dim1

Executes a single dimensioning command, then returns to the Command prompt (*short for DIMension once; an undocumented command in Release 13*).

Command	Alias	Side Menu	Pull-down	Tablet
dim1	. . .	. . .	. . .	. . .

```
Command: dim1
Dim:
```

COMMAND OPTIONS

*All "old" dimension commands; see **Dim** command for list.*

RELATED AUTOCAD COMMANDS

- **DDim**   Displays dialogue box for setting dimension variables.
- **Dim**   Switches to "old" dimensioning mode and remains there.

RELATED DIM VARIABLES

- **DimAso** Determines whether dimensions are drawn associatively.
- **DimTxt** Determines the height of text.
- **DimScale** Determines the dimension scale.

RELATED DIM BLOCK

- **Dot**   **Dim** uses a dot in place of the arrow head.

TIP

- Use the **Dim1** command when you need to use just a single "old" dimension command.

DimAligned

Draws linear dimensions aligned with an object (*formerly the Dim:ALigned command*).

Command	Alias	Side Menu	Pull-down	Tablet
dimaligned	dimali	[DRAW DIM]	[Draw]	Y 5
		[Aligned:]	[Dimensioning]	
			[Aligned]	

```
Command: dimaligned
First extension line origin or RETURN to select: [Enter]
Select object to dimension: [pick]
Dimension line location (Text/Angle): T
Dimension text <>: [Enter]
```

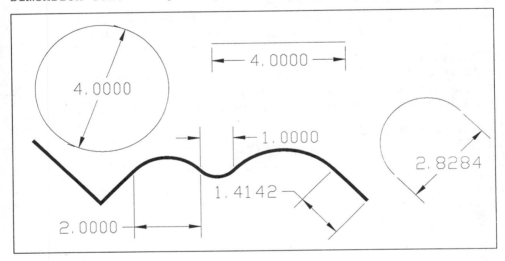

COMMAND OPTIONS

[Enter]	Displays the submenu for selecting objects:
[pick line]	Dimensions line.
[pick arc]	Dimensions arc.
[pick circle]	Dimensions circle.
[pick pline]	Dimensions an individual segment.
Text	Specifies dimension text.
Angle	Indicates dimension angle.

RELATED DIM COMMAND

■ **DimRotated** Draws angular dimension line with perpendicular extension line.

RELATED DIM VARIABLE

■ **DimExo** Dimension line offset distance.

DimAngular

Draws a dimension that measures an angle (*formerly the Dim:ANgular command*).

Command	Alias	Side Menu	Pull-down	Tablet
dimangular	dimang	[DRAW DIM] [Angular:]	[Draw] [Dimensioning] [Angular]	Y 3

```
Command: dimangular
Select arc, circle, line, or RETURN: [pick]
Second angle endpoint: [pick]
Dimension line arc location (Text/Angle): T
Dimension text <>: [Enter]
```

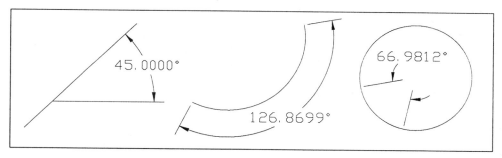

COMMAND OPTIONS

[pick arc]	Measures the angle of the arc.
[pick circle]	Prompts you to pick two points on the circle.
[pick line]	Prompts you to pick two lines.
[Enter]	Prompts you to pick points to make an angle.
Text	Specifies dimension text.
Angle	Indicates dimension angle.

DimBaseline

Draws linear dimension from the previous starting point (*formerly the Dim:Baseline command*).

Command	Alias	Side Menu	Pull-down	Tablet
dimbaseline	dimbase	[DRAW DIM]	[Draw]	X 2
		[Baselin:]	[Dimensioning]	
			[Baseline]	

```
Command: dimbaseline
Second extension line origin or RETURN to select: [pick]
Dimension text:
```

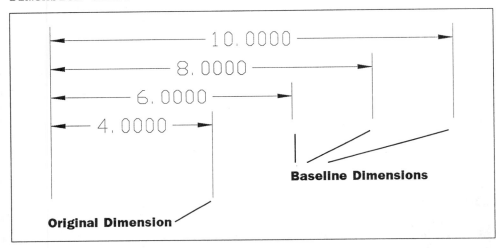

COMMAND OPTION
[Enter]   Prompts to select original dimension (*see figure, above*).

RELATED DIM COMMAND
■ **Continue** Continues linear dimensioning from last extension point.

RELATED DIM VARIABLES
■ **DimDli** Specifies the distance between baseline dimension lines.
■ **DimSe1** Suppresses first extension line.

DimCenter

Draws center lines on arcs and circles (*formerly the **Dim:CEnter** command*).

Command	Alias	Side Menu	Pull-down	Tablet
dimcenter	...	[DRAW DIM]	[Draw]	W 1
		[Center:]	[Dimensioning]	
			[Center Mark]	

Command: **dimcenter**
Select arc or circle: **[pick]**

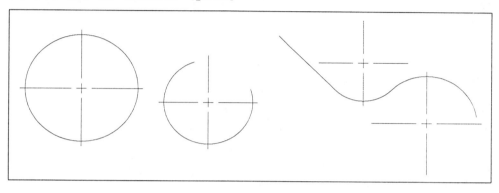

COMMAND OPTIONS
None

RELATED DIM COMMANDS
- **DimAligned** Dimensions arcs and circles.
- **DimDiameter** Dimensions arcs and circles by diameter value.
- **DimRadius** Dimensions arcs and circles by radius value.

RELATED DIM VARIABLE
- **DimCen** Size of the center mark.

DimContinue

Continues a dimension from the second extension line of the previous dimension (*formerly the Dim:COntinue command*).

Command	Alias	Side Menu	Pull-down	Tablet
dimcontinue	dimcont	[DRAW DIM]	[Draw]	X 3
		[Continu:]	[Dimensioning]	
			[Continue]	

```
Command: dimcontinue
Select continued dimension: [pick]
Second extension line origin or RETURN to select:  [pick]
Dimension text:
```

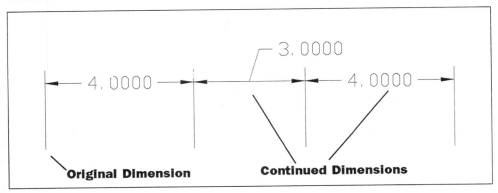

Original Dimension   **Continued Dimensions**

COMMAND OPTION
[Enter]   Prompts you to select the original dimension.

RELATED DIM COMMAND
■ **DimBaseline** Continues dimensioning from first extension point.

RELATED DIM VARIABLES
■ **DimDli**   The distance between continuous dimension lines.
■ **DimSe1**   Suppresses first extension line.

DimDiameter

Draws a diameter dimension on arcs, circles, and polyline arcs (*formerly the **Dim:Diameter** command*).

Command	Alias	Side Menu	Pull-down	Tablet
dimdiameter	dimdia	[DRAW DIM]	[Draw]	Y 2
		[Diametr:]	[Dimensioning]	
			[Radial]	
			[Diameter]	

```
Dim: diameter
Select arc or circle: [pick]
Dimension text: [Enter]
Enter leader length for text: [pick]
```

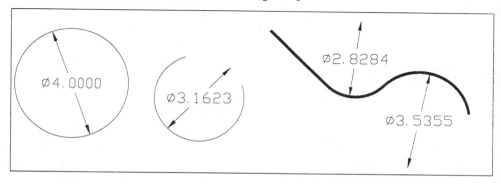

COMMAND OPTIONS
None

RELATED DIM COMMANDS
- **DimCenter** Marks the center point of arcs and circles.
- **DimRadius** Draws the radius dimension of arcs and circles.

RELATED DIM VARIABLE
- **DimCen** Controls the size of the center mark.

DimEdit

Edits dimension text (*formerly the **Dim:HOMetext**, **Dim:Newtext**, **Dim:OBlique**, and **Dim:TRotate** commands*).

Command	Alias	Side Menu	Pull down	Tablet
dimedit	dimed	[MOD DIM] [DimEdit:]	...	W 2

```
Command: dimedit
Dimension Edit (Home/New/Rotate/Oblique) <Home>:
```

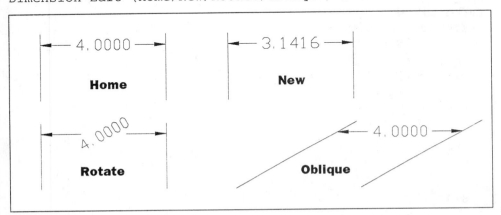

COMMAND OPTIONS

Angle   Rotates the dimension text.
Home   Returns dimension text to original position.
Left   Moves dimension text to the left.
Right   Move dimension text to the right.

RELATED DIM COMMANDS

■ *All*

RELATED DIM VARIABLES

■ *Most*

TIPS

■ When entering dimension text with **DimEdit**'s New option, AutoCAD recognizes the following metacharacters:

[Square brackets]   Alternate units format string.
< Angle brackets >   Prefix and suffix text format string.

■ Use the **Oblique** option to angle dimension lines by 30 degrees, suitable for isometric drawings. Use the **Style** command to oblique text by 30 degrees.

DimLinear

Draws horizontal dimensions *(formerly the **Dim:HORizontal,
Dim:ROtated,** and **Dim:VErtical** commands).*

Command	Alias	Side Menu	Pull-down	Tablet
dimlinear	dimlin	[DRAW DIM] [Linear:]	[Draw] [Dimensioning] [Linear]	X 4-5

```
Command: dimlinear
First extension line origin or RETURN to select: [Enter]
Select line, arc or circle: [pick]
Dimension line location(Text/Angle/Horizontal/Vertical/
Rotated): T
Dimension text <>: [Enter]
```

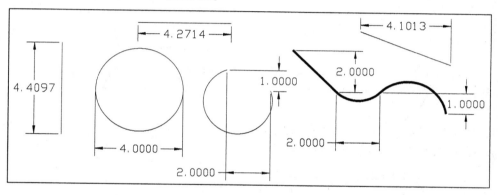

COMMAND OPTIONS

[Enter]   Displays the submenu for dimensioning objects:
  Select line, arc or circle
          Select a line, arc, or circle object to automatically dimension.
Text   Allows you to change the text of the dimension.
Angle   Specifies the angle of the text.
Horizontal Forces dimension to be horizontal.
Vertical   Forces dimension to be vertical.
Rotated   Force dimension to be rotated.

RELATED DIM COMMAND

■ **DimAligned** Draws linear dimensions aligned with objects.

DimOrdinate

Draws an x- or y-ordinate dimension (*formerly the **Dim:ORdinate** command*).

Command	Alias	Side Menu	Pull-down	Tablet
dimordinate	dimord	[DRAW DIM]	[Draw]	Y 4
		[Ordinat:]	[Dimensioning]	
			[Ordinate]	

```
Command: dimordinate
Select Feature: [pick]
Leader endpoint (Xdatum/Ydatum/Text): [pick]
Leader endpoint: [pick]
```

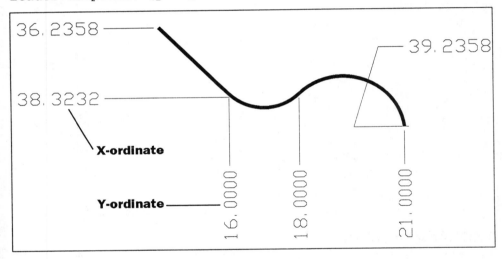

COMMAND OPTIONS

Text   Places text, rather than dimension.
Xdatum   Forces x-ordinate dimension.
Ydatum   Forces y-ordinate dimension.

RELATED DIM COMMANDS

■ **DimLinear** Draws regular horizontal and vertical dimensions.
■ **Leader**   Draws leader dimensions.

DimOverride

Overrides the currently set dimension variables (*formerly the Dim:OVerride command*).

Command	Alias	Side Menu	Pull-down	Tablet
dimoverride	dimover	[MOD DIM]	. . .	. . .
		[Overrid:]		

Command: **dimoverride**
Dimension variable to override:
Current value *xxx* New Value:
Select objects: **[pick]**

COMMAND OPTIONS
None

RELATED DIM COMMAND
- **DimStyle** Creates and modifies dimension styles.

RELATED DIM VARIABLES
- *All dimension variables*

DimRadius

Draws radial dimensions on circles, arcs, and polyline arcs (*formerly the Dim:RAdius command*).

Command	Alias	Side Menu	Pull-down	Tablet
dimradius	dimrad	[DRAW DIM]	[Draw]	Y 1
		[Radius:]	[Dimensioning]	
			[Radial]	
			[Radius]	

```
Command: dimradius
Select arc or circle: [pick]
Dimension line location (Text/Angle): T
Dimension text <>:
```

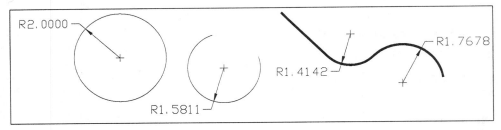

COMMAND OPTIONS

Text   Places text.
Angle   Changes angle of dimension text.

RELATED DIM COMMANDS

- **DimCenter**   Draws center mark on arcs and circles.
- **DimDiameter** Draws diameter dimensions on arcs and circles.

RELATED DIM VARIABLE

- **DimCen**   Determines the size of the center mark.

TIP

- To include the diameter symbol, use the mtext control code \U+2205.

DimStyle

Creates and edits dimstyles (*short for DIMension STYLEs; formerly the Dim:REStore, Dim:SAve, Dim:STAtus, and Dim:VAriables commands*).

Command	Alias	Side Menu	Pull-down	Tablet
dimstyle	dimsty	[MOD DIM]	...	V 2-3
		[DimStyl:]		

Command: **dimstyle**
Dimension style STANDARD
Dimension style overrides: *dimvar list*
Dimension Style Edit (Save/Restore/STatus/Variables/Apply/?):

COMMAND OPTIONS

Save	Saves current dimvar settings as a named dimstyle.
Restore	Sets dimvar settings from a named dimstyle.
STatus	Lists dimvars and current settings, then exits the **DimStyle** command.
Variables	Lists dimvars and their current settings.
Apply	Updates selected dimension objects with current dimstyle settings.
?	Lists names of dimstyles stored in drawing.

INPUT OPTIONS

~dimvar	(Tilde prefix) Lists differences between current and selected dimstyle.
[Enter]	Lists dimvar settings for selected dimension object.

RELATED DIM COMMANDS

- **DDim**   Changes dimvar settings.
- **DimScale** Determines the scale of dimension text.

RELATED DIM VARIABLES

- *All*
- **DimStyle** Name of the current dimstyle.

TIPS

- At the **Dim:** prompt, the **Style** command sets the text style for dimension text and does *not* select a dimension style.

- Dimstyles cannot be stored to disk, except in a drawing.

- Read dimstyles from other drawings with the **XBind Dimstyld** command.

- Dimstyles stored in prototype drawings:
  - AutoCAD default: Acad.Dwg
  - American architectural: Us_Arch.Dwg
  - American mechanical: Us_Mech.Dwg
  - ISO: AcadIso.Dwg
  - JIS J rchitecturJJ: Jis_Arch.Dwg
  - JIS mechJ nicJ J: Jis_Mech.Dwg

DimTEdit

Edits the location and orientation of text in associative dimensions (*formerly the **Dim:TEdit** command*).

Command	Alias	Side Menu	Pull-down	Tablet
dimtedit	dimted	[MOD DIM]	[Modify]	W 3-5
		[DimTEdt:]	[Dimension ing]	
			[AlignText]	

```
Command: dimtedit
Select dimension: [pick]
Enter text location (Left/Right/Home/Angle):
```

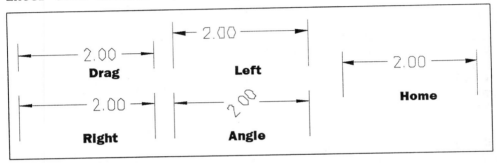

COMMAND OPTIONS

Angle	Rotates the dimension text.
Home	Returns dimension text to original position.
Left	Moves dimension text to the left.
Right	Moves dimension text to the right.
[Drag]	Drag the dimension text and lines to a new location.

RELATED DIM COMMANDS

- **DDim** Changes dimvar values.
- **DimEdit** Edits associative dimension text.
- **DimStyle** Creates and sets associative dimension styles.

RELATED DIM VARIABLES

- **DimSho** Toggles wheter dimension text dynamically updates while dragged.
- **DimTih** Toggles wether dimension text is drawn horizontally or aligned with dimension line.
- **DimToh** Toggles whether dimension text is forces inside dimension lines.

TIPS

■ Use the **DdEdit** command to edit text in non-associative dimensions.

■ An angle of 0 returns dimension text to its default orientation.

■ When entering dimension text with **DimTEdit**'s New option, AutoCAD recognizes the following metacharacters:

[Square brackets]   Alternate units format string.

< Angle brackets >   Prefix and suffix text format string.

■ Use the **Oblique** option to angle dimension lines by 30 degrees, suitable for isometric drawings. Use the **Style** command to oblique text by 30 degrees.

'Dist

Ver. 1.0

Lists the 3D distance and angles between two points (*short for DISTance*).

Command	Alias	Side Menu	Pull-down	Tablet
'dist	. . .	[ASSIST]	[Assist]	R 2
		[INQUIRY]	[Inquiry]	
		[Dist:]	[Distance]	

```
Command: dist
First point: [pick]
Second point: [pick]
```

Example result:
```
Distance=17.38, Angle in X-Y Plane=358, Angle from X-Y Plane=0
Delta X = 16.3000, Delta Y = -7.3000,  Delta Z = 0.0000
```

COMMAND OPTIONS
None

RELATED AUTOCAD COMMANDS
- **Area**   Calculates the area and perimeter of objects.
- **Id**   Lists the 3D coordinates of a point.
- **List**   Lists information about selected objects.

RELATED SYSTEM VARIABLE
- **Distance** Holds last measured distance.

TIP
- Use object snaps to precisely measure between two geometric features; for example, use CENter object snap to measure the distance between the centers of two circles.

Divide

Places points or blocks at an equally-divided distance along lines, arcs, and polylines.

Command	Alias	Side Menu	Pull-down	Tablet
divide	...	[DRAW 2]	[Draw]	W 22
		[Divide:]	[Point]	
			[Divide]	

```
Command: divide
Select object to divide: [pick]
<Number of segments>/Block: B
Block name to insert:
Align block with object? <Y>:
Number of segments: 10
```

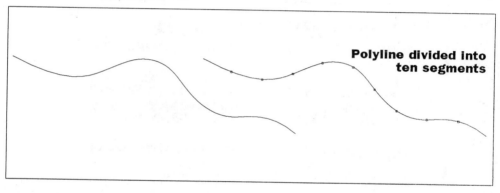

Polyline divided into ten segments

COMMAND OPTION

Block   Specifies the name of the block to insert along the object.

RELATED AUTOCAD COMMANDS

- **Block**   Creates the block to use with the Divide command.
- **Insert**   Places a single block in the drawing.
- **MInsert** Places an array of blocks in the drawing.
- **Measure** Divides an object into measured distances.

RELATED SYSTEM VARIABLES

- **PdMode**   Sets the style of point drawn.
- **PdSize**   Sets the size of the point, in pixels.

TIPS

- Use **PdSize** and **PdMode** to make points visible along object.
- Minimum number of segments is 2; maximum is 32,767.

DlgColor

Redefines the colors of dialogue boxes (*short for DiaLoGue COLOR; an external command in DlgColor.Exp*).

Command	Alias	Side Menu	Pull-down	Tablet
dlgcolor	...	[OPTIONS]	[Options]	...
		[DlgClr:]	[Dialog Box Colors]	

Command: **dlgcolor**

Displays dialogue box.

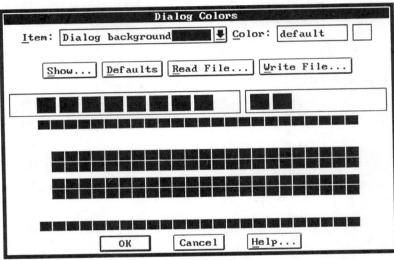

COMMAND OPTIONS

Item	Selects dialogue box feature to change.
Color	Selects new color.
Defaults	Returns colors to default values.
Read file	Read a DCC dialogue color configuration file.
Write file	Saves a color scheme in a DCC dialog color configuration file.

Show   Shows dummy dialog box with selected color scheme.

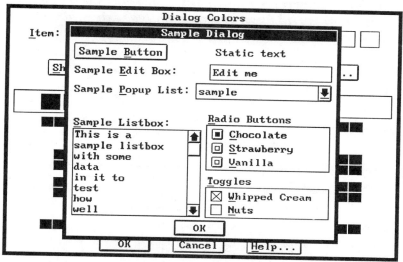

RELATED AUTOCAD COMMANDS
- **Config**   Configures the display with different colors.
- **DlxConfig** Configures display-list driver.

RELATED FILE
- ***.DCC**   Dialogue color configuration files.

TIPS
- In addition to the default color scheme, AutoCAD comes with two pre-defined color schemes, found in subdirectory \Acad13\Dos\Support:
  - **Bright**   A garish color scheme.
  - **DarkGrey** Stately shades of grey.

- Either **DlgClr**, **Config**, or **DlxConfig** can be used to specify the color of dialogue box element.

'DlxHelp

Displays the help screen for AutoCAD's display-list driver (*short for Display List eXpress HELP; an undocumented, external command in DL153100.Res*).

Command	Alias	Side Menu	Pull-down	Tablet
'dlxhelp	dlx	...	...	...

Command: **dlxhelp**

Displays dialogue box.

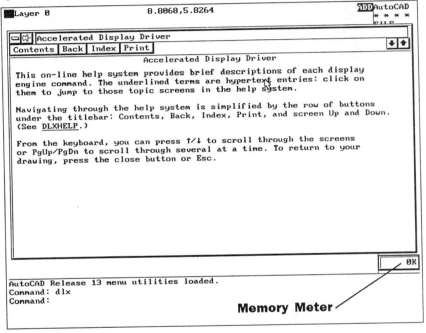

COMMAND OPTIONS

'AV Turns on the Aerial View window:

  AV=D Turns on Aerial View in default location.

  AV=T Temporarily turns on Aerial View (default).

  AV=P Turns on Aerial View until turned off.

  AV=0 Turns off Aerial View.

  AV=+ Enables real-time pan and zoom (default).

  AV=- Disables real-time pan and zoom.

'DlxCol Save menu color scheme:

  DlxCol=S Saves to DL153100.Cfg configuration file.

  DlxCol=W Writes to an AutoCAD-format script file.

'DlxConfig Configures the display-list driver (*alias: DlxCfg*).
'DlxDl Toggles display-list processing and true erase:
    DlxDl=Y Turns on display-list processing (*default*).
    DlxDl=N Turns off display-list processing.
    DlxDl=Y,Y Also turns on true erase.
    DlxDl=N,N Also turns off true erase.
'DlxHelp Display the help screens for Dlx (*alias: Dlx*).
'DlxMeter Toggles display of the memory meter (*alias: DlxMtr*).
    DlxMeter=Y Turns on meter (*default*).
    DlxMeter=N Turns off meter.
    DlxMeter=D Move meter to its default position.
'DlxPalette Changes color palette (*alias: DlxPal*).
'DlxScr Controls the screen capture feature
'DlxStatus Displays the driver name, version, serial number, and memory use (*alias: 'DlxStat*).
    DlxStatus= Displays status on command line.
    DlxStatus=V Displays draw-code version date.
'DlxText Displays AutoCAD's text screen in a window:
    DlxText=G Text window displays in graphics mode.
    DlxText=T Text window displays in text mode.
    DlxText=F Next flipscreen occurs in text mode.
    DlxText=D Moves text window to default position.
'GC Cleans up the display list for current viewport:
    GC Requests a new display list from AutoCAD.
    GC=Y Enables true erase.
    GC=N Disables true erase.
'GCAll Cleans up display list for all viewports; alias: GCA.
    GCA Requests a new display list from AutoCAD.
    GCA=Y Enables true erase.
    GCA=N Disables true erase.
'RD Alias for AutoCAD's **Redraw** command.
'RDA Alias for AutoCAD's **RedrawAll** command.
RegenMax Displays the **Zoom VMax** view; maximum zoom out (*alias: RGX*).
RegenMin Opposite to the **RegenMax** command: maximum zoom in.
'ZV Alias for the Release 11 version of the **Zoom VMax** command.

RELATED AUTOCAD COMMANDS
- **Config** Selects display driver.
- **Pan** AutoCAD's built-in panning command.
- **Redraw** Redraws the screen to clean up artifacts.
- **Regen** Regenerates the drawing from the database.
- **Zoom** AutoCAD's built-in zooming command.

RELATED DOS ENVIRONMENT VARIABLE

- **VibScr**   Toggles the screen grab feature:
  - **VibScr=On**   Default.
  - **VibScr=Off**   Turns off feature.

RELATED FILES

- **RcpDlx.Exp**   AutoCAD Release 13 for DOS's display-list driver.
- **DL153100.Cfg**   Display-list driver's configuration file.
- **DL153100.Res**   Display-list driver's help and message file.
- **Acad.Cfg**   AutoCAD's configuration file.
- **Render.Cfg**   **Render** command's configuration file.

TIPS

- Use the **ZV** command to perform the **Zoom Extents** command without a regeneration.

- Most **Dlx**-related commands are transparent commands; they can be used during another AutoCAD command.

- The benefit to the display-list driver is a significant speed-up in redraws, zooms, and pans; the drawback is that it uses a significant amount of memory to store the display list. To reduce the memory requirement:
  - Reduce the bit-size from 32 bits to 16 bits with the **DlxConfig** command; or
  - Turn off display-list processing with the **DlxDl=N** command.

- "True erase" automatically removes erased objects from the display list; true erase should be left on, unless you are working with CAD Overlay. In that case, use the **GCA=N** command.

- Press the **[Prt Scr]** key to save the graphics and the windowed text screen to a BMP (Windows bitmap) format file with the default name \Vibscrn.Bmp. Because the file is overwritten with the next screen grab, use the **DlxScr=***filename* command to change the filename.

- The **DlxText** command supports the Ansi.Sys driver.

- See the **AV** command for more details on using the Aerial View.

- **DlxHelp** is not documented by Autodesk. To print out a copy of the documentation, use the **DlxHelp=W,Dlxcmnds.Txt** command.

Donut *or* Doughnut

Draws solid circles with a pair of wide polyline arcs.

Command	Alias	Side Menu	Pull-down	Tablet
donut	. . .	[DRAW 1]	[Draw]	O 9
		[Dnut:]	[Circle]	
			[Donut]	
doughnut				

```
Command: donut
Inside diameter <0.5000>:
Outside diameter <1.0000>:
Center of doughnut: [pick]
Center of doughnut: [Enter]
```

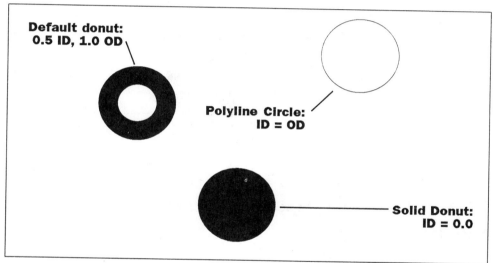

Default donut:
0.5 ID, 1.0 OD

Polyline Circle:
ID = OD

Solid Donut:
ID = 0.0

COMMAND OPTION
[Enter]   Exits the **Donut** command.

RELATED AUTOCAD COMMAND
■ Circle   Draws a circle.

RELATED SYSTEM VARIABLES
■ **DonutId** The current donut internal diameter.
■ **DonutOd** The current donut outside diameter.

TIP
■ Command automatically repeats itself until cancelled.

'Dragmode

Controls the display of an image during dragging operations.

Command	Alias	Side Menu	Pull-down	Tablet
dragmode	...	...	...	...

```
Command: dragmode
ON/OFF/Auto <Auto>:
```

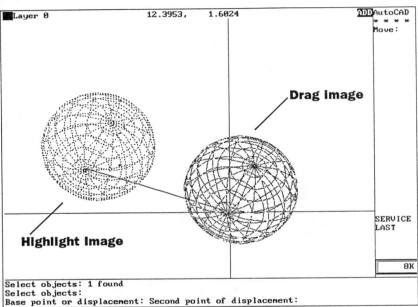

```
Select objects: 1 found
Select objects:
Base point or displacement: Second point of displacement:
```

COMMAND OPTIONS

ON   Enables dragging display only with the Drag option.

OFF   Turns off all dragging displays.

Auto   Have AutoCAD determine when to display dragging.

COMMAND MODIFIER

Drag   Displays drag image when Dragmode=On.

RELATED SYSTEM VARIABLES

■ **Dragmode** Current dragmode setting:
   - **0** No drag image.
   - **1** On if required.
   - **2** Automatic.
■ **Drag1**   Drag regeneration rate (default=10).
■ **Drag2**   Drag redraw rate (default=25).

DText

Enters text in the drawing in a visual mode (*short for Dynamic TEXT*).

Command	Alias	Side Menu	Pull-down	Tablet
dtext	...	[DRAW]	[Draw]	T1 - U3
		[DText:]	[Text]	
			[Dynamic Text]	

```
Command: dtext
Justify/Style/<Start point>: J
Align/Fit/Center/Middle/Right/TL/TC/TR/ML/MC/MR/BL/BC/BR:
Height:
Rotation Angle:
Text:
```

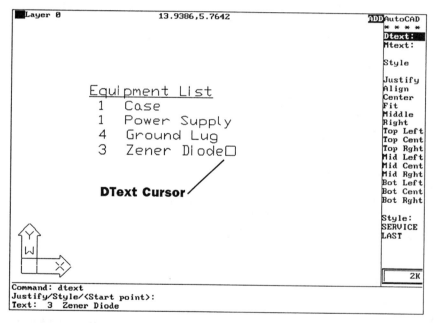

COMMAND OPTIONS

Justify	Displays the justification submenu:
Align	Aligns the text between two points with adjusted text height.
Fit	Fits the text between two points with fixed text height.
Center	Centers the text along the baseline.
Middle	Centers the text horizontally and vertically.
Right	Right-justifies the text.
TL	Top-left justification.
TC	Top-center justification.

TR	Top-right justification.
ML	Middle-left justification.
MC	Middle-center justification.
MR	Middle-right justification.
BL	Bottom-left justification.
BC	Bottom-center justification.
BR	Bottom-right justification.

<Start point> Left-justify the text.
Style Displays the style submenu:
  Style name Indicates a different style name.
  ? Lists the currently loaded styles.
[Enter] Exits the **DText** command.

COMMAND MODIFIERS

%%c	Draws diameter symbol: Ø.
%%d	Draws degree symbol: °.
%%o	Starts and stops overlining.
%%p	Draw the plus-minus symbol: ±.
%%u	Starts and stops underlining.
%%%	Draws the percent symbol: %.

RELATED AUTOCAD COMMANDS

- **DdEdit** Edits the text.
- **Change** Change the text height, rotation, style, and content.
- **Style** Create new text styles.
- **Text** Add new text to the drawing.
- **MText** Places paragraph text in drawings.

RELATED SYSTEM VARIABLES

- **TextSize** The current height of text.
- **TextStyle** The current style.
- **ShpName** The default shape name

TIPS

- Use the **DText** command to easily place text in many locations on the drawing.

- Be careful: the spacing between lines of text does not necessarily match the current snap spacing.

- The popdown menus are not available during the **DText** command.

- Transparent commands do not work during the **DText** command.

- You can enter any justification mode at the '<Start point>:' prompt.

- The command automatically repeats until cancelled with **[Enter]**.

DView

Dynamically zooms and pans 3D drawings, and turns on perspective mode (*short for Dynamic VIEW*).

Command	Alias	Side Menu	Pull-down	Tablet
dview	dv	[VIEW]	[View]	J3 - K3
		[Dview:]	[3D Dynamic View]	

```
Command: dview
Select objects: ]Enter]
CAmera/TArget/Distance/POints/PAn/Zoom/TWist/CLip/Hide/Off/
    Undo/<eXit>:
```

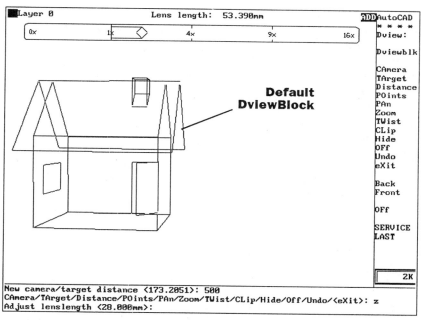

Default DviewBlock

COMMAND OPTIONS

CAmera	Indicates the camera angle relative to the target:
Toggle	Switches between input angles.
TArget	Indicates the target angle relative to the camera.
Distance	Indicates camera-to-target distance; turns on perspective mode.
POints	Indicates both the camera and target points.
PAn	Dynamically pans the view.
Zoom	Dynamically zooms the view.
TWist	Rotates the camera.
CLip	Displays the submenu for view clipping:
Back	Displays the submenu for back clipping:
ON	Turns on the back clipping plane.

OFF	Turns off the back clipping plane.
\<Distance from target\>	
	Indicates the location of the back clipping plane.
Front	Displays the submenu for front clipping:
Eye	Positions the front clipping plane at the camera.
\<Distance from target\>	
	Indicates the location of the front clipping plane.
\<Off\>	Turns off view clipping.
Hide	Performs hidden-line removal.
Off	Turns off the perspective view.
Undo	Undoes the most recent **DView** action.
\<eXit\>	Exit the **DView** command.

RELATED AUTOCAD COMMANDS

- **Hide**   Removes hidden-lines from a non-persepctive view.
- **Pan**   Pans a non-perspective view.
- **VPoint**   Selects an non-perspective viewpoint of a 3D drawing.
- **Zoom**   Zoom a non-perspective view.

RELATED SYSTEM VARIABLES

- **BackZ**   Back clipping plane offset.
- **FrontZ**   Front clipping plane offset.
- **LensLength** Perspective view lens length, in millimeters.
- **Target**   UCS 3D coordinates of target point.
- **ViewCtr**   2D coordinates of current view center.
- **ViewDir**   WCS 3D coordinates of camera offset from target.
- **ViewMode** Perspective and clipping settings.
- **ViewSize** Height of view.
- **ViewTwist** Rotation angle of current view.

RELATED SYSTEM BLOCK

- **DViewBlock** Alternate viewing object during **DView** command.

TIPS

- The view direction is from 'camera' to 'target'.

- To help set the dview of a complex object, either select a part of it or press **[Enter]** at the 'Select objects:' prompt to display the house.

- You replace the house block with a symbol of your own design by redefining the DVIewBlock block.

- To view a 3D drawing in one-point perspective, use the **DView Zoom** command.

- The pull-down menus, transparent zoom and pan are not available during the **DView** command.

- Once the view is in perspective mode, you cannot use the **Sketch, Zoom,** or **Pan** commands.

Dxbin

Imports a DXB-format file into the current drawing (*short for Drawing Exchange Binary INput*).

Command	Alias	Side Menu	Pull-down	Tablet
dxbin	. . .	[FILE]	[File]	. . .
		[IMPORT]	[Import]	
		[DXBin:]	[DXB]	

```
Command: dxbin
DXB file:
```

COMMAND OPTIONS
None

RELATED AUTOCAD COMMANDS
- **DxfIn**   Reads DXF-format files.
- **Plot**   Writes DXB-format files when configured for ADI plotter.

RELATED SYSTEM VARIABLES
- *None*

TIP
- Configure AutoCAD with the ADI plotter driver to produce a DXB file.

Dxfin

Reads a DXF-format file into a drawing (*short for Drawing inter-change Format INput*).

Command	Alias	Side Menu	Pull-down	Tablet
dxfin	. . .	[FILE]	[File]	. . .
		[IMPORT]	[Import]	
		[DXFin:]	[DXF]	

Command: **dxfin**
File name:

COMMAND OPTIONS
None

RELATED AUTOCAD COMMANDS
- **DxbIn** Reads a DXB-format file.
- **DxfOut** Writes a DXF-format file.

RELATED SYSTEM VARIABLES
- *None*

TIP
- The **IGESin** command was removed from Release 13.

DxfOut

Writes a DXF-format file of part or all of the current drawing (*short for Drawing interchange Format OUTput*).

Command	Alias	Side Menu	Pull-down	Tablet
dxfout	. . .	[FILE]	[File]	. . .
		[EXPORT]	[Export]	
		[DXFout:]	[DXF]	

```
Command: dxfout
File name:
Enter decimal places of accuracy (0 to 16)/Objects/Binary
   <6>: e
Select objects: [pick]
Select objects: [Enter]
Enter decimal places of accuracy (0 to 16)/Binary <6>:
```

COMMAND OPTIONS

0 — 16	For ASCII binary files, indicates decimal places of accuracy.
Objects	Selects objects to export in DXF format.
Binary	Creates binary DXF file.

RELATED AUTOCAD COMMANDS

■ **DxfIn**   Reads a DXF-format file.
■ **Save**   Writes the drawing in DWG format.

RELATED SYSTEM VARIABLES

■ *None*

TIPS

■ Use the ASCII DXF format to exchange drawings with other CAD and graphics programs.

■ A binary DXF file is much smaller and is created much faster than an ASCII binary file; however, few applications read a binary DXF file.

■ There is no facility to create Release 12-compatible DXF files, as there is for DWG files (via the **SaveAsR12** command).

■ The **IGESout** command was removed from Release 13.

Edge

Toggles the visibility of 3D faces (*an external command in Edge.Lsp*).

Command	Alias	Side Menu	Pull-down	Tablet
edge	...	...	[Draw] [Surfaces] [Edge]	...

```
Command: edge
Display/<Select edge>: D
Select/<All>: S
Select objects: [pick]
Display/<Select edge>: [Enter]
```

COMMAND OPTIONS

<Select edge> Selected edge is no longer visible.
Display   Highlights invisible edges.
Select   Regenerates selected hidden edges.
All   Selects all hidden edges and regenerates them.

RELATED AUTOCAD COMMAND
■ **3dFace**   Creates 3D faces.

RELATED SYSTEM VARIABLE
■ **SplFrame** Toggles visibility of 3D face edges.

TIPS
■ Make edges invisible to make 3D objects look nicer.

■ The **Edge** command repeats itself until you press **[Enter]** at the 'Display/<Select Edge>:' prompt.

EdgeSurf

Draws a 3D polygon mesh as a Coons surface patch between four boundaries (*short for EDGE-defined SURFace*).

Command	Alias	Side Menu	Pull-down	Tablet
edgesurf	...	[DRAW 2]	[Draw]	O 8
		[SURFACES]	[Surfaces]	
		[Edgsurf:]	[Edge Surface]	

```
Command: edgesurf
Select edge 1: [pick]
Select edge 2: [pick]
Select edge 3: [pick]
Select edge 4: [pick]
```

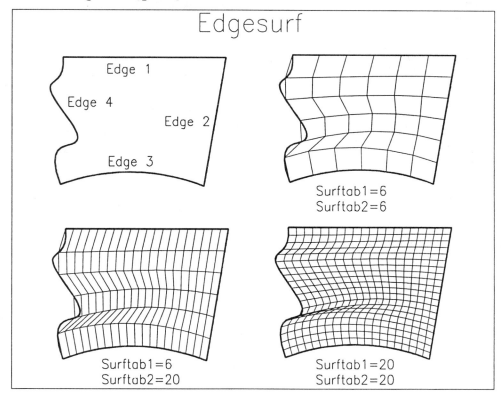

COMMAND OPTIONS
None

RELATED AUTOCAD COMMANDS

- **3Dmesh** Creates a 3D mesh by specifying every vertex.
- **3Dface** Creates a 3D mesh of irregular vertices.
- **Pedit** Edits the mesh created by Edgesurf.
- **Tabsurf** Creates a tabulated 3D surface.
- **Rulesurf** Creates a ruled 3D surface.
- **Revsurf** Creates a 3D surface of revolution.

RELATED SYSTEM VARIABLES

- **Surftab1** The current M density of meshing.
- **Surftab2** The current N density of meshing.

TIPS

- The Coons surface created by the **EdgeSurf** command is an interpolated bi-cubic surface.

- The four boundary edges can be made from lines, arcs, and open 2D and 3D polylines; the edges must meet at their endpoints.

- The maximum mesh density is 32,767.

'Elev

Sets elevation and thickness of extruded 3D objects (*short for ELEVation*).

Command	Alias	Side Menu	Pull-down	Tablet
'elev	...	[SETTINGS]	...	...
		[ELEV:]		

```
Command: elev
New current elevation <0.0000>:
New current thickness <0.0000>:
```

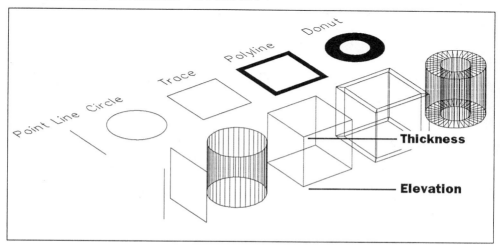

COMMAND OPTIONS

None

RELATED AUTOCAD COMMANDS

- **Change** Changes the thickness and elevation of objects.
- **Chprop** Changes the thickness of objects.
- **Move** Moves objects, including in the z-direction.

RELATED SYSTEM VARIABLES

- **Elevation** Stores the current elevation setting.
- **Thickness** Stores the current thickness setting.

TIPS

■ The current value of elevation is used whenever a z-coordinate is not supplied.

■ The thickness is measured up from the current elevation in the positive z-direction.

Ellipse

Draws an ellipse by four different methods, elliptical arcs, and isometric circles.

Command	Alias	Side Menu	Pull-down	Tablet
ellipse	...	[DRAW 1]	[Draw]	N 10
		[Ellipse:]	[Ellipse]	

```
Command: ellipse
Arc/Center/Isocircle/<Axis endpoint 1>: [pick]
Axis endpoint 2: [pick]
<Other axis distance>/Rotation: [pick]
```

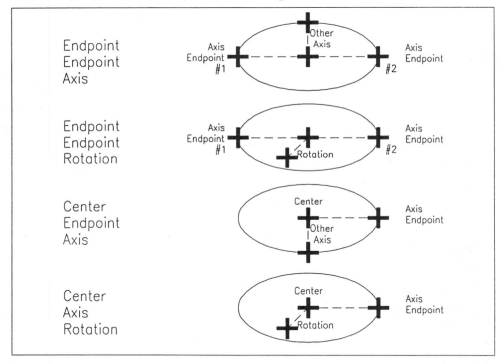

COMMAND OPTIONS

Axis endpoint 1
> Indicates the first endpoint of the major axis.

Axis endpoint 2
> Indicates the second endpoint of the major axis.

Center   Indicatse the center point of the ellipse.

Arc   Draws an elliptical arc.

Rotation   Selects a rotation angle around the major axis.

Isocircle   Draws isometric circles; appears only when **Snap** is set to isometric mode.

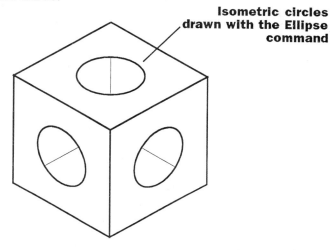

Isometric circles drawn with the Ellipse command

RELATED AUTOCAD COMMANDS

- **Isoplane** Sets the current isometric plane.
- **Pedit** Edits ellipses and other polyline objects.
- **Snap** Controls the setting of isometric mode.

RELATED SYSTEM VARIABLES

- **PEllipse** Ellipse-creation mode:
  0 Draw true ellipse (*Default*).
  1 Draw ellipse with a polyline (*R12 compatible*).
- **SnapIsoPair** Current isometric plane:
  0 Left (*Default*).
  1 Top.
  2 Right.
- **Snapstyl** Regular or isometric drawing mode:
  0 Standard (*Default*).
  1 Isometric.

TIPS

- Previous to Release 13, the **Ellipse** command constructed the ellipse as a series of short polyline arcs; thus, ellipses translated by the **SaveAsR12** command are not mathematically exact.

- When **PEllipse** = 1, the Arc option is not available.

- Use ellipses to draw circles in isometric mode. When **Snap** is set to isometric mode, the **Ellipse** command's Isocircle option projects a circle into the working isometric drawing plane. Use **[Ctrl]+E** to toggle isoplanes.

End

Saves the drawing and exits AutoCAD to the operating system.

Command	Alias	Side Menu	Pull-down	Tablet
end	. . .	. . .	. . .	. . .

Command: **end**

COMMAND OPTIONS
None

RELATED AUTOCAD COMMANDS
■ **Saveas**   Saves read-only drawings by another name.
■ **Quit**   Leaves AutoCAD without saving the drawing.

RELATED SYSTEM VARIABLES
■ **Dbmod**   Determines whether the drawing has been modified since loaded.

TIPS
■ AutoCAD renames the drawing file to .BAK before saving the contents of the drawing.

■ The **End** command does not work with drawings set to read-only; use the **SaveAs** command instead.

Erase

Erases objects from the drawing.

Command	Alias	Side Menu	Pull-down	Tablet
erase	e	[MODIFY]	[Modify]	V 7-8
		[Erase:]	[Erase]	

```
Command: erase
Select objects: [pick]
```

COMMAND OPTIONS
None

RELATED AUTOCAD COMMANDS
- **Break**   Removes a portion of a line, circle, arc, or polyline.
- **Change** Changes the length of a line.
- **Oops**   Returns the most-recently erased objects to the drawing.
- **Trim**   Reduces the length of a line, polyline, or arc.
- **Undo**   Returns the erased objects to the drawing.

TIPS
- The **Erase L** command combination erases the last-drawn item visible on the screen.

- The **Oops** command brings back the most-recently erased objects; use the **U** command to bring back other erased objects.

Explode

Explodes a polyline, block, associative dimension, hatch, multiline, 3D
solid, region, body, or polyface mesh into its constituent objects.

Command	Alias	Side Menu	Pull-down	Tablet
explode	...	[MODIFY]	[Modify]	...
		[Explode:]	[Explode]	

Command: **explode**
Select objects: **[pick]**

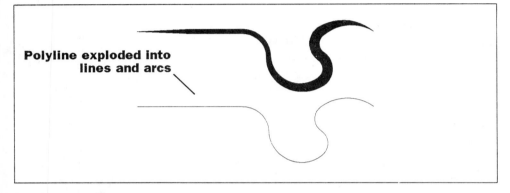

**Polyline exploded into
lines and arcs**

COMMAND OPTIONS
None

RELATED AUTOCAD COMMANDS
- **Block**   Recreates a block after an explode.
- **PEdit**   Converts a line into a polyline.
- **Region**   Converts 2D objects into a region.
- **Undo**   Reverses the effects of explode.
- **Xplode**   Allows greater control over the exploding process.

RELATED SYSTEM VARIABLE
- **ExplMode** Toggles whether non-uniformly scaled blocks can be exploded:
  - **0** Does not explode (*R12-compatible*)
  - **1** Does explode (*Default*)

TIPS

- The **Explode** command has the following effect:
  - Blocks reduced to their constituent parts.
  - Associative dimensions become lines, solids, and text.
  - 2D polylinesbecome lines and arcs; width and tangency information is lost.
  - 3D polylines reduced to lines.
  - Multilines reduced to lines.
  - Polygon meshes reduced to 3D faces.
  - Polyface meshes reduced to 3D faces, lines, and points.
  - 3D solids reduced to regions and bodies.
  - Regions reduced to lines, arcs, ellipses, and splines.
  - Bodies reduced to single bodies, regions, and curves.

- With Release 13, you can explode blocks inserted with unequal scale factors, mirrored blocks, and blocks created by the **MInsert** command

- You cannot explode xrefs and dependent blocks.

- The parts making up exploded blocks and associative dimensions may change color and linetypes.

- Resulting objects become the previous selection set.

- A circle within a non-uniformly scaled block explodes into an ellipse; an arc into an elliptical arc.

Extend

Extends the length of a line, open polyline, or arc to a boundary.

Command	Alias	Side Menu	Pull-down	Tablet
extend	...	[MODIFY]	[Modify]	X 16
		[Extend:]	[Extend]	

```
Command: extend
Select boundary edges:(Projmode=UCS,Edgemode=No extend)
Select objects: [pick]
Select objects: [Enter]
<Select object to extend>/Project/Edge/Undo: P
None/Ucs/View:
```

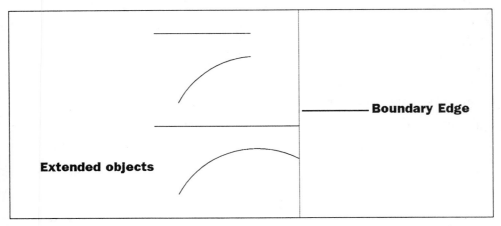

Boundary Edge

Extended objects

COMMAND OPTIONS

Project   Specifies projection mode (*new to Release 13*):
  None   Extends objects to boundary (*Release 12 compatible*).
  Ucs   Boundary is x,y-plane of current UCS.
  View   Boundary is current view plane.
Edge   Toggles actual or implied edge (*new to Release 13*):
  Extend   Extends to implied boundary.
  No extend   Extends only to actual boundaries (*Release 12 compatible*).
Undo   Undoes the most recent extend operation.

RELATED AUTOCAD COMMANDS

- **Change**   Changes the length of lines.
- **Lengthen** Changes the length of open objects.
- **Stretch**   Stretches objects wider or narrower.
- **Trim**   Reduces the length of lines, polylines ,and arcs.

RELATED SYSTEM VARIABLES

- **EdgeMode** Toggles boundary mode for **Extend** and **Trim** commands:
  - **0** Use actual edges (*Release 12 compatible; default*).
  - **1** Use implied edge.
- **ProjMode** Toggles projection mode for **Extend** and **Trim** commands:
  - **0** None (*Release 12 compatible*).
  - **1** Current UCS (*Default*).
  - **2** Current view plane.

TIPS

- The following objects can be used as edges:
  - Lines, rays, xlines, and multilines.
  - Arcs, circles, ellipses, and elliptical arcs.
  - 2D and 3D polylines, and splines.
  - Text and regions.

- Pick the object a second time to extend it to a second boundary line.

- Circles and other closed objects are valid edges: object is extended in direction nearest to the pick point.

- Extending a variable-width polyline widens it proportionately; extending a splined polyline adds a vertex.

Extrude

Creates a 3D solid by extruding a 2D object with optional tapered sides *(formerly the SolExt command; an external command in Acis.Dll).*

Command	Alias	Side Menu	Pull-down	Tablet
extrude	...	[DRAW 2]	[Draw]	K 8
		[SOLIDS]	[Solids]	
		[Extrude:]	[Extrude]	

```
Command: extrude
Select objects: [pick]
Path/<Height of extrusion>:
Extrusion taper angle <0>:
```

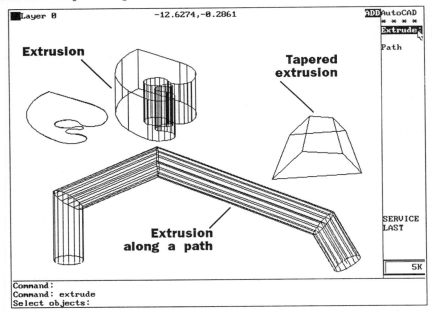

COMMAND OPTIONS

Path   Selects an open object for the extusion path.
Height   Specifies the extrusion height.
Extrusion taper angle
              Specifies the taper angle, -90 to +90 degrees.

RELATED AUTOCAD COMMAND

■ **Revolve**   Creates a 3D solid by revolving a 2D object.

TIPS

- You can extrude the following objects:
  - Circles, ellipses, and donuts.
  - Closed polylines, polygons, closed splines, and regions.

- You *cannot* extrude the following objects:
  - Objects within a block; the the **Explode** command first.
  - Polylines with less than 3 vertices, or more than 500 vertices.
  - Crossing and self-intersecting polylines.

- The taper angle:
  - Must between 0 (*Default*) and 90 degrees.
  - Positive angle tapers in from base; negative angle taper out.

- The **Extrude** command does not work when:
  - The taper angles less than -90 degrees, or more than +90 degrees.
  - If the combination of angle and height makes the object's extrusion walls intersect.

- You can use the following objects as extrusion paths:
  - Lines and polylines.
  - Arcs and elliptical arcs.
  - Circles and ellipses.

- Contrary to Autodesk's documentation,the **Extrude** command *cannot*:
  - Use a spline as a path.
  - Use a path in the plane of the profile.

'Files

Displays the **File Utilities** dialogue box to list, copy, rename, delete, and unlock files.

Command	Alias	Side Menu	Pull-down	Tablet
'files	...	[FILE]	[File]	V 24
		[MANAGE}	[Management]	
		[Files:]	[Utilities]	

Command: **files**

Displays dialogue box.

COMMAND OPTIONS

List files   Lists files sorted by user-defined extension.
Copy file   Copies a file to another location.
Rename file Renames a file with a different name.
Delete file   Deletes files.
Unlock file Erases lock files created by AutoCAD; sample dialogue box:

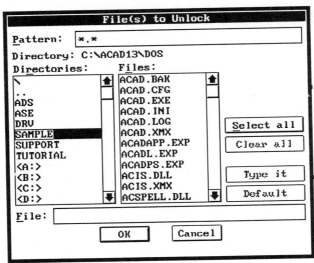

Exit   Returns to Command prompt.

RELATED AUTOCAD COMMAND

■ Shell   Returns temporarily to the operating system to perform file functions.

RELATED SYSTEM VARIABLE

■ FileDia   Toggles display of dialogue box:
   0 Functions display on text screen:
      0. Exit File Utility menu
      1. List drawing files.
      2. List user specified files
      3. Delete files
      4. Rename files
      5. Copy files
      6. Unlock files

   1 Display dialogue box (*Default*).

TIPS

■ Do not delete AutoCAD's temporary files while AutoCAD is running:
   ■ *.AC$ and *.$A   Temporary files.
   ■ *.SWR   Swap files.
   ■ *.??K   Lock files.

■ When AutoCAD crashes, the files listed above are often left behind and should be erased to recover disk space. Use the DOS **Erase** command after exiting AutoCAD.

■ Use the **Config** command to turn off file locking when your AutoCAD is not networked.

'Fill

Toggles wide objects (traces, multilines, solids, or polylines) to be displayed and plotted as solid-filled or as outlines.

Command	Alias	Side Menu	Pull-down	Tablet
'fill	. . .	[OPTIONS]	[Options]	. . .
		[DISPLAY]	[Display]	
		[Fill:]	[Solid Fill]	

```
Command: fill
ON/OFF <On>:
```

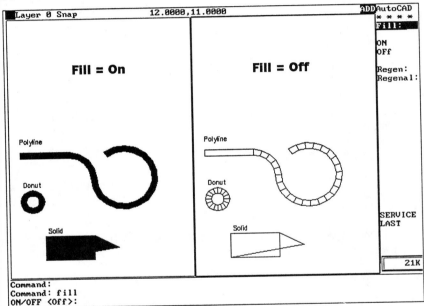

COMMAND OPTIONS

ON	Turns fill on, after next regeneration.
OFF	Turns fill off, after next regeneration.

RELATED SYSTEM VARIABLES

- **FillMode** Current setting of fill status:
  - 0 Fill mode is off.
  - 1 Fill mode is on (*Default*).
- **TextFill** Toggles whether PostScript and TrueType fonts are filled:
  - 0 Fonts not filled (*Default*).
  - 1 Fonts filled.

RELATED AUTOCAD COMMAND

■ **Regen**   Adjustss display to reflect fill-nofill status.

TIPS

■ The state of fill (or no fill) does not come into effect until the next regeneration.

■ Traces, solids, and polylines are not filled when the view is *not* in plan view, regardless of the setting of the **Fill** command.

■ Since filled objects take longer to regenerate, redraw and plot, consider leaving fill off during editing and plotting. During plotting, use a wide pen for filled areas.

■ **Fill** affects objects derived from polylines, including:
   ■ Donuts and polygons.
   ■ Ellipses created with PEllipse = 1.

Fillet

Joins two intersecting lines, polylines, arcs, circles, or 3D solids with a radius.

Command	Alias	Side Menu	Pull-down	Tablet
fillet	...	[CONSTRCT] [Fillet:]	[Construct] [Fillet]	X 19-20

```
Command: fillet
Polyline/Radius/Trim/<Select first object>: [pick]
Select second object: [pick]
```

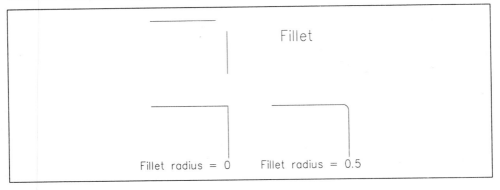

Fillet

Fillet radius = 0   Fillet radius = 0.5

COMMAND OPTIONS

Polyline Fillets all vertices of a polyline.
Radius Indicates the filleting radius.
Trim Toggless whether objects are trimmed (*new to Release 13*).

RELATED AUTOCAD COMMAND

- **Chamfer** Bevel intersecting lines or polyline vertices.

RELATED SYSTEM VARIABLES

- **FilletRad** The current filleting radius.
- **TrimMode** Toggles whether objects are trimmed.

TIPS

- Pick the end of the object you want filleted; the other end will remain untouched.

- The lines, arcs, or circles need not touch.

- As a faster substitute for the **Extend** and **Trim** commands, use the **Fillet** command with the radius of zero.

- If the lines to be filleted are on two different layers, the fillet is drawn on the current layer.

- The fillet radius must be smaller than the length of the lines. For example, if the lines to be filleted are 1.0m long, the fillet radius can be no more than 0.9999m.

- Use the **Close** option of the **Polyline** command to ensure a polyline is filleted at all vertices.

- You cannot fillet polyline segments from different polylines.

- Filleting a pair of circles does not trim them.

- As of Release 13, you can fillet parallel lines; the fillet radius is half the offset distance.

Removed Command: Filmroll

The **Filmroll** command, which creates FLM files read by AutoShade, was removed from Release 13. The workaround is to use AutoVision in place of AutoShade.

'Filter

Creates a filter list applied to selection sets (*an external command in Filter.Lsp*).

Command	Alias	Side Menu	Pull-down	Tablet
'filter	...	[ASSIST]	[Assist]	...
		[Filter:]	[Selection Filters]	

Command: filter
Displays dialogue box.

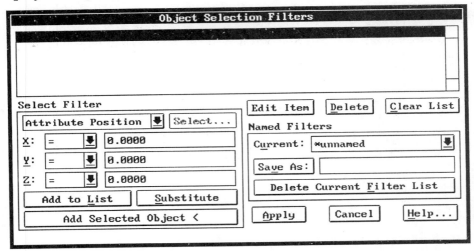

COMMAND OPTIONS

Select Filter Selects filter based on object properties.
Select   Displays all items of specified type in drawing.
X:, Y:, Z: Specifies object coordinates.
Add to List Adds current select-filter option to filter list.
Substitute   Replaces a highlighted filter with selected filter.
Add selected Object
          Selects object from drawing.
Edit Item   Lets you edit highlighted filter item.
Delete   Deletes highlighted filter item.
Clear list   Clears entire filter list.
Current named filter
          Selects named filter from list.
Save as: Saves filter list with name and .NFL extension.
Delete current Filter list
          Deletes named filter.
Apply   Applies filter operation.

RELATED AUTOCAD COMMANDS

■ *Any AutoCAD command with a 'Select objects:' prompt.*

RELATED FILE

■ ***.NFL**   Named filter list.

RELATED SYSTEM VARIABLES

■ *None*

TIPS

■ The selection set created by the **Filter** command is accessed via the 'P' (previous) selection option; alternatively, **'Filter** is used transparently at the 'Select objects:' prompt.

■ Filter cannot find objects with the following parameters:
  ■ Color is set to BYLAYER.
  ■ Linetype is set to BYLAYER.

■ You save selection sets by name to an NFL (*short for Named FiLter*) file on disk for use in other drawings or editing sessions.

■ The **Filter** command uses the following grouping operators:
  ■ **Begin OR   *and*   **End OR
  ■ **Begin AND   *and*   **End AND
  ■ **Begin XOR   *and*   **End XOR
  ■ **Begin NOT   *and*   **End NOT

■ The **Filter** command uses the following relational operators:
  ■ <   Less than.
  ■ <=   Less than or equal to.
  ■ =   Equal.
  ■ !=   Not equal to.
  ■ >   Greater than.
  ■ >=   Greater than or equal to.
  ■ *   All values.

'Gifin

Imports GIF raster files into the drawing as a block; converts pixels into solids (*an external file in RasterIn.Exp*).

Command	Alias	Side Menu	Pull-down	Tablet
'gifin	. . .	[FILE]	[File]	. . .
		[IMPORT]	[Import]	
		[GIFin:]	[Raster]	
			[GIF]	

```
Command: gifin
GIF file name:
Insertion point:
Scale factor:
```

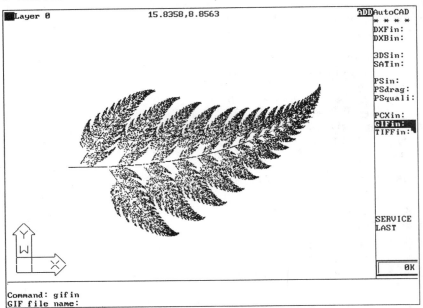

COMMAND OPTIONS

None

RELATED AUTOCAD COMMANDS

- **Pcxin**   Imports PCX raster files.
- **PsIn**   Imports EPS files.
- **Tiffin**   Imports TIFF raster files.

RELATED SYSTEM VARIABLES

- **RiAspect** Adjusts image's aspect ratio.
- **RiBackG** Change the image's background color.
- **RiEdge** Outlines edges.
- **RiGamut** Specifies number of colors.
- **RiGrey** Imports as a grey scale image.
- **RiThresh** Controls brightness threshold.

TIPS

- The GIF format (*short for Graphics Interchange Format*) was invented by CompuServe as a compressed graphics format that can be displayed on different hardware platforms.

- **GifIn** is limited to displaying a maximum of 255 colors.

- Exploding an imported GIF block greatly increases the drawing file size, since each pixel is defined as a solid.

- Turn off system variable **GripBlock** (*set it to 0*) to avoid highlighting all the solid objects making up the block.

'GraphScr

Switches the text screen back to the graphics screen in single-screen systems.

Command	Alias	Side Menu	Function Key	Tablet
'graphscr	...	...	[F1]	V 18

Command: **graphscr**

COMMAND OPTIONS

None

RELATED AUTOCAD COMMANDS

- **Script**   Runs script files, which can use the **GraphScr** command.
- **TextScr**   Switches from graphics screen to text screen.

RELATED AVE RENDER COMMAND

- **RendScr**   Switches back to rendering display.

RELATED SYSTEM VARIABLE

- **Screenmode** Indicates whether current screen is text or graphics:
  - **0** Text screen.
  - **1** Graphics screen.
  - **2** Dual screen displaying both text and graphics.

TIP

- The **GraphScr** and **TextScr** commands do not work on a dual screen display.

'Grid

Displays a grid of reference dots within the currently set limits.

Command	Ctrl+	Side Menu	Pull-down	Function	Tablet
'grid	G	[ASSIST]	. . .	[F7]	V 20
		[Grid:]	. . .		

```
Command: grid
Grid spacing(X) or ON/OFF/Snap/Aspect <1.0000>:
```

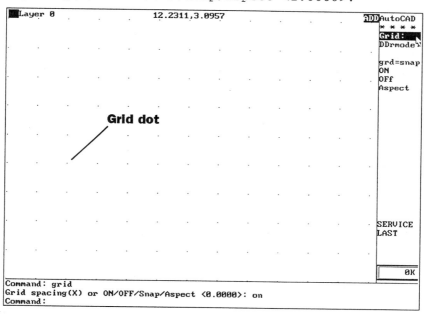

COMMAND OPTIONS

Aspect   Indicates different spacing for the x- and y-direction.

Grid spacing(X)

      Sets the x- and y-direction spacing; an *x* following the value sets the grid spacing a multiple of the current snap setting.

OFF   Turns grid markings off.

ON   Turns grid markings on.

Snap   Makes the grid spacing the same as the snap spacing.

RELATED AUTOCAD COMMANDS

- **Ddrmodes** Sets the grid via a dialogue box.
- **Limits**   Sets the limits of the grid in WCS.
- **Snap**   Sets the snap spacing.

RELATED SYSTEM VARIABLES

■ **Gridmode** Current grid visibility:
> **0** Grid is off.
> **1** Grid is on.

■ **Gridunit** Current grid x,y-spacing.

TIPS

■ The grid is most useful when set to the snap spacing, or to a multiple of the snap spacing.

■ You can set a different grid spacing in each viewport and a different grid spacing in the x- and y-directions.

■ Rotate the grid with the **Snap** command's **Rotate** option; **Snap**'s **Isometric** option creates an isometric grid.

■ If a very dense grid spacing is selected, the grid will take a long time to display; press **[Esc]** to cancel the display.

■ AutoCAD does not display a too-dense grid and gives the message, "Grid too dense to display."

■ Grid markings are not plotted; to create a plotted grid, use the **Array** command to place an array of points.

Group

Creates a named selection set of objects.

Command	Ctrl+	Side Menu	Pull-down	Tablet
group	A	[ASSIST]	[Assist]	V 12
		[Group:]	[Group Objects]	

Command: **group**

Displays dialogue box.

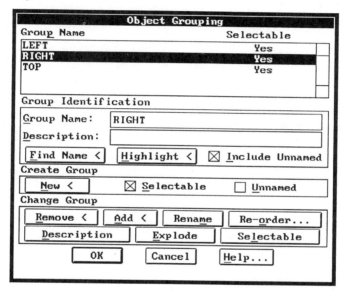

Command: **-group**
?/Order/Add/Remove/Explode/REName/Selectable/<Create>:

COMMAND OPTIONS

?	Lists names and descriptions of currently-defined groups.
Order	Changes the order of objects within the group.
Add	Add objects to group.
Remove	Removes objects from group.
Explode	Removes group definition from drawing.
REName	Renames the group.
Selectable	Toggles whether group is selectable.
Create	Creates a new named group from objects selected.

RELATED AUTOCAD COMMANDS

- **Block** Creates a named symbol from a group of objects.
- **Select** Creates a selection set.

RELATED SYSTEM VARIABLE

■ **PickStyle** Toggles whether groups are selected by the usual selection process:

    0 Groups and associative hatches are not selected.

    1 Groups are included in selection sets.

    2 Associate hatches are included in selection sets.

    3 Both are selected (*Default*).

TIPS

■ Use **[Ctrl]+A** to toggle groups.

■ Consider a group as a named selection set; unlike a regular selection set, a group is not "lost" when the next group is created.

■ Group names are up to 31 characters long, including $, _ , and - .

■ Group descriptions are up to 64 characters long.

■ Anonymous groups are unnamed; AutoCAD refers to them as *A*n.

REMOVED COMMAND: Handles

The **Handles** command has been removed from Release 13.
The system variable **Handles** is always turned on.

Hatch

Draws a non-associative cross-hatch pattern within a closed boundary.

Command	Alias	Side Menu	Pull-down	Tablet
hatch	. . .	. . .	. . .	. . .

```
Command: hatch
Pattern (? or name/U,style):
Scale for pattern <1.0000>:
Angle for pattern <0>:
Select hatch boundaries or RETURN for direct hatch option,
Select objects: [Enter]
Retain polyline <N>:
From point: [pick]
Arc/Close/Length/Undo/<Next Point>: [pick]
From point or RETURN to apply hatch: [Enter]
```

COMMAND OPTIONS

Pattern	Indicates name of hatch pattern.
?	Lists the hatch pattern names.
U	Creates a user-defined hatch pattern.
style	Displays the sub-menu of hatching styles:
N	Hatches alternate boundaries (*short for Normal*).
O	Hatchs only outermost boundaries (*short for Outermost*).
I	Hatchs everything within boundary (*short for Ignore*).

Direct hatch options:

Retain polyline

> **Yes:** leaves boundary in place after hatch is complete.
> **No:** erases boundary after hatching.

From point	Begins drawing the hatch boundary.
Next point	Draws straight line.
Arc	Draws an arc hatch boundary.
Close	Closes the hatch boundary.
Length	Continues the boundary by specified distance.
Undo	Undoes last-drawn segment

RELATED AUTOCAD COMMANDS

- **BHatch** Creates automatic, associative hatching.
- **Boundary** Automatically creates polyline or region boundary.
- **Explode** Reduces hatch pattern to its constituent lines.
- **PsFill** Fills closed polyline with a PostScript pattern.
- **Snap** Changes the hatch pattern's origin.

RELATED SYSTEM VARIABLES

- **HpAng** Hatch pattern angle.
- **HpDouble** Doubled hatch pattern.
- **HpName** Hatch pattern name.
- **HpScale** Hatch pattern scale.
- **HpSpace** Hatch pattern spacing.
- **SnapBase** Controls the origin of the hatch pattern.
- **SnapAng** Controls the angle of the hatch pattern.

RELATED FILE

- **Acad.Pat** Hatch pattern definition file.

TIPS

- The **Hatch** command draws non-associative hatch patterns; the pattern remains in place when its boundary is edited.

- For complex hatch areas, you may find it easier to outline the area with a polyline (using object snap) or to use the **BHatch** command.

- By default, the hatch is created as a block; the name begins with the letter "X" followed by a consecutive number. To create the hatch as line objects, precede the pattern name with * (asterisk).

- AutoCAD includes the following hatch patterns in the file Acad.Pat:

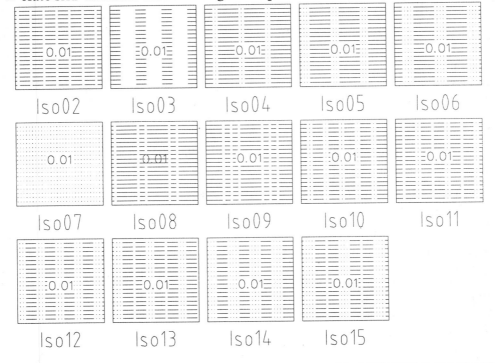

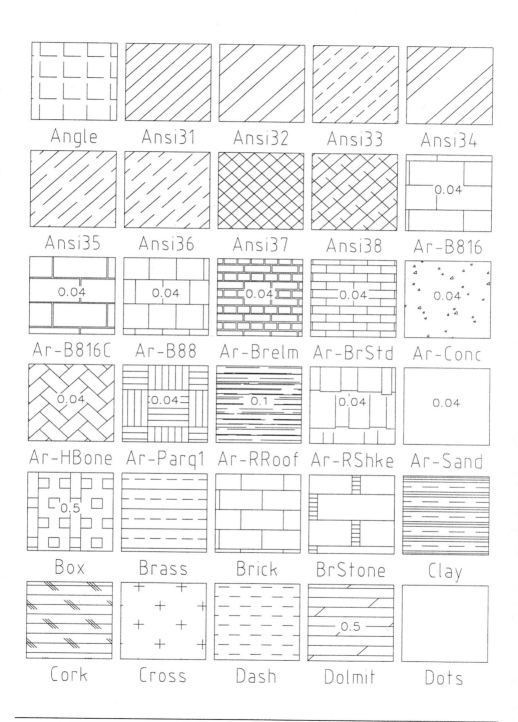

Angle	Ansi31	Ansi32	Ansi33	Ansi34
Ansi35	Ansi36	Ansi37	Ansi38	Ar-B816
Ar-B816C	Ar-B88	Ar-Brelm	Ar-BrStd	Ar-Conc
Ar-HBone	Ar-Parq1	Ar-RRoof	Ar-RShke	Ar-Sand
Box	Brass	Brick	BrStone	Clay
Cork	Cross	Dash	Dolmit	Dots

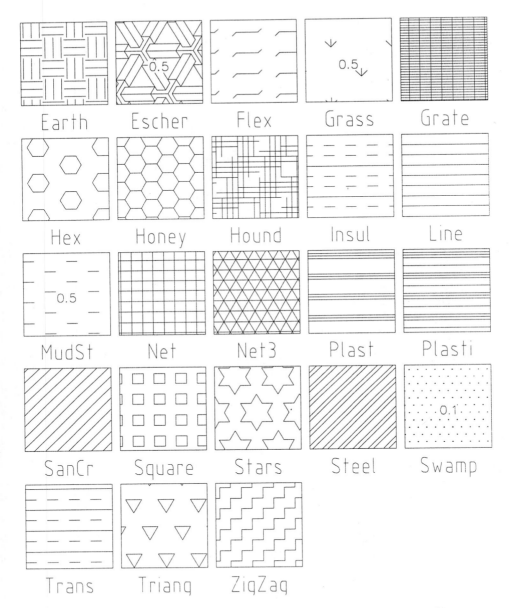

Earth	Escher	Flex	Grass	Grate
Hex	Honey	Hound	Insul	Line
MudSt	Net	Net3	Plast	Plasti
SanCr	Square	Stars	Steel	Swamp
Trans	Triang	ZigZag		

■ Patterns are drawn at scale factor 1.0; those marked with a scale number (0.01, 0.5, etc) are shown at a smaller scale.

HatchEdit

Edits associative hatch patterns.

Command	Alias	Side Menu	Pull-down	Tablet
hatchedit	...	[MODIFY]	[Modify]	W 17
		[HatchEd:]	[Edit Hatch]	

Command: **hatchedit**

Displays dialogue box.

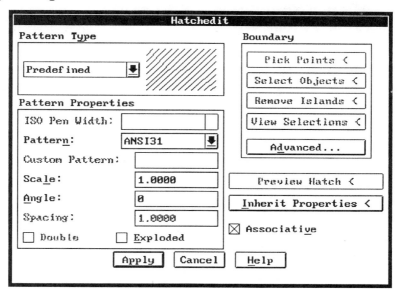

COMMAND OPTIONS

Pattern Type   Toggles between 'Predefined' in Acad.Pat, 'User-defined' on the fly, and 'Custom' in another PAT file.

Pattern Properties:

  ISO Pen Width

          Specify plotting width for ISO hatch patterns.

  Pattern   Name of hatch pattern in Acad.Pat.

  Custom Pattern

          Name of custom hatch pattern.

  Scale   Hatch pattern scale.

  Angle   Global hatch pattern angle.

  Spacing   Spacing between pattern lines.

  Double   Double hatch (apply at 90 degrees).

  Exploded   Place hatch pattern as lines, rather than as a block.

Inherit Properties

Select another hatch pattern to match parameters.

Associative Toggle associativity of hatch pattern.

RELATED AUTOCAD COMMANDS

- **BHatch**   Applies associative hatch pattern.
- **Hatch**   Applies non-associative hatch pattern.
- **Explode**   Explodes a hatch pattern block into lines.

RELATED SYSTEM VARIABLES

- **HpAng**   Hatch pattern angle.
- **HpDouble** Doubled hatch pattern.
- **HpName** Hatch pattern name.
- **HpScale** Hatch pattern scale.
- **HpSpace** Hatch pattern spacing.

'Help or '?

Lists text screens of information for using AutoCAD's commands.

Command	Alias	Side Menu	Pull-down	Tablet
'help	'?	[INQUIRY]	[Help]	T 7-8
		[HELP:]	[Help]	

Command: **help**

Displays dialogue box.

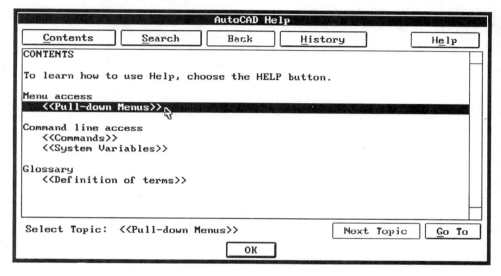

COMMAND OPTIONS

Contents	Displays the table of contents for the help screens.
Search	Searches for key words in the help file.
Back	Moves back to the previoys help screen.
History	Displays list of most-recently accessed help topics.
Help	Displays help on using the **Help** command.
Next Topic	Accesses next help topic, if more than one per line of text.
Go To	Goes to highlighted help topic.
OK	Cancel **Help** command.

RELATED AUTOCAD COMMANDS

■ *All*
■ WhatsNew Describes commands new to Release 13.

RELATED SYSTEM VARIABLES

All

RELATED FILES

- **Acad.Ahp** The AutoCAD help file, located in \Acad13\Common\Support.
- **HelpHelp.Ahp**
  The Help help file.
- ***.HDX**   The help index file.

TIPS

- Since **Help** and **?** are transparent commands, you can use it during another command to get help on the command's options.

- The text of the help file is stored in the file **Acad.Ahp**; as of Release 13, this file is no longer ASCII and cannot be edited or customized.

Hide

Removes hidden lines from 3D drawings.

Command	Alias	Side Menu	Pull-down	Tablet
help	...	[TOOLS]	[Tools]	N1
		[Hide:]	[Hide]	
		[TOOLS]		
		[SHADE]		
		[Hidden]		

```
Command: hide
Regenerating drawing.
Removing hidden lines: 25
```

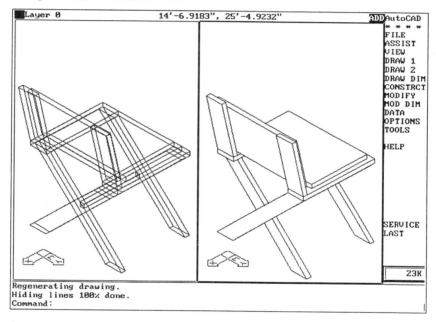

COMMAND OPTIONS
None

RELATED AUTOCAD COMMANDS.

- **DView** Removes hidden lines of perspective 3D views.
- **MView** Removes hidden lines during plots of paper space drawings.
- **Plot** Removes hidden lines during plotting of 3D drawings.
- **Regen** Returns the view to wireframe.
- **Render** Performs realistic renderings of 3D models.
- **Shade** Performs quick renderings and quick hides of 3D models.
- **VPoint** Select the 3D viewpoint.

RELATED SYSTEM VARIABLES
- *None*

TIPS
- The **Hide** command considers the following objects as opaque:
  - Circle.
  - Solid, trace, and wide polyline.
  - 3D face and polygon mesh.
  - The extrusion of any object with thickness.

- Use the **MSlide** command to save the hidden-line view as an SLD file; view the saved image with the **VSlide** command.

- Use the **SaveImg** command to save the hidden-line view as a TIFF, TGA, or GIF file; view the saved image with the **Replay** command.

- The **Shade** command simulates hidden-line removal when **ShadEdge** system variable is set to 2.

- Freezing layers speeds up the hide process since **Hide** ignores those objects.

- **Hide** does not consider the visibility of text and attributes.

- To create a hidden-line view when plotting in paper space, select the **HidePlot** option of the **MView** command.

- Use the **Regen** command to return to the wireframe view.

- As of Release 13, AutoCAD no longer supports the "Release 11" hidden-line algorithm.

HpMPlot

Allows HPGL/2 plotters to plot one rendered viewport in paper space (*short for Hewlett-Packard Mixed PLOT; an external command in HpMPlot.Exp*).

Command	alias	Side Menu	Pull-down	Tablet
hpmplot	...	...	...	...

Command: **hpmplot**

Displays dialogue box.

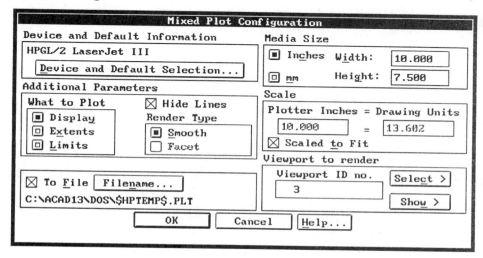

COMMAND OPTIONS

Device and Default Information
    Selects HPGL/2 output device.

Additional Parameters
    Selects the view, type of rendering, and determines whether hidden lines are removed from wireframe viewports.

To File   Option to plot to an HPGL/2-format plot file.

Media Size Specifies size of media.

Scale   Specifies plot scale.

Viewport to Render
    Selects the one viewport to be rendered.

RELATED AUTOCAD COMMANDS

- **Config**   Configures AutoCAD for output devices.
- **Plot**   Plots non-rendered paper space and model space drawings.
- **RConfig** Configures AutoCAD for rendering plots and displays.
- **Render** Displays renderings to screen or common file formats.

TIPS

■ **HpMPlot** is useful for plotting both a rendering and regular wireframe on a single sheet.

■ "Only HPGL/2 devices are valid for mixed plots."

■ The **HpRender** command renders a single viewport to the output device; displays dialogue box:

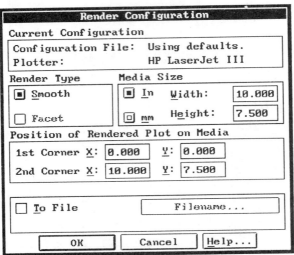

QUICK START: Using HpMPlot

To set up AutoCAD for using **HpMPlot**, follow these steps:

1. Configure AutoCAD for an HPGL/2 plotter with the **Config** command.

2. Configure **Render** for an HPGL/2 hardcopy rendering device with the **RConfig** command, as follows:

   ■ When AutoCAD complains about a missing rendering driver, supply 'RHpRtl.Exp' as the driver name.

   ■ Select from one of the following HPGL/2 plotters:
      ■ HP DesignJet 650C, 600, 200.
      ■ HP PaintJet XL300.
      ■ HP 7600 Series, Monochrome or Color.
      ■ HP LaserJet III and 4.

3. Use the **HpConfig** command to configure the output parameters; displays a dialogue box:

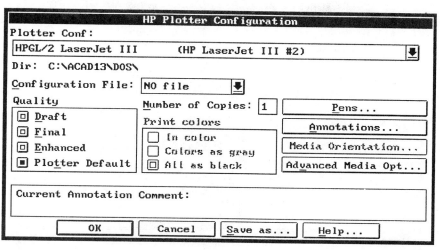

The **Pens** button displays the following dialogue box:

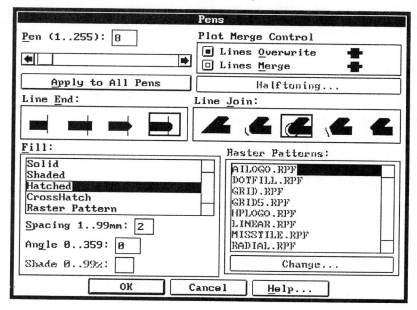

The **Annotations** button displays the following dialogue box:

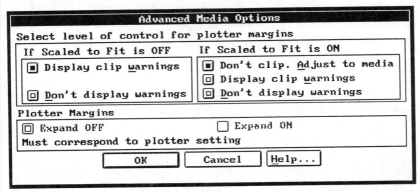

The **Advanced Media** button displays the following dialogue box:

4. Save the output parameters to an HPC file with the **Save As** button.

5. Set **TileMode = 0**.

6. Use the **MView** command to create a pair paperspace viewports.

7. Start the **HpMPlot** command:
   ■ Select the one viewport to be the rendered viewport.
   ■ Create the mixed plot.

RELATED FILES
■ *.HPC   Stores configuration parameters of the **HpConfig** command.
■ *. PLT   HPGL/2 plot files.
■ *.RPF   Raster pattern files used by **HpMPlot**, found in subdirectory
            \Acad13\Dos\Support:
                AiLogo, DotFill, Grid, Grid5, HpLogo, Linear, MissTile,
                Radial, Rivrston, Sediment, Shingle, and SwampGrs.

'Id

Identifies the 3D coordinates of a point (*short for IDentify*).

Command	Alias	Side Menu	Pull-down	Tablet
'id	...	[ASSIST]	[Assist]	Q 1
		[INQUIRY]	[Inquiry]	
		[Id:]	[Locate Point]	

Command: **id**
Point: **[pick]**

Example output:
X = 1278.0018   Y = 1541.5993   Z = 0.0000

COMMAND OPTIONS
None

RELATED AUTOCAD COMMANDS
- **List** Lists information about a picked object.
- **Point** Draws a point.

RELATED SYSTEM VARIABLES
- **LastPoint** Contains the 3D coordinates of the last picked point.

TIPS
- The **Id** command stores the picked point in the **LastPoint** system variable. Access that value by entering '@' at the next prompt for a point value.

- Use the **Id** command to set the value of the **Lastpoint** system variable, which can be used as relative coordinates in another command.

- The z-coordinate displayed by the **Id** command is the current elevation setting; if you use the **Id** command with an object snap, then the z-coordinate is the osnap'ed value.

- The **Id** command used in a menu macro or AutoLISP routine can quickly label points on the screen.

REMOVED COMMANDS: IgesIn and IgesOut

The **IgesIn** and **IgesOut** commands were removed from Release 13.

Insert

Inserts a previously-defined block into the drawing.

Command	Alias	Side Menu	Pull-down	Tablet
insert	. . .	. . .	. . .	. . .

```
Command: insert
Block name (or ?):
Insertion point: [pick]
X scale factor <1> / Corner / XYZ: [Enter]
Y scale factor (default=X): [Enter]
Rotation angle <0>: [Enter]
```

COMMAND OPTIONS

Block name Indicates the name of the block to be inserted.

? Lists the names of blocks stored in the drawing.

X scale factor <1>

Indicates the x-scale factor.

Corner Indicates the x- and y-scale factors by pointing on the screen.

XYZ Displays the x-, y-, and z-scale submenu.

P Supplies predefined block name, scale, and rotation values.

INPUT OPTIONS

- In response to the 'Block Name:' prompt, you can enter:
    - **~** *(Tilde)* Displays a dialogue box of blocks stored on disk, as in:
        ```
        Block name: ~
        ```
    - **=** *(Equals)* Redefines existing block with a new block, as in:
        ```
        Block name: oldname=newname
        ```
    - ***** *(Asterisk)* Explodes block upon insertion, as in:
        ```
        Block name: *name
        ```

- In response to the 'Insertion point:' prompt, you can enter:
    - **Scale** Specifies x-, y-, z-scale factors.
    - **PScale** Presets the x-, y-, and z-scale factors.
    - **Xscale** Specifies x-scale factor.
    - **PsScale** Presets x-scale factor.
    - **Yscale** Specifies y-scale factor.
    - **PyScale** Presets y-scale factor.
    - **Zscale** Specifies z-scale factor.
    - **PzScale** Presets the z-scale factor.
    - **Rotate** Specifies the rotation angle.
    - **PRotate** Presets the rotation angle.

RELATED AUTOCAD COMMANDS

- **Block** Creates a block of a group of objects.
- **DdInsert** Displays dialogue box for inserting blocks.
- **Explode** Reduces an inserted block to its constituent objects.
- **MInsert** Inserts blocks as a blocked rectangular array.
- **Rename** Renames blocks.
- **WBlock** Writes blocks to disk.
- **XRef** Displays drawings stored on disk in the drawing.

RELATED SYSTEM VARIABLES

- **ExplMode** Toggles whether non-uniformly scaled blocks can be exploded:
  - **0** Cannot explode (Release 12 compatible).
  - **1** Can be exploded (default).
- **InsBase** Name of most-recently inserted block.

TIPS

- You can insert any other AutoCAD drawing into the current drawing.

- A "preset" scale factor or rotation means the dragged image is shown at that factor.

- Drawings are normally inserted as a block; prefix the filename with an * (*asterisk*) to insert the drawing as separate objects.

- Redefine an existing block by adding the suffix = (*equal*) after its name at the 'Block name:' prompt.

- Insert a mirrored block by supplying a negative x- or y-scale factor (*such as 'X scale factor: -1'*); AutoCAD converts negative z-scale factors into their absolute value (*makes them always positive*).

- As of Release 13, you can explode a mirrored block and a block inserted with different scale factors when system variable **ExplMode** is turned on.

Interfere

Determines the interference of two or more 3D solid objects; creates a 3D solid body of the volumes in common (*formerly the SolInterf command; an external command in Acis.Dll*).

Command	Alias	Side Menu	Pull-down	Tablet
interfere	...	[DRAW 2]	[Draw]	Y 15
		[SOLIDS]	[Solids]	
		[Interfr:]	[Interference]	

```
Command: interfere
Select the first set of solids: [pick]
Select the second set of solids: [pick]
Create interference solids? <N>: Y
Highlight pairs of interfering solids? <N>: Y
eXit/<Next pair>: X
```

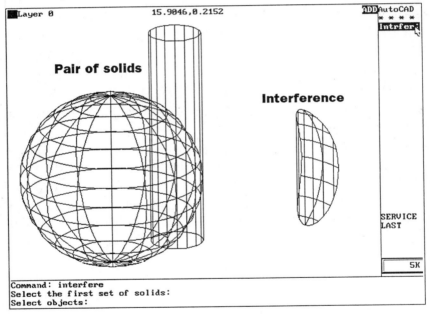

COMMAND OPTIONS

Select first set of solids

All solids in a single selection set are checked for interference against each other.

Select second set of solids

All solids in the one selection set are checked for interference with solids in the second selection set.

Create interference solids

Creates a solid representing the volume of interference.

Highlight pairs of interfering solids

Useful when the drawing contains many interferences.

RELATED AUTOCAD COMMANDS

■ **Intersect** Creates a new volume from the intersection of two volumes.
■ **Section** Creates a 2D region from a 3D solid.
■ **Slice** Slices a 3D solid with a plane.

TIP

One primary difference between the **Interfere** and **Intersect** commands is that the **Interfere** command works with more than two objects, while the **Intersect** command works with just two objects.

Intersect

Creates a 3D solid of 2D region from the intersection of two or more solids or regions; (formerly the **SolInt** command; an external command in Acis.Dll).

Command	Alias	Side Menu	Pull-down	Tablet
intersect	. . .	[DRAW 2]	[Draw]	Y 12
		[SOLIDS]	[Solids]	
		[Intersct:]	[Intersection]	

```
Command: intersect
Select objects: [pick]
```

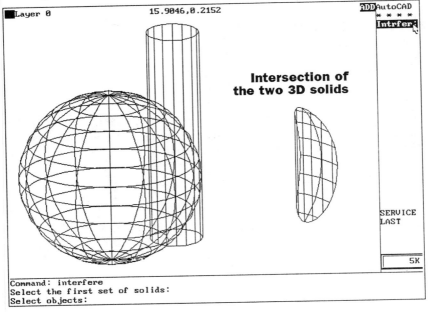

Intersection of the two 3D solids

COMMAND OPTIONS

None

RELATED AUTOCAD COMMANDS

- **Interfere** Creates a new volume from the interference of two or more volumes.
- **Subtract** Subtracts one 3D solid from another.
- **Union** Joins D solids into a single body.

TIP

One primary difference between the **Interfere** and **Intersect** commands is that the **Interfere** command works with more than two objects, while the **Intersect** command works with just two objects.

'Isoplane

Switches the crosshairs between the three isometric drawing planes.

Command	Ctrl+	Side Menu	Pull-down	Tablet
'isoplane	E	...	...	V 19

```
Command: isoplane
Left/Top/Right/<Toggle>: [Enter]
Current Isometric plane is: Left
```

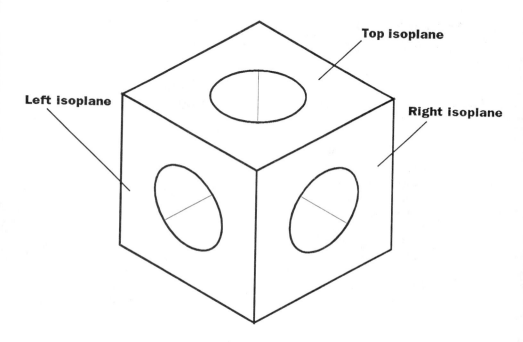

Top isoplane

Left isoplane

Right isoplane

COMMAND OPTIONS

Left   Switches to the left isometric plane.
Top   Switches to the top isometric plane.
Right   Switchs to the right isometric plane.
<Toggle> Switch to the next isometric plane in the order of left, top, right.

RELATED AUTOCAD COMMANDS

- **Ddrmodes** Displays dialogue box for setting isometric mode and planes.
- **Snap**   Turns isometric drawing mode on.

RELATED SYSTEM VARIABLE

- **SnapIsoPair** Contains the current isometric plane.

'Layer

Controls the creation and visibility of layers.

Command	Alias	Side Menu	Pull-down	Tablet
'layer	la	. . .	. . .	L 3
				M3 – O4

Command: **layer**
?/Make/Set/New/ON/OFF/Color/Ltype/Freeze/Thaw/LOck/Unlock:

COMMAND OPTIONS

Color	Indicates the color for all objects drawn on the layer.
Freeze	Disables the display of the layer.
LOck	Locks the layer.
Ltype	Indicates the linetype for all objects drawn on the layer.
Make	Creates a new layer and make it the working layer.
New	Creates a new layer.
OFF	Turns the layer off.
ON	Turns the layer on.
Set	Makes the layer the working layer.
Thaw	Un-freezes the layer.
Unlock	Unlocks the layer.
?	Lists the names of layers currently in the drawing.

RELATED AUTOCAD COMMANDS

- **Change** Moves objects to a different layer.
- **ChProp** Moves objects to a different layer.
- **DdLModes** Uses a dialogue box to control layers.
- **Purge** Removes unused layers from the drawing.
- **Rename** Renames layer names.
- **VpLayer** Controls the visibility of layers in paper space viewports.
- **Xplode** Explodes blocks, hatches, meshes, and polylines, and places them on a new layer.

RELATED SYSTEM VARIABLES

- **CLayer** Contains the name of the current layer.

TIP

- Layer **DimPts** is a non-plotting layer.

Leader

Draws a leader line with a single line of text (*formerly the Dim:LEAder command*).

Command	Alias	Side Menu	Pull-down	Tablet
leader	lead	[DRAW DIM]	[Draw]	X 1
		[Leader:]	[Dimensioning]	
			[Leader]	

```
Command: leader
From point: [pick]
To point: [pick]
To point (Format/Annotation/Undo) <Annotation>: F
Spline/STraight/Arrow/None/<eXit>:
Tolerance/Copy/Block/None/<MText>:
```

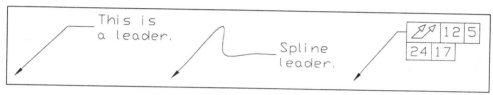

COMMAND OPTIONS

Format Specifies the style of leader:
  Spline Draws leader line as a NURBs curve.
  STraight Draws straight leader line (default).
  Arrow Draws leader with arrowhead (default).
  None Draws leader with no arrowhead.
Annotation Specifies the type of annotation:
  Tolerance Places one or more tolerance symbols.
  Copy Copies text from another part of the drawing.
  Block Places a block in the manner of the **Insert** command.
  None No annotation.
  <MText> Places an MText note at the end of the leader line.
Undo Undoes the leader line to the previous vertex.

RELATED DIM VARIABLES

- **DimAsz** Arrowhead and hookline size.
- **DimBlk** Type of arrowhead.
- **DimClrd** Color of leader line and arrowhead.
- **DimGap** Gap between hookline and annotation; gap between box and text.
- **DimScale** Overall scale of leader.

TIPS

- The text in a leader is an MText (multiline text) object.
- Use the '\P' metacharacter to create line breaks in leader text.

Lengthen

Lengthens and shortens open objects by four methods.

Command	Alias	Side Menu	Pull-down	Tablet
lengthen	...	[MODIFY]	[Modify]	Y 18
		[Lengthn:]	[Lengthen]	

```
Command: lengthen
DElta/Percent/Total/DYnamic/<Select object>: [pick]
Current length: <>, included angle: <>
```

DElta option:
```
Angle/<Enter delta length>: A
Enter delta angle:
<Select angle to change>/Undo:
```

Percent option:
```
Enter percent length:
<Select angle to change>/Undo:
```

Total option:
```
Angle/<Enter total length>: A
Enter delta angle:
<Select angle to change>/Undo:
```

DYnamic option:
```
<Select angle to change>/Undo:
```

COMMAND OPTIONS

<Select object> Displays length and included angle; does not change object.
DElta   Changes length by incremental length.
Percent   Changes length by a percentage of the original length.
Total   Changes by absolute value.
DYnamic   Dynamically changes length by dragging.
  Angle   Sets the angle of the selected arc.
  Undo   Undoes the most-recent lengthening operation.

RELATED AUTOCAD COMMANDS

■ **Extend**   Lengths an open object to a cutting edge.
■ **Trim**   Trims a open and closed objects back to a cutting edge.

TIPS

■ Unlike the **Extend** and **Trim** commands, the **Lengthen** command does not require an object to work as a cutting edge.

■ **Lengthen** command only works with open objects, such as lines, arcs, and polylines

■ **Lengthen** does not work with closed objects, such as circles, polygons, and regions.

■ **DElta** option changes the length or angle using the following measurements:
   ■ Distance from endpoint of the selected object to the pick point.
   ■ For arc angles, changes by the incremental length measured from the endpoint of the arc..
   ■ Positive values lengthen; negative values shorten.

■ **Percent** option works relative to 100%:
   ■ Less than 100% shortens the object; for example, 50% shortens object by half.
   ■ 100%: length does not change.
   ■ More than 100% lengthens the object; for example, 200% doubles the length.

Light

Places four types of lights for the **Render** command (*an external command in Render.Arx*).

Command	Alias	Side Menu	Pull-down	Tablet
light	...	[TOOLS]	[Tools]	M 2
		[RENDER]	[Render]	
		[Lights:]	[Lights]	

Command: **light**

Displays dialogue box.

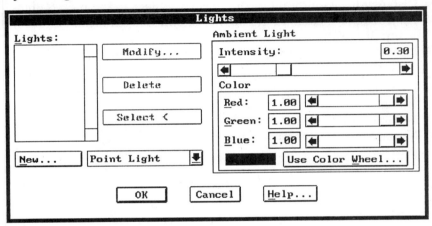

COMMAND OPTIONS

Modify	Modifiesy an existing light in the drawing.
Delete	Deletes the selected light.
Select	Selects a light from the drawing.
Intensity	Adjusts intensity of ambient light.
Color	Adjusts color of ambient light; displays dialogue box:

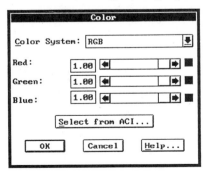

New Create a new light; displays dialogue box, depending on light type:

New point light:

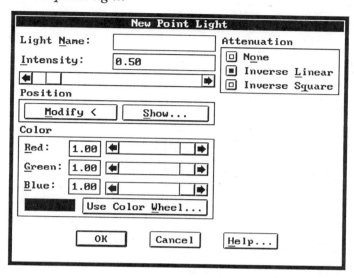

New distant light:

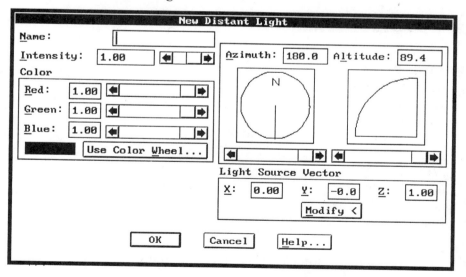

New spot light:

```
┌──────────────────────────────────────────────────────────────┐
│                         New Spotlight                          │
├──────────────────────────────────────────────────────────────┤
│  Light Name:  [          ]      Hotspot: [44.00]               │
│                                                                │
│  Intensity:  [5.45      ]       [◄|  |  |          |►]         │
│                                                                │
│  [◄|        |              |►]  Falloff: [45.00]               │
│  Position                       [◄|    |  |        |►]         │
│    [   Modify <   ] [  Show... ]                               │
│  Color                                                         │
│    Red:   [1.00] [◄|        |►]                                │
│                                   Attenuation                  │
│    Green: [1.00] [◄|        |►]   ┌──────────────────────┐     │
│                                   │ ▢ None               │     │
│    Blue:  [1.00] [◄|        |►]   │ ▣ Inverse Linear     │     │
│    [▬▬▬▬] [  Use Color Wheel...]  │ ▢ Inverse Square     │     │
│                                   └──────────────────────┘     │
│                                                                │
│           [   OK   ]  [  Cancel  ]  [ Help... ]                │
└──────────────────────────────────────────────────────────────┘
```

RELATED AUTOCAD COMMANDS

- **Render**   Renders the drawing.
- **Scene**   Specifies lights and view to use in rendering.

RELATED SYSTEM VARIABLE

- **Target**   Cntains the coordinates of light's target point.

RELATED FILES

In \Acad13\Common\Support subdirectory:
- **Direct.Dwg**   Direct light block
- **Overhead.Dwg** Overhead drawing block.
- **Sh_Spot.Dwg** Spotlight drawing block.

In \Acad13\Dos subdirectory:
- **Render.Cfg**   Render device configuration file.
- **Render.Mli**   Rendering material library.
- **Render.Xmx**   External message file for **Render**.
- **ReadMe.Ren**   Last-minute updates concerning **Render**.

TIPS

- When you use the **Render** command with no lights defined, AutoCAD assumes a single light source located at your eye.

- While it is not necessary to define any lights to use the **Render** command, a light must be included in a **Scene** definition for the **Render** command to make use of the light.

- The light beam travels from the *light location* (light block placement) to the *light target*.
- Ambient light:
  - Ensures every object in the scene has illumination.
  - Is an omnipresent light source.
  - Should be set to 0 (*turned off*) for night scenes.
- Distant lights:

- Place one Distant light to simulate the sun.
- Parallel light beams with constant intensity.
- Azimuth ranges from -180 to 180 degrees.
- Altitude ranges from -90 to 90 degrees (*use the text box for values down to -90 degrees*).

- Point lights:

- Place several Point lights as light bulbs (*lamps*).
- Beams light in all directions, with inverse linear, inverse square, or constant intensity.

- Spot lights:

- Beams light in a cone.
- "*Hotspot*" is the brightest cone of light; beam angle ranges from 0 to 160 degrees (default: 45 degrees).
- "*Falloff*" is the angle of the full light cone; field angle ranges from 0 to 160 (default: 45 degrees).
- Intensity of 0 turns light off.

DEFINITIONS

Constant light:
- Attenuation is 0.
- Default intensity is 1.0.

Inverse linear light:
- Light strength decreases to ½-strength two units of distance away, and ¼-strength four units away.
- Default intensity is ½-extents distance.

Inverse square light:
- Light strength decreases to ¼-strength two units away, and $1/_8$-strength four units away.
- Default intensity is ½ the square of the extents distance.

Extents distance:
- Distance from minimum lower-left coordintate to the maximum upper-right coordinate.

RGB color:
- The three primary colors — red, green, blue — shaded from black to white.

HLS color:
- Changes each color by hue (color), lightness (more white or more black), and saturation (less grey).

'Limits

Defines the 2D limits in the WCS for the grid markings and the **Zoom All** command.

Command	Alias	Side Menu	Pull-down	Tablet
'limits	. . .	[DATA]	[Data]	. . .
		[Limits:]	[Drawing Limits]	

```
Command: limits
Reset Model space limits:
ON/OFF/<Lower left corner> <0.0000,0.0000>: [pick]
Upper right corner <12.0000,9.0000>: [pick]
```

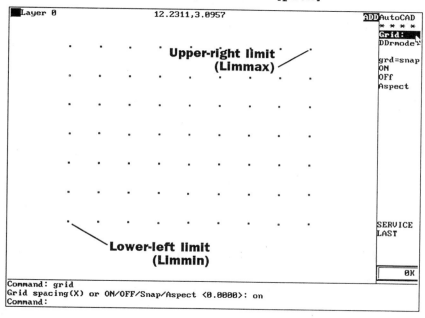

COMMAND OPTIONS

OFF	Turns limits checking off.
ON	Turns limits checking on.
[Enter]	Retains limits values.

RELATED AUTOCAD COMMANDS

- **Grid** Grid dots are bounded by limits.
- **Status** Lists the current drawing limits.
- **Zoom** **Zoom All** displays the drawing's extents or limits.

RELATED SYSTEM VARIABLES

- **LimCheck** Toggle for limit's drawing check:
    - 0 Off (*Default*).
    - 1 On.
- **LimMin** Lower-right 2D coordinates of current limits.
- **LimMax** Upper-left 2D coordinates of current limits.

TIPS

- Use the **Limits** command to define the extents of grid markings.

- The limits determine the extents displayed by the **Zoom All** command.

- If limits checking is turned on, AutoCAD will complain with an outside-limits error. Use this to limit drawing to the drawing extents.

- There are no limits in the z-direction.

- Model space and paper space have separate limits.

Line

Draws straight 2D and 3D lines.

Command	Alias	Side Menu	Pull-down	Tablet
line	1	[DRAW 1]	[Draw]	J 10
		[Line:]	[Line]	
	3dline			

```
Command: line
From point: [pick]
To point: [pick]
To point: [Enter]
```

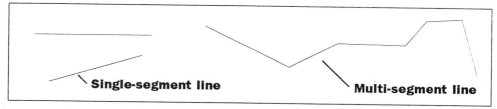

Single-segment line   **Multi-segment line**

COMMAND OPTIONS

C	Closees the line from the current point to the starting point.
U	Undos the last line drawn.
[Enter]	At the 'From point:' prompt, continues the line from the last endpoint.
[Enter]	At the 'To point:' prompt, terminates the **Line** command.

RELATED AUTOCAD COMMANDS

- **MLine**   Draws up to 16 parallel polylines.
- **PLine**   Draws polylines and polyline arcs.
- **Trace**   Draws lines with width.
- **Ray**   Creates a semi-infinite construction line.
- **Xline**   Creates an infinite construction line.

RELATED SYSTEM VARIABLES

- **Elevation** Distance above (or below) the x,y-plane a line is drawn.
- **Lastpoint** Last-entered coordinate triple.
- **Thickness** Determines thickness of the line.

TIPS

- To draw a 2D line, enter x,y-coordinate pairs; the z-coordinate takes on the value of the Elevation system variable.

- To draw a 3D line, enter x,y,z-coordinate triples.

- When system variable **Thickness** is not zero, the line has thickness, which makes it a plane.

'Linetype

Loads linetype definitions into the drawing, creates new linetypes, and sets the working linetype.

Command	Alias	Side Menu	Pull-down	Tablet
'linetype	lt	...	...	Y 15

Command: **linetype**
?/Create/Load/Set:

COMMAND OPTIONS

Create	Creates a new user-defined linetype.
Load	Loads a linetype from an LIN linetype definition file.
Set	Sets the working linetype.
?	Lisst the linetypes loaded into the drawing.

RELATED AUTOCAD COMMANDS

- **Change**   Changes objects to a new linetype; changes linetype scale.
- **ChProp**   Changes objects to a new linetype.
- **DdEModes** Sets the working linetype via a dialogue box.
- **DdLModes** Set the linetype for all objects on a layer.
- **DdLtype** Sets the linetype via a dialogue box.
- **LtScale** Sets the scale of the linetype.
- **Rename**   Changes the name of the linetype.

RELATED SYSTEM VARIABLES

- **CeLtype** The current linetype setting.
- **LtScale**   The current linetype scale.
- **PsLtScale** Linetype scale relative to paper scale.
- **PlineGen** Controls how linetypes are generated for polylines.

TIPS

- The only linetype initially defined in an AutoCAD drawing is the CONTINUOUS linetype.

- Linetypes must be loaded from LIN definition files before being used in a drawing. When loading one or more linetypes, it's faster to load all linetypes, then use the **Purge** command to remove linetype definitions the drawing has not used.

- As of Release 13, objects can have independent linetype scales.

RELATED FILES

■ Linetypes stored in \Acad13\Common\Suppport\LTypeShp.Lin (*new in Release 13*):

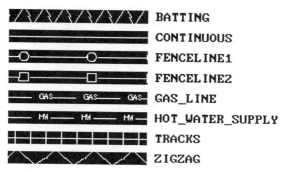

	BATTING
	CONTINUOUS
	FENCELINE1
	FENCELINE2
	GAS_LINE
	HOT_WATER_SUPPLY
	TRACKS
	ZIGZAG

The following ISO-standard linetypes (*new to Release 13*) are stored in \Acad13\Common\Support\Acad.Lin:

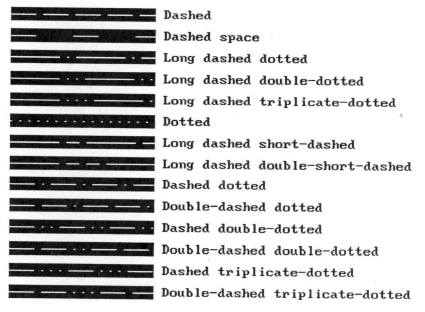

	Dashed
	Dashed space
	Long dashed dotted
	Long dashed double-dotted
	Long dashed triplicate-dotted
	Dotted
	Long dashed short-dashed
	Long dashed double-short-dashed
	Dashed dotted
	Double-dashed dotted
	Dashed double-dotted
	Double-dashed double-dotted
	Dashed triplicate-dotted
	Double-dashed triplicate-dotted

■ The following standard linetypes are supplied with AutoCAD; their definitions are stored in file \Acad13\Common\Support\Acad.Lin:

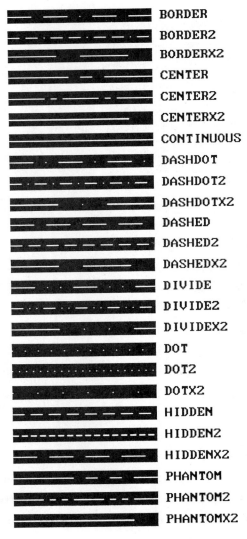

BORDER
BORDER2
BORDERX2
CENTER
CENTER2
CENTERX2
CONTINUOUS
DASHDOT
DASHDOT2
DASHDOTX2
DASHED
DASHED2
DASHEDX2
DIVIDE
DIVIDE2
DIVIDEX2
DOT
DOT2
DOTX2
HIDDEN
HIDDEN2
HIDDENX2
PHANTOM
PHANTOM2
PHANTOMX2

QUICK START: Creating a Custom Linetype

To create a custom linetype on-the-fly:

1. Type the **Linetype Create** command:
   ```
   Command: linetype
   ?/Create/Load/Set: C
   ```

2. Name the linetype in three steps:
   - First, the linetype name:
     ```
     Name of linetype to create: [enter up to 31 characters]
     ```
   - Second, the LIN filename.
     ```
     Append linetype description to Acad.Lin or create
     new LIN file.
     ```
   - Third, describe the linetype:
     ```
     Descriptive text: [enter up to 47 characters]
     ```

3. Define the linetype pattern by using five codes:
   - Positive number for dashes; 0.5 is a dash 0.5 units long.
   - Negative number for gaps; -0.25 is a gap 0.25 units long.
   - Zero is for dots; 0 is a single dot.
   - "A" forces the linetype to align between two endpoints, since linetypes start and stop with a dash).
   - Commas (,) separate values.

Example:
```
*DASHDOT,__ . __ . __ . __ . __ . __ . __ . __ .
A,.5,-.25,0,-.25 [Enter]
```

4. Press **[Enter]** to end linetype definition.

5. Use the **Linetype Load** command to load pattern into drawing.
   ```
   Linetype to load: [type name]
   ```

6. Use the **Linetype Set** command to set the linetype.
   ```
   New object linetype (or ?) <>: [type name]
   ```

   Alternatively, use the **Change** command to change objects to the linetype.

List

List information about selected objects in the drawing.

Command	Alias	Side Menu	Pull-down	Tablet
list	. . .	[ASSIST]	[Assist]	Q 2
		[INQUIRY]	[Inquiry]	
		[List:]	[List]	

```
Command: list
Select objects: [pick]
Select objects: [Enter]
```

Example output:

```
        LINE        Layer: 36
                    Space: Model space
        Color: BYLAYER      Linetype: CONTINUOUS
        Handle = 24A6
  from point, X=  10.0000  Y=   6.0000  Z=   0.0000
    to point, X=   9.0000  Y=   4.0000  Z=   0.0000
Length =    2.2361,  Angle in X-Y Plane =     243
Delta X =  -1.0000, Delta Y =   -2.0000, Delta Z =    0.0000
```

COMMAND OPTIONS

[Esc]	Cancels the list display.
[Ctrl]+S	Pauses the display; press any key to continue.
[F1]	Returns to graphics screen.

RELATED AUTOCAD COMMANDS

- **Area** — Calculates the area and perimeter of some objects.
- **DbList** — Lists information about all objects in the drawing.
- **Dist** — Calculates the 3D distance and angle between two points.

RELATED SYSTEM VARIABLES

- *None*

TIPS

- Use the **List** command as a faster alternative to using the **Dist** and **Area** commands for finding lengths and areas of objects.

- Conditional information listed by the **List** command:
  - Object's color and linetype, if not set BYLAYER.
  - Thickness, if not 0.
  - Extrusion direction, if different from z-axis of current UCS.

- The elevation is not listed and must interpolated from the z-coordinate.

- Object handles are described by hexadecimal numbers.

Load

Loads SHX-format shape files into the drawing via a dialogue box.

Command	Alias	Side Menu	Pull-down	Tablet
load	. . .	[DRAW 2]	[Data]	. . .
		[Shape:]	[Shape File]	
		[Load:]		

Command: **load**
Name of shape file to load (or ?):

COMMAND OPTION

?   Lists the currently loaded shape files.

RELATED AUTOCAD COMMAND

- **Shape**   Inserts shapes into the current drawing.

TIP

- Shapes are more efficient than blocks but are harder to create.

RELATED FILES

- *.SHP   Source code for shape files.
- *.SHX   Compile shape files.

In \Acad13\Common\Sample subdirectory:
- **Es.Shx** and **Es.Shp**   Electronic component shapes.
- **Pc.Shx** and **Pc.Shp**   Printed circuit board shapes.
- **St.Shx** and **St.Shp**   Surface texture shapes for mechanical part drawings.

In \Acad13\Common\Support subdirectory:
- **Gdt.Shx** and **Gdt.Shp**
  Tolerancing shapes used by the **Tolerance** command.
- **LtypeShp.Shx** and **LtypeShp.Shp**
  Linetype shapes used by the **Linetype** command.

QUICK START: Using shapes in your drawing.

1. (*If required*) Use the **Compile** command to compile the source code SHP file into an SHX file.

2. Use the **Load** command to load the SHX shape file into the drawing.

3. Use the **Shape** command to place shapes. The **?** option lists the names of shapes defined by the SHX file.

LogFileOff

Closes the **Acad.Log** file.

Command	Alias	Side Menu	Pull-down	Tablet
logfileoff	...	...	[Options]	...
			[Log Files]	
			[Session Log]	

Command: **logfileoff**

COMMAND OPTIONS
None

RELATED AUTOCAD COMMANDS
- **LogFileOn** Turns on recording Command prompt text to file Acad.Log.
- **[Ctrl]+Q** Echos Command prompt text to the printer.

RELATED FILE
- **Acad.Log** Log file.

TIP
- AutoCAD places a line of dashes at the end of each log file session.

LogFileOn

Opens Acad.Log file and records Command: prompt text to the file.

Command	Alias	Side Menu	Pull-down	Tablet
logfileon	...	...	[Options]	...
			[Log Files]	
			[Session Log]	

Command: logfileon

COMMAND OPTIONS
None

RELATED AUTOCAD COMMANDS
■ **LogFileOff** Turns off recording Command prompt text to file Acad.Log.
■ **[Ctrl]+Q** Echos Command prompt text to the printer.

RELATED FILES
■ **Acad.Log** Log file.

TIPS
■ If log file recording is left on, it resumes when AutoCAD is next loaded.

■ AutoCAD places a line of dashes at the end of each log file session.

'LtScale

Sets the scale factor of linetypes (*short for Line Type SCALE*).

Command	Alias	Side Menu	Pull-down	Tablet
'ltscale	...	...	[Options]	Y 19
			[Linetypes]	
			[Global Linetype Scale]	

Command: **ltscale**
New scale factor <1.0000>:
Regenerating drawing.

```
—  —  —  —  —        — — — — — — — —        —   —    —

    Dashed            Dashed2           DashedX2
```

COMMAND OPTIONS
None

RELATED AUTOCAD COMMANDS
■ **Change**   Changes linetype scale of objects.
■ **Linetype** Loads, creates and sets the working linetype.

RELATED SYSTEM VARIABLES
■ **LtScale**   Contains the current linetype scale factor.
■ **PlineGen** Controls how linetypes are generated for polylines.
■ **PsLtScale** Sets linetype scale relative to paper space.

TIPS
■ If the linetype scale is too large, the linetype appears solid.

■ If the linetype scale is too small, the linetype appears as a solid line that redraws very slowly.

■ In addition to setting the scale with the **LtScale** command, the Acad.Lin contains each linetype in three scales (*see figure, above*):
  ■ Normal.
  ■ Half-size with 2 suffix).
  ■ Double-size with 2X suffix.

MakePreview

Creates BMP-format thumbnail image of drawing.

Command	Alias	Side Menu	Pull-down	Tablet
makepreview ...	...		...	...

Command: **makepreview**
Sample image:

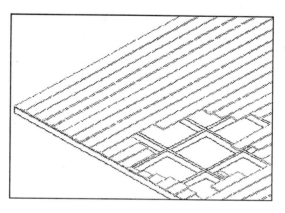

COMMAND OPTIONS
None

RELATED AUTOCAD COMMANDS
- **SaveAsR12** Save drawing in Release 12 format.
- **SaveImg** Save rendering in TIFF, Targa, or GIF format.
- **Plot** Output drawing in one of many raster formats.

RELATED SYSTEM VARIABLE
- **RasterPreview**
  Controls output of the **MakePreview** command.

RELATED FILES
- ***.DWG** Bitmap can be created for any AutoCAD drawing file loaded into Release 13.
- ***.BMP** Bitmap file created by **MakePreview** command.

TIPS

■ **MakePreview** creates a compressed BMP file (short for bitmap, a raster image) in 255x188 pixels by 256 colors.

■ The BMP file created by Release 13 is an compressed format, unable to be read by most common graphics programs; for example, Windows Paintbrush complains, "The format of this file is not supported."

■ The two programs that read **MakePreview**'s BMP files are PaintShop Pro and Graphic Viewer (*both are shareware*); once loaded into either program, use the Windows Clipboard to move the image into other applications.

■ AutoCAD automatically stores a preview image of the drawing in Release 13 drawings, displayed by the **Open File** dialogue box.

■ Use the **MakePreview** command to provide preview images of drawings saved in formats other than Release 13 DWG; the BMP files can be used by other programs to display a snapshot image of the drawing.

MassProp

Reports the mass properties of a 3D solid model, body, or 2D region (*short for MASS PROPerties; an external command in Acis.Dll; formerly the SolMassP command; .*).

Command	Alias	Side Menu	Pull-down	Tablet
massprop	. . .	[ASSIST]	[Assist]	P 1
		[INQUIRY]	[Inquiry]	
		[MassPro:]	[Mass Properties]	

```
Command: massprop
Select objects: [pick]
Select objects: [Enter]
```

Example output of a solid sphere:

```
———————— SOLIDS ————————
Mass:               112.6241
Volume:             12.6241
Bounding box:       X: 4.7910  —  10.7826
                    Y: -1.0540  —   4.9376
                    Z: -2.9958  —   2.9958
Centroid:           X: 7.7868
                    Y: 1.9418
                    Z: 0.0000
Moments of inertia: X: 828.9818
                    Y: 7233.2389
                    Z: 7657.9057
Products of inertia: XY: 1702.9437
                     YZ: 0.0000
                     ZX: 0.0000
Radii of gyration:  X: 2.7130
                    Y: 8.0140
                    Z: 8.2459
Principal moments and X-Y-Z directions about centroid:
             I: 404.3150 along [1.0000 0.0000 0.0000]
             J: 404.3150 along [0.0000 1.0000 0.0000]
             K: 404.3150 along [0.0000 0.0000 1.0000]
Write to a file <N>? y
```

COMMAND OPTIONS

Y   Writes mass property report to an MPR file.

N   Does not write report to file.

RELATED AUTOCAD COMMAND

■ **Area**   Calculates area of non-ACIS objects.

RELATED FILE

■ *.MPR   MassProp writes its results to an MPR mass properties report file.

TIPS

■ As of Release 13, AutoCAD's solid modeling no longer allows you to apply a material density to any solid model. Solids and bodies have a density of 1.0.

■ AutoCAD only analyzes regions coplanar with the first region selected.

DEFINITIONS

Area

■ Total surface area of selected 3D solids, bodies, or 2D regions.

Bounding Box

■ The lower-right and upper-left coordinates of a rectangle enclosing the 2D region.

■ The x,y,z-coordinate pair of a 3D box enclosing the 3D solid or body.

Centroid

■ The x,y,z-coordinates of the center of the 2D region.

■ The center of mass for 3D solids and bodies.

Mass

■ Not calculated for regions.

■ Ten times the volume, since density = 10.

Moment of Inertia

■ For 2D regions:

```
Moment of Inertia = Area * Radius²
```

■ For 3D solids and bodies:

```
Moment of Inertia = Mass * Radius²
```

Perimeter

- Total length of inside and outside loops of 2D regions.
- Not calculated for 3D solids and bodies.

Product of Inertia

- For 2D regions:

  ```
  Product of Inertia = Mass * Distance (of centroid to y,z-
       axis) * Distance (of centroid to x,z-axis)
  ```

- For 3D solids and bodies:

  ```
  Product of Inertia = Mass * Distance (of centroid to y,z-
       axis) * Distance (of centroid to x,z-axis)
  ```

Radius of Gyration

- For 2D regions and 3D solids:

  ```
  Radiua of Gyration = (MomentOfInertia / Mass)
  ```
  $^{1/2}$

Volume

- Not calculated for regions.
- The amount of 3D space occupied by a 3D solid or body.

MatLib

Imports and exports material-look definitions for use by the RMat command (*short for MATerial LIBrary; an external command in Render.Arx*).

Command	Alias	Side Menu	Pull-down	Tablet
matlib	...	[TOOLS]	[Tools]	M 1
		[RENDER]	[Render]	
		[MatLib:]	[Materials Library]	

Command: **matlib**

Displays dialogue box.

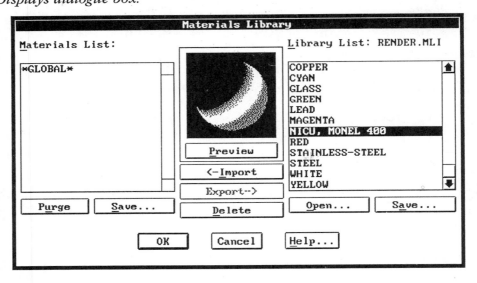

COMMAND OPTIONS

Preview	Previews the selected material mapped to a sphere object.
Import	Brings a material definition into the drawing.
Export	Adds material definition to MLI library fil.
Purge	Deletes unattached material definitions from the **Materials** list.
Save	Saves to an MLI file.
Delete	Deletes selected material definitions from the **Materials** or **Library** lists.
Open	Loads material definitions from an MLI file.

RELATED AUTOCAD COMMAND

■ RMat   Attaches a material definition to objects, colors, and layers.

RELATED FILES

■ Render.Mli Material LIbrary; contains the material definitions.
■ AutoVis.Mli AutoVision material library file.

TIPS

■ MatLib only loads and purges material definitions; use RMat to attach the definitions to objects.

■ "Materials" define the look of a rendered object: coloring, reflection (shinyness), roughness, and ambient reflection.

■ When you import materials from an AutoVision MLI file, only the following parameters are read: Color, Ambient, Reflection, and Roughness.

■ Materials do not define the density of 3D solids and bodies.

■ By default, a drawing contains a single material definition, called *GLO-BAL*, with the default parameters for color, roughness, ambient, and reflection.

■ The AutoVis.Mli file contains 144 additional material definitions; you can find the file in subdirectory \Autovis\Avis_sup of the Release 13 distribution CD-ROM.

Measure

Divides lines, arcs, circles, and polylines into equi-distant segments, placing a point or a block at each segment.

Command	Alias	Side Menu	Pull-down	Tablet
measure	...	[DRAW 2]	[Draw]	X 22
		[Measure:]	[Point]	
			[Measure]	

```
Command: measure
Select object to measure: [pick]
<Segment length>/Block: B
Block name to insert:
Align block with object? <Y>
Segment length:
```

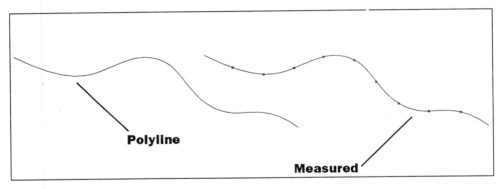

Polyline

Measured

COMMAND OPTIONS

Block   Indicates the name of the block to use as a marker.
<Segment length>
          Indicates the distance between markers.

RELATED AUTOCAD COMMANDS

- **Block**   Creates blocks that can be used with **Measure**.
- **Divide**   Divides an object into a number of segments.

RELATED SYSTEM VARIABLES

- **PdMode**   Controls the shape of a point.
- **PdSize**   Controls the size of a point.

TIPS

■ You must define the block before it can be used with the **Measure** command.

■ The **Measure** distance does not place a point or block at the beginning of the measured object.

Menu

Loads an MNX menu file into the drawing editor; compiles the MNU and MNL source files.

Command	Alias	Side Menu	Pull-down	Tablet
menu	. . .	[TOOLS]	[Tools]	X 25
		[Menu:]	[Menus]	

```
Command: menu
Menu file name or . for none <acad>:
```

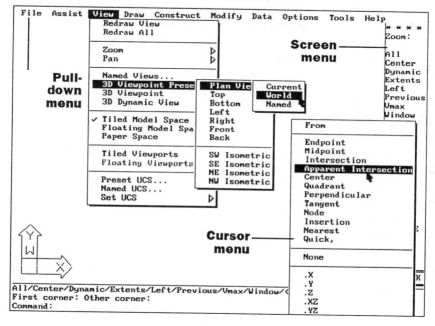

COMMAND OPTIONS

.	*(Period)* Removes current menu from AutoCAD.
[Enter]	Reloads current menu.

RELATED AUTOCAD COMMAND
■ **Tablet**   Configures digitizing tablet for use with overlay menus.

RELATED AUTODESK PROGRAM
■ **MC.Exe**   Stand-alone menu compiler.

RELATED SYSTEM VARIABLES
■ **MenuName** The currently loaded menu file.
■ **MenuEcho** Suppresses menu echoing.
■ **ScreenBoxes** Specifies the number of menu lines displayed on the side menu.

RELATED FILES

Files are located in the \Common\Support or \Dos\Support subdirectories:

- **Acad.Mnu** Default menu file.
- **Acad.Mnx** Compiled menu file.
- **Acad.Mnl** AutoLISP routines used by menu files.
- ***.XMX** External message file.
- ***.DCL** Dialogue box definition files.
- ***.DCC** Dialogue box color definitions.
- ***.INI** Initialization files.
- ***.LSP** AutoLISP routines for external commands.
- ***.EXP** ADS routines used by external commands.
- ***.Arx** *and* ***.Dll**

     ARx routines used by external commands.

TIPS

- AutoCAD automatically compiles MNU files into MNX files for faster loading.
- The MNU file defines the function of:
  - The screen menu (*see figure*).
  - Pull-down menu (*see figure*).
  - Cursor menu (*see figure*).
  - Icon menus.
  - Digitizing tablet menus.
  - Pointing device buttons.
  - AUX: device.

- To create a large drawing area, use the **Config** command to remove the screen menu area.

- The DOS version of Release 13 does not support the Toolbar and Toolbox icons found in the Windows version.

- The DOS version of Release 13 does not support the **MenuLoad** and **MenuUnload** commands, for loading (and unloading) part of the menu file.

MInsert

Inserts an array of blocks as a single block (*short for Multiple INSERT*).

Command	Alias	Side Menu	Pull-down	Tablet
minsert	. . .	[DRAW 2]	[Draw]	. . .
		[Minsert:]	[Insert]	
			[Multiple Blocks]	

```
Command: minsert
Block name (or ?) <>:
Insertion point: [pick]
X scale factor <1> / Corner / XYZ: [pick]
Y scale factor (default=X): [pick]
Rotation angle <0>: [pick]
Number of rows (- - -) <1>:
Number of columns (| | |) <1>:
Unit cell or distance between rows (—):
Distance between columns (| | |):
```

COMMAND OPTIONS

Block name Indicates the name of the block to be inserted.

?   Lists the names of blocks stored in the drawing.

X scale factor <1>

        Indicates the x-scale factor.

Corner   Indicates the x- and y-scale factors by pointing on the screen.

XYZ   Displays the x-, y- and z-scale submenu.

P   Supplies predefined block name, scale, and rotation values.

INPUT OPTIONS

■ In response to the 'Block Name:' prompt, you can enter:

    ■ ~   (*Tilde*) Displays a dialogue box of blocks stored on disk.

    ■ =   (*Equals*) Redefines existing block with a new block, as in:

        Block name: **oldname=newname**

- In response to the 'Insertion point:' prompt, you can enter:
  - **Scale**   Specifies x-, y-, z-scale factors.
  - **PScale**   Presets the x-, y-, and z-scale factors.
  - **Xscale**   Specifies x-scale factor.
  - **PsScale**   Presets x-scale factor.
  - **Yscale**   Specifies y-scale factor.
  - **PyScale**   Presets y-scale factor.
  - **Zscale**   Specifies z-scale factor.
  - **PzScale**   Presets the z-scale factor.
  - **Rotate**   Specifies the rotation angle.
  - **PRotate**   Presets the rotation angle.

RELATED AUTOCAD COMMANDS

- **3dArray**   Creates 3D rectangular and polar arrays.
- **Array**   Creates 2D rectangular and polar arrays.
- **Block**   Creates a block.

TIP

- The array placed by the **MInsert** command is a single block.

Mirror

Creates a mirror copy of a group of objects in 2D space.

Command	Alias	Side Menu	Pull-down	Tablet
mirror	. . .	[Constrct]	[Construct]	X 12
		[Mirror:]	[Mirror]	

```
Command: mirror
Select objects: [pick]
Select objects: [Enter]
First point of mirror line: [pick]
Second point: [pick]
Delete old objects? <N>
```

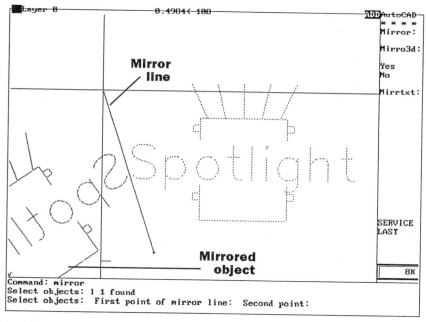

COMMAND OPTIONS
N   Does not delete selected objects.
Y   Deletes selected objects.

RELATED AUTOCAD COMMANDS
- **Copy**   Creates a non-mirrored copy of a group of objects.
- **Mirror3d** Mirrors objects in 3D space.

RELATED SYSTEM VARIABLE
- **MirrText** Determines whether text is mirrored by the **Mirror** command:
        0 Text is not mirrored about horizontal axis.
        1 Text is mirrored.

Mirror3d

Mirrors objects about a plane in 3D space (*an external command in Geom3d.Exp*).

Command	Alias	Side Menu	Pull-down	Tablet
mirror3d	...	[CONSTRCT]	[Construct]	Y 21
		[Mirr3D:]	[3D Mirror]	

```
Command: mirror3d
Select objects: [pick]
Select objects: [Enter]
Plane by Object/Last/Zaxis/View/XY/YZ/ZX/<3 points>:
Delete old objects? <N>
```

COMMAND OPTIONS

Object   Selects object to specify mirroring plane:
  Pick a circle, arc or 2D-polyline segment:

Last   Selects last-picked mirroring plane.
View   Current view plane is the mirror plane:
  Align on view plane <0,0,0>:

XY/YZ/ZX   X,y-, y,z- or z,x-plane is the mirror plane:
  Point on XY plane <0,0,0>:

Zaxis   Defines mirroring plane by a point on the plane and on the normal to the plane (*z-axis*):
  Point on plane:
  Point on Z-axis (normal) of the plane:

<3 points> Defines three points on mirroring plane:

RELATED AUTOCAD COMMANDS

■ **Mirror**   Mirrors objects in 2D space.
■ **Rotate3d** Rotates objects in 3D space.

RELATED SYSTEM VARIABLE

■ **MirrText** Determines whether text is mirrored by the **Mirror3D** command.

MlEdit

Edits multilines (*short for MultiLine EDITor; replaces the DLine command*).

Command	Alias	Side Menu	Pull-down	Tablet
mledit	. . .	[MODIFY]	[Modify]	. . .
		[MlEdit:]	[Edit Multiline]	

Command: **mledit**
Displays dialogue box.

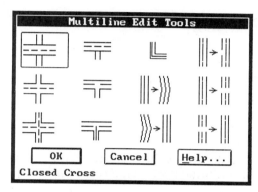

COMMAND OPTIONS

U   Undoes the most recent multiline edit.

Closed Cross

Closes the intersection of two multilines.

Open Cross

Opens the intersection of two multilines.

Merged Cross

Merges a pair of multilines (open exterior lines; closes interior lines).

Closed Tee

Closes a T-intersection.

Open Tee

Opens a T-intersection.

Merged Tee

Merges a T-intersection: opens exterior lines; closes interior lines.

Corner Joint

Creates a corner joint of a pair of intersecting multilines.

Add Vertex

Adds a vertex (*joint*) to a multiline segment.

〉⟩·‖ **Delete Vertex**
Removes a vertex from a multiline segment.

‖·‖ **Cut Single**
Places a gap in a single line of a multiline.

‖·‖ **Cut All**
Places a gap in all lines of a multiline.

‖·‖ **Weld All**
Removes a gap in a multiline.

RELATED AUTOCAD COMMANDS

- **MLine**   Draws up to 16 parallel lines.
- **MlProp**   Defines the properties of a multiline.

RELATED SYSTEM VARIABLES

- **CMlJust**   Current multiline justification:
  - **0** Top (*Default*)
  - **1** Middle
  - **2** Bottom
- **CMlScale** Current multiline scale factor (*Default = 1.0*).
- **CMlStyle** Current multiline style name (*Default = " "*).

RELATED FILE

- ***.MLN**   Multiline style definition file is in \Acad13\Common\Support.

TIPS

- Use the **Cut All** option to open up a gap before placing door and window symbols in a multiline wall.

- Use the **Weld All** option to close up a gap after removing the door or window symbol in a multiline.

- Use the **Stretch** command to move a door or window symbols in a multiline wall.

MLine

Draws up to 16 parallel lines (*short for Multiple LINE; replaces the
DLine command*).

Command	Alias	Side Menu	Pull-down	Tablet
mline	...	[DRAW 1]	[Draw]	J 9
		[Mline:]	[Multiline]	

```
Command: mline
Justification=Top, Scale=1.0000, Style=STANDARD
Justification/Scale/STyle/<From point>: [pick]
Undo/<To point>: [pick]
Close/Undo/<To point>:
```

COMMAND OPTIONS

Undo   Back up by one segment.

Close   Close the multiline to its start point.

Justification options:

Top   Draws top line of multiline at cursor; remainder of multiline
            is "below" cursor.

Zero   Draws along the zero-offset point of multiline.

Bottom Draws bottom line of multiline at cursor; remainder of
            multiline is "above" cursor.

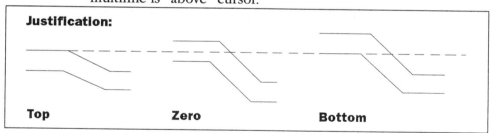

Justification:

Top   **Zero**   **Bottom**

Scale option examples:

1.0   Default scale factor.

2.0   Draws multiline twice as wide

-1.0   Flips multiline.

0   Collapses multiline to a single line.

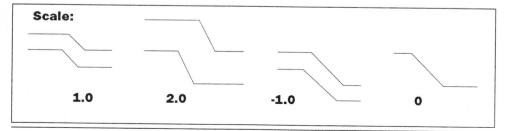

Scale:

1.0   **2.0**   **-1.0**   **0**

STyle options:
Multiline style name:
> Specifies the name of multiline style.

? Lists names of multiline styles defined in drawing.

RELATED AUTOCAD COMMANDS

- **MlEdit** Edits multilines.
- **MlProp** Defines the properties of a multiline.

RELATED SYSTEM VARIABLES

- **CMlJust** Current multiline justification:
  > **0** Top (*Default*)
  > **1** Middle
  > **2** Bottom
- **CMlScale** Current multiline scale factor (*Default = 1.0*).
- **CMlStyle** Current multiline style name (*Default = " "*).

RELATED FILE

- ***.MLN** Multiline style definition file is in \Acad13\Common\Support.

TIP

- Multiline styles are stored in MLN files in a DXF-like format.

MlStyle

Defines the characteristics of multilines (*short for MultiLine STYLE*).

Command	Alias	Side Menu	Pull-down	Tablet
mline	...	[DATA]	[Data]	...
		[MlStyle:]	[Multiline Style]	

Command: **mlstyle**

Displays dialogue box.

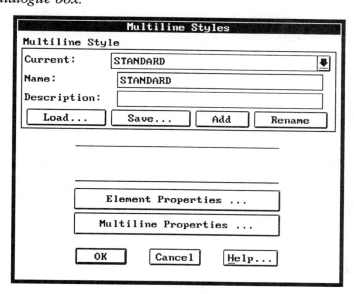

COMMAND OPTIONS

Current   Lists currently loaded multiline style names (*Default = STANDARD*)

Name   Gives a name to a new multiline style, or renames an existing style.

Description Describes the multiline style, with up to 255 characters.

Load   Loads style from the multiline library file Acad.Mln;
                displays dialogue box:

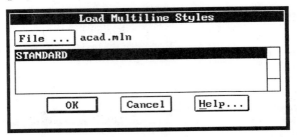

Save   Saves a multiline style or rename a style.
Add   Adds the multiline style (taken from the **Name** box) to the
                Current list.
Remove   Removes the multiline style from the **Current** list.
Element Properties
                Specifies the properties for the multiline style; displays dialogue box:

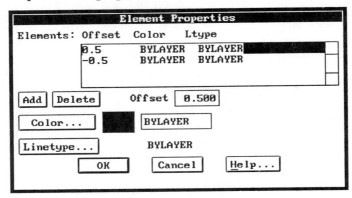

This dialogue box controls:
■ Adding and removing lines (*maximum = 16*).
■ The offset distance (*negative and positive distance from
   origin*).
■ Color of each line.
■ Linetype of each line.

Multiline Properties

Specifies additional properties for multilines; displays dialogue box:

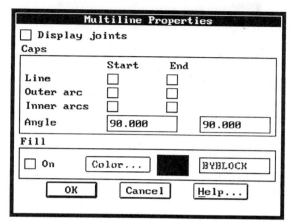

This dialogue box controls:
- Toggling the display of joints (*cross-segment at vertices*).
- Displaying the endcaps at start and endpoints (*line, angled line, outer arc, and/or inner arc*).
- Toggling the fill of multiline.
- Selecting the color for solid fill.

RELATED AUTOCAD COMMANDS
- **MlEdit**   Edits multilines.
- **MLine**   Draws up to 16 parallel lines.

RELATED SYSTEM VARIABLES
- **CMlJust**   Current multiline justification:
    - 0 Top (*Default*)
    - 1 Middle
    - 2 Bottom
- **CMlScale** Current multiline scale factor (*Default = 1.0*).
- **CMlStyle** Current multiline style name (*Default = " "*).

RELATED FILE
- **Acad.Mln** Multiline style definition file in \Acad13\Common\Support.

TIPS
- Use the **MlEdit** command to create (or close up) gaps to place door and window symbols in multiline walls.

- The multiline scale factor has the following effect on the look of a multiline:
  - **1.0**   Default scale factor.
  - **2.0**   Draws multiline twice as wide, not twice as long.
  - **-1.0**   Flips multiline about its origin.
  - **0**   Collapse multiline to a single line.

- The MLN file describes multiline styles in a DXF-like format:

```
MLSTYLE
2
 STANDARD
70
 0
3

62
 0
51
 90.00000000000000
52
 90.00000000000000
71
 2
49
 0.50000000000000
62
 256
6
 BYLAYER
49
 -0.50000000000000
62
 256
6
```

Move

Moves a group of objects to a new location.

Command	Alias	Side Menu	Pull-down	Tablet
move	m	[MODIFY]	[Modify]	W 15
		[Move:]	[Move]	

```
Command: move
Select objects: [pick]
Select objects: [Enter]
Base point or displacement: [pick]
Second point of displacement: [pick]
```

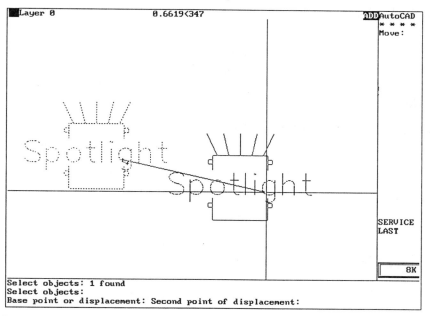

COMMAND OPTIONS

Base point Indicates the starting point for the move.
Displacement Indicates the distance to move.

RELATED AUTOCAD COMMANDS

- **Copy** Makes a copy of selected objects.
- **MlEdit** Moves the vertices of a multiline.
- **PEdit** Moves the vertices of a polyline.

TIP

- You can move objects without using the **Move** command; click twice on the object, then press the spacebar to toggle through the editing options until ** MOVE ** appears.

MSlide

Save the current view as an SLD-format slide file on disk (*short for Make SLIDE*).

Command	Alias	Side Menu	Pull-down	Tablet
mslide	. . .	[TOOLS]	[Tools]	. . .
		[SLIDES]	[Slide]	
		[MSlide:]	[Save]	

Command: **mslide**
Slide file:

COMMAND OPTIONS
None

RELATED AUTOCAD COMMANDS
- **Save**   Saves the current drawing as a DWG-format drawing file.
- **SaveImg** Saves the current view as a TIFF, Targa, or GIF raster file.
- **VSlide**   Displays an SLD-format slide file in AutoCAD.

RELATED AUTODESK PROGRAM
- **Slidelib.Exe** Compiles a group of slides into an SLB-format slide library file.

MSpace

Switches the drawing from paper space back to model space (*short for Model SPACE*).

Command	Alias	Side Menu	Pull-down	Tablet
mspace	ms	[VIEW]	[View]	V 14
		[MSpace:]	[Tiled Model Space]	
			[View]	
			[Floating Model Space	

Command: **mspace**

COMMAND OPTIONS
None

RELATED AUTOCAD COMMANDS
- **MView**   Creates viewports in paper space.
- **MvSetup**   Sets up the configuration of a new drawing.
- **PSpace**   Switches from model space to paper space.
- **VpLayer**   Sets independent visibility of layers.

RELATED SYSTEM VARIABLES
- **MaxActVp**   Maximum number of viewports with visible objects (*Default = 16*).
- **PsLtScale**   Linetype scale relative to paper space.
- **Tilemode**   The current setting of tilemode:
    - 0 Off (*Default*).
    - 1 On.

TIPS
- **Tilemode** must be set to zero before switching to paper space and using the **MSpace** command.

- To switch from paper space back to model space, at least one viewport must be active; create the viewport with the **MView** command.

- Objects in the current selection set are ignored if they were not collected in the current space.

- AutoCAD clears the selection set when moving between paper and model space.

MText

Places paragraph text in a boundary box (*short for Multline TEXT*).

Command	Alias	Side Menu	Pull-down	Tablet
mtext	t	[DRAW 1]	[Draw]	. . .
		[MText]	[Text]	

```
Command: mtext
Attach/Rotation/Style/Height/Direction/<Insertion point>:
   [pick]
Attach/Rotation/Style/Height/Direction/Width/2Points/<Other
   corner>: [pick]
Height <>:
```

Loads user-supplied text editor, Edit by default.

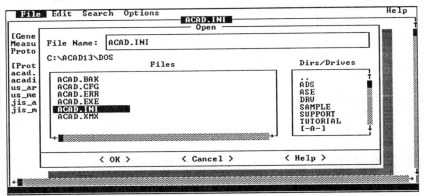

COMMAND OPTIONS

Attach boundary box options:

TL	Top left.
TC	Top center.
TR	Top right.
ML	Middle left.
MC	Middle center.
MR	Middle right.
BL	Bottom left.
BC	Bottom center.
BR	Bottom right.

Rotation   Rotation angle of boundary box.
Style   Text style for multiline text (*Default = STANDARD*).
Height   Height of UPPERCASE text (*Default = 0.2 units*).
Direction   Drawing direction of multiline text: horizontal or vertical.

| Width | Width of boundary box. |
| 2Points | Pick two points to define the boundary box. |

RELATED AUTOCAD COMMANDS

- **DdEdit** Edits multiline text via external text editor.
- **DText** Places several lines of text.
- **MtProp** Changes properties of multiline text.
- **Style** Creates a named text style from a font file.
- **Text** Places a single line of text.

RELATED SYSTEM VARIABLE

- **MTextEd** Name of external text editor to place and edit multiline text.

TIPS

- By default, the DOS version of the **MText** command attempts to load Edit, the DOS v5/6 text editor.

- Use the **MTextEd** system variable to define a different text editor.

- The **MText** command fails when:
    - Your computer does not have QuickBasic; or
    - Your computer does not have Edit, the DOS text editor, which requires QuickBasic to run; or
    - The text editor you specify with **MTextEd** does not accept filenames at the command line.

- Use the **Direction** option for languages that read vertically, such as Chinese and Japanese.

- The control codes recognized by **MText**:
    - \~ Places a non-breaking space.
    - \P Forces a line break.
    - \\ Places a backslash.
    - \{ Places an opening brace.
    - \} Places a closing brace.
    - \L Turns underLinning on.
    - \l Turns underlinning off (*Default*).
    - \O Turns Overlinning on.
    - \o Turns overlinning off (*Default*).
    - \S$n$^m Stack n over m.
    - \F$x$; Changes Font to filename x; uses any valid SHX, PFB, and TTF font file (*Default = current Style*).
    - \C$n$; Changes text to Color n (*Default = BYLAYER*).
    - \H$n$; Changes text to Height n (*Default = current height*).
    - \Q$n$; Changes to obliQuing angle n (*Default = 0 degrees*).
    - \T$n$; Changes Tracking n from 0.75 to 4.0 (*Default = 1.0*).
    - \W$n$; Changes text Width to value n (*Default = 1.0*).

'MtProp

Changes the properties of multiline text (*short for Multline Text PROPerties*).

Command	Alias	Side Menu	Pull-down	Tablet
'mtprop	. . .	. . .	. . .	. . .

Command: **mtprop**
Select an MText object: **[pick]**

Displays dialogue box.

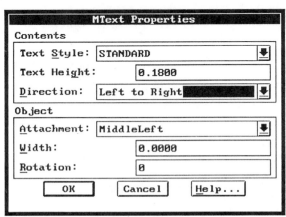

COMMAND OPTIONS

Text Style Selects a named text style (*default = STANDARD*).
Text Height Sets height of UPPERCASE text (*default = 0.2 units*).
Direction Sets direction of text (*default = left to right*).
Attachment Sets alignment of text boundary box at the insertion point.
Width Sets width of text boundary box.
Rotation Sets rotation of text boundary box.

RELATED AUTOCAD COMMANDS

- **DdEdit** Edits multiline text via external text editor.
- **DText** Places several lines of text.
- **MText** Places multiline text.
- **Style** Creates a named text style from a font file.
- **Text** Places a single line of text.

TIP

- Use the **Direction** option for languages that read vertically, such as Chinese and Japanese.

Multiple

A command modifier to automatically repeat commands.

Command	Alias	Side Menu	Pull-down	Tablet
multiple	...	...	...	...

Exampe usage:
Command: **multiple circle**
3P/2P/TTR/<Center point>: **[pick]**
Diameter/<Radius>: **[pick]**
circle 3P3P/2P/TTR/<Center point>: **[pick]**
Diameter/<Radius>: **[pick]**
circle 3P3P/2P/TTR/<Center point>: **[Esc]**

COMMAND OPTION

[Esc]   Stops the command from automatically repeating itself.

COMMAND INPUT OPTIONS

[Space]   Press the spacebar to repeat any previous command.
[Click]   Click on any blank spot on the tablet menu to repeat a command.

RELATED AUTOCAD COMMANDS

■ **Redo**   Undoes an undo.
■ **U**   Undoes the previous command.

RELATED COMMAND MODIFIERS

■ **'**   *(Apostrophe)* Allows use of certain transparent commands in another command.
■ **~**   *(Tilde)* Forces display of dialogue box.
■ **-**   *(Dash)* Forces display of prompts on command line.

TIPS

■ **Multiple** is not a command but a command modifier; it does nothing on its own.

■ **Multiple** only repeats the command name; it does not repeat command options.

■ Some commands automatically repeat, including **Point** and **Donut**.

MView

Creates and manipulates overlapping viewports (*short for Make VIEWports*).

Command	Alias	Side Menu	Pull-down	Tablet
mview	...	[VIEW]	[View]	P 3-5
		[MView:]	[Floating Viewports]	
				Q 3-5
				R4

```
Command: mview
ON/OFF/Hideplot/Fit/2/3/4/Restore/<First Point>: [pick]
Other corner: [pick]
Regenerating drawing.
```

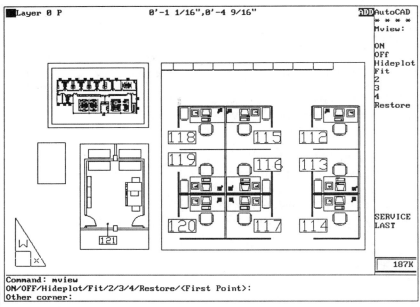

COMMAND OPTIONS

<First Point>	Indicates the first point of a single viewport.
Fit	Creates a single viewport that fits the screen.
Hideplot	Creates a hidden-line view during plotting and printing.
OFF	Turns a viewport off.
ON	Turns a viewport on.
Restore	Restore a saved viewport configuration.

2   Displays the submenu of viewport orientations:
Horizontal Stacks the two viewports.
‹Vertical›   Side-by-side viewports.

3   Displays the submenu of viewport orientations:
Horizontal Stacks the three viewports.
Vertical   Side-by-side viewports.
Above   Two viewports above the third.
Below   Two viewports below the third.
Left   Two viewports to the left of the third.
‹Right›   Two viewports to the right of the third.

4   Displays the submenu of viewport orientations:
Fit   Creates four same-size viewports to fit the screen.
‹First Point› Indicates the area for the four viewports.

RELATED AUTOCAD COMMANDS

- **[Ctrl]+V** Switches to the next viewport.
- **MSpace** Switches to model space.
- **MvSetup** Sets the up configuration of a drawing in paper space.
- **PSpace** Switchs to paper space before creating viewports.
- **Redrawall** Redraws all viewports.
- **RegenAll** Regenerates all viewports.
- **VpLayer** Controls the visibility of layers in each viewport.
- **VPorts** Creates tiled viewports in model space.
- **Zoom** The **XP** option zooms a viewport relative to paper space.

RELATED SYSTEM VARIABLES

- **CvPort** Current viewport.
- **MaxActVp** Controls the maximum number of visible viewports:
  - 1 Minimum.
  - 16 Default.
  - 32767 Maximum.
- **Tilemode** Controls the availability of overlapping viewports:
  - 0 Off.
  - 1 On.

TIPS

- Although system variable **MaxActVp** limits the number of simultaneously visible viewports, the **Plot** command plots all viewports.

- **Tilemode** must be set to zero to switch to paper space and use the **MSpace** command.

- **Snap, Grid, Hide, Shade**, etc, can be set separately in each viewport.

MvSetup

Inserts predefined title blocks, creates a set of viewports, sets a global scale factor (*short for Model View SETUP; an external command in MvSetup.Lsp*).

Command	Alias	Side Menu	Pull-down	Tablet
mvsetup	mvs	...	[View] [Floating Viewports] [MV Setup]	...

Command: **mvsetup**

Command prompt when Tilemode = 1:
Enable paper space? (No/<Yes>): **N**
Units type (Scientific/Decimal/Engineering/Architectural/Metric):
Enter the scale factor:
Enter the paper width:
Enter the paper height:

Command prompt when Tilemode = 0:
Align/Create/Scale viewports/Options/Title block/Undo: **A**
Angles/Horizontal/Vertical alignment/Rotate view/Undo: **A**
Base point: **[pick]**
Other point: **[pick]**
Distance from basepoint:
Angle from basepoint:

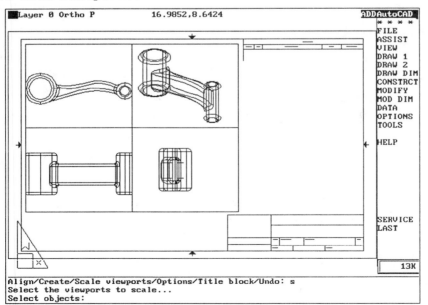

COMMAND OPTIONS

Align   Aligns new viewport with base point of existing viewport.
Create   Creates viewports in four layouts:
       0 No layout.
       1 Single viewport.
       2 Standard engineering layout.
       3 Array viewports along x- and y-axes.

Scale viewports Scales border with respect to drawing objects.
Options   Select an option:
  Set layer Specifies layer for title block.
  Limits   Specifies whether to reset limits after title block insertion.
  Units   Specifies inch or millimeter paper units.
  Xref   Specifies whether title is inserted as a block or as an xref.
Title block Specifies title block style.
Undo   Undoes **MvSetup** operations in reverse order.

RELATED SYSTEM VARIABLE

■ **Tilemode** The current setting of tilemode:
    0 Off (*Default*).
    1 On.

RELATED FILES

■ **MvSetup.Dfs** The **MvSetup** default settings file.
■ **AcadIso.Dwg** Prototype drawing with ISO defaults.

TIPS

■ When option 2 (Std. Engineering) is selected at the **Create** option, the following views are created (counterclockwise from upper left):
  ■ Top view.
  ■ Isometric view.
  ■ Front view.
  ■ Right view.

■ To create the title block, **MvSetup** searches the path specified by the AcadPrefix variable. If the appropriate drawing cannot be found, **MvSetup** creates the default border.

■ **MvSetup** produces the following predefined title blocks:
  ■ None.
  ■ ISO A0 through A4 (mm, metric).
  ■ ANSI A through E, ANSI V (in, imperial).
  ■ Architectural and engineering D-size.
  ■ Generic D-size.

- The metric A0 size is similar to the imperial E-size, while the metric A4 is similar to A-size.

- You can add your own title block with the **Add** option. Before doing so, create the title block as an AutoCAD drawing.

QUICK START: Adding a Border and Views

MvSetup has many options but does not present them in a logical fashion. To set up a drawing with **MvSetup**, follow these steps:

1. Start the **MvSetup** command:
   ```
   Command: mvsetup
   ```

2. Place the title block with the **Title** option.

3. Set up the viewports with the **Create** option. For standard drawings, select option #2, Std. Engineering.

4. Make the object the same size in all four viewports with the **Scale** option. When you are prompted to 'Select objects:', select the four viewports, not the objects in the drawing.

5. You can interrupt the **MvSetup** command at any time with the [Esc] key, then resume the command to complete the setup.

New

Names and starts a new drawing.

Command	Alias	Side Menu	Pull-down	Tablet
new	. . .	[FILE]	[File]	U 24
		[New:]	[New]	

Command: new

Displays dialogue box.

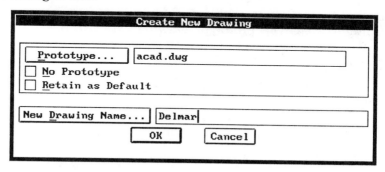

COMMAND OPTIONS

Prototype   Specifies the name of the prototype drawing.

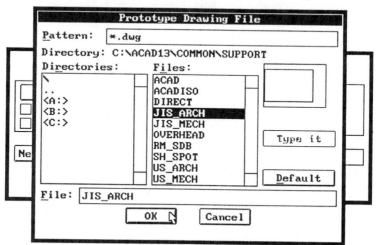

No prototype   Does not use a prototype drawing.
Retain as default
            Retains drawing as the default prototype drawing.
New drawing name
            Specifies the filename of the new drawing.

RELATED AUTOCAD COMMANDS

■ **SaveAs**   Saves drawing with a different name.

RELATED SYSTEM VARIABLES

■ **DbMod**   Indicates whether drawing has changed since being loaded.
■ **DwgName**   Filename of current drawing.

RELATED FILES

Found in \Acad13\Common\Support subdirectory:
■ **Acad.Dwg**   The default prototype drawing.
■ **AcadIso.Dwg** The ISO/DIN prototype drawing.
■ **Jis_Arch.Dwg** The JIS architectural prototype drawing.
■ **Jis_Mech.Dwg** The JIS mechanical prototype drawing.
■ **Us_Arch.Dwg** The US architectural prototype drawing.
■ **Us_Mech.Dwg** The US mechanical prototype drawing.

TIPS

■ AutoCAD allows you to save your work before using the **New** command.

■ Until you give the drawing a name, AutoCAD names it 'Unnamed.Dwg.'

■ Picking the **OK** button without naming the drawing leaves the name unchanged.

■ The **Prototype** button lets you select a different prototype drawing from a dialogue box.

■ The default prototype drawing is Acad.Dwg; edit and save Acad.Dwg to change the defaults in new drawings.

Offset

Draws parallel lines, arcs, circles, and polylines; repeats automatically until cancelled.

Command	Alias	Side Menu	Pull-down	Tablet
offset	. . .	[CONSTRCT]	[Construct]	W 14
		[Offset:]	[Offset]	

```
Command: offset
Offset distance or Through <Through>: t
Select object to offset: [pick]
Through point: [pick]
Select object to offset: [Esc]
```

COMMAND OPTIONS

Through Indicates the offset distance.
[Esc] Exits the **Offset** command.

RELATED AUTOCAD COMMANDS

- **Copy** Creates copies of a group of objects.
- **Mirror** Creates a mirror copy of a group of objects.
- **MLine** Draws up to 16 parallel lines.

RELATED SYSTEM VARIABLE

- **OffsetDist** Current offset distance.

Oops

Unerases the last-erased group of objects; returns the group of objects after the **Block** command.

Command	Alias	Side Menu	Pull-down	Tablet
oops	...	[MODIFY]	[Modify]	W 18
		[Oops:]	[Erase]	
			[Oops!]	

Command: **oops**

COMMAND OPTIONS
None

RELATED AUTOCAD COMMAND
- **Undo**   Undoes the most recent command.

RELATED SYSTEM VARIABLES
- *None*

TIPS
- **Oops** only unerases the most-recently erased object; use the **Undo** command to unerase earlier objects.

- Use **Oops** to bring back objects after turning them into a block with the **Block** and **WBlock** commands.

Open

Loads a drawing into AutoCAD.

Command	Alias	Side Menu	Pull-down	Tablet
open	. . .	[FILE]	[File]	U 25
		[Open:]	[Open]	

Command: open

Displays dialogue box.

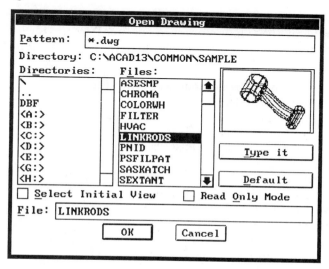

COMMAND OPTIONS

Default   Loads current drawing again.
Pattern   Specifies the filename pattern.
Read only mode
              Displays drawing but you cannot edit it.
Select initial view
              Selects a named view from a dialogue box:

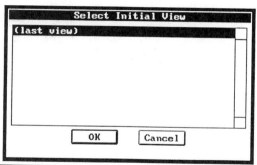

RELATED AUTOCAD COMMANDS

- **New** Starts a new drawing.
- **SaveAs** Saves drawing with a new name.

TIPS

- The **Open** command loads DWG drawing files for Release 13 and earlier.

- When a pre-Release 13 drawing is loaded, it is converted with the message, "Converting old drawing."

- To retain a drawing in a pre-Release 13 DWG format, use the **SaveAs** comamnd to rename the file or store it in another subdirectory. As an alternative, use the **SaveAsR12** command to save the drawing in Release 12 format.

- The **Open** command does not load any other file format into AutoCAD. Instead, use these commands:
  - **DxfIn** ASCII and binary DXF file format.
  - **DxbIn** DXB file format.
  - **PsIn** EPS, encapsulated PostScript.
  - **TiffIn** TIFF, tagged image file format.
  - **PcxIn** PCX
  - **GifIn** GIF, graphics interchange format.
  - **Replay** TIFF, GIF, and TGA (Targa).
  - **AcisIn** ASCII-format SAT (save as text) ACIS (*new to Release 13*).
  - **VlConv** Visual Link files (*new to Release 13*).
  - **3dsIn** 3D Studio files (*new to Release 13*).
  - **VSlide** SLD (slide) files.

'Ortho

Constrains drawing and editing commands to the vertical and horizontal directions only (*short for ORTHOgraphic*).

Command	Ctrl+	Function Key	Pull-down	Tablet
'ortho	O	[F8]	[Assist]	V 15
			[Ortho]	

Command: **ortho**
ON/OFF <Off>:

COMMAND OPTIONS

OFF   Turns ortho mode off.
ON   Turn ortho mode on.

RELATED AUTOCAD COMMAND

■ **DdRModes** Toggles ortho mode via a dialogue box.

RELATED SYSTEM VARIABLE

■ **OrthoMode** The current state of ortho mode.

TIPS

■ Use ortho mode when you want to constrain your drawing and editing to right angles.

■ Rotate the angle of ortho with the **Snap** command's **Rotate** option.

■ In isoplane mode, ortho mode constrains the cursor to the current isoplane.

■ Ortho mode is ignored when entering coordinates by the keyboard and in perspective mode.

'OSnap

Sets and turns off object snap modes (*short for Object Snap*).

Command	Button	Side Menu	Pull-down	Tablet
'osnap	[#2]	[* * * *]	[Assist]	T 12-22
		[Osnap:]	[Object Snap]	
		[SERVICE]	[Options]	U 12-13
		[Osnap:]	[Running Object Snap]	

```
Command: osnap
Object snap modes:
```

COMMAND OPTIONS

As abbreviation, enter only the first three letters:

APParent intersection
> Snaps to the imaginary intersection of two objects.

CENter   Snaps to center point of arcs and circles.

ENDpoint   Snaps to endpoint of lines, polylines, traces, and arcs.

from   Extends from a point by a given distance.

INSertion   Snaps to insertion point of blocks, shapes, and text.

INTersection Snaps to intersection of two objects.

MIDpoint   Snaps to middle point of lines and arcs.

NEArest   Snaps to object nearest to crosshairs.

NODe   Snaps to a point object.

NONe   Temporarily turns off all object snap modes.

OFF   Turns off all object snap modes.

PERpendicular
> Snaps perpendicularly to objects.

QUAdrant   Snaps the quadrant points of circles and arcs.

QUIck   Snaps to the first object found in the database.

TANgent   Snaps tangent to arcs and circles.

RELATED AUTOCAD COMMANDS

- **Aperture** Controls the size of the object snap cursor up to 50 pixels.
- **DdOSnap** Dialogue box for selecting object snap modes.

RELATED SYSTEM VARIABLES

■ **Aperture** Controls the size of the object snap cursor to any size.

■ **OsMode** Current object snap mode settings:

- 0 No object snap modes set.
- 1 ENDpoint.
- 2 MIDpoint.
- 4 CENter.
- 8 NODe.
- 16 QUAdrant.
- 32 INTersection.
- 64 INSertion point.
- 128 PERpendicular.
- 256 TANgent.
- 512 NEArest.
- 1024 QUIck.
- 2048 APPint (*new to Release 13*).

TIPS

■ The **Aperture** command controls the snap area AutoCAD searches through.

■ If AutoCAD finds no snap mode that can be used on the selected entities, the pick point is selected.

■ The **APPint** and **from** object snap modes are new to Release 13.

Examples of object snap modes:

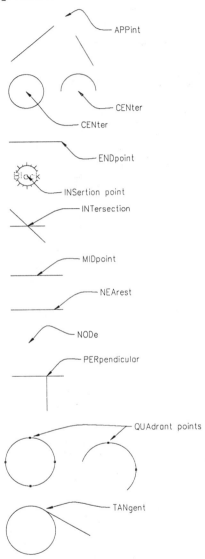

- APPint
- CENter
- CENter
- ENDpoint
- INSertion point
- INTersection
- MIDpoint
- NEArest
- NODe
- PERpendicular
- QUAdrant points
- TANgent

'Pan

Moves the view in the current viewport to a different position.

Command	Alias	Side Menu	Pull-down	Tablet
'pan	p	[VIEW]	[View]	Q 10
		[Pan:]	[Pan]	

```
Command: pan
Displacement: [pick]
Second point: [pick]
```

Before panning left:

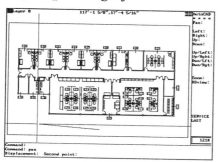

After panning to the left:

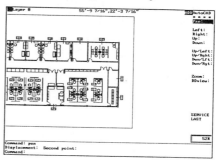

COMMAND OPTIONS

None

RELATED AUTOCAD COMMANDS

- **AV**   Aerial View pans in an independent window.
- **DView**   Pans during perspective mode.
- **View**   Saves and restores named views.
- **ViewRes** Toggles whether pans are redrawn or regenerated.
- **Zoom**   The **Dynamic** option includes a pan option.

RELATED SYSTEM VARIABLES

- **RegenAuto** Determines how regenerations are handled.
- **ViewCtr** The x,y-coordinate of the view's center.
- **ViewDir** View direction relative to UCS.
- **ViewSize** Height of view in units.

TIPS

- The pan command moves the drawing (not the viewport) in the direction you indicate.

- You pan each viewport independently.

■ You can use the **Pan** command transparently to start drawing an object in one area of the drawing, pan over, then continue drawing in another area of the drawing.

■ In the Aerial View window, change the **Static** button to **Dynamic** to perform 'real-time' panning: the drawing pans as quickly as you move the mouse.

■ The **Pan** command is a semi-transparent command: you cannot use transparent pan during:
   ■ Paper space.
   ■ Perspective mode created by the **DView** command.
   ■ **VPoint** command.
   ■ **DView** command.
   ■ Another **Pan, View,** or **Zoom** command.

■ The **DView** command has its own **Pan** option.

'Pcxin

Imports PCX raster files into the drawing as a block *(an external file in Raster.Exp)*.

Command	Alias	Side Menu	Pull-down	Tablet
'pcxin	...	[FILE]	[File]	...
		[IMPORT]	[Import]	
		[PCXin:]	[Raster]	
			[PCX]	

```
Command: pcxin
PCX filename:
Insertion point <0,0,0>:
Scale factor:
```

COMMAND OPTIONS

None

RELATED AUTOCAD COMMANDS

- **PsIn**   Imports EPS files.
- **GifIn**   Imports GIF raster files.
- **Replay**   Displays GIF, TIFF, and Targa files.
- **TiffIn**   Imports TIFF raster files.

RELATED SYSTEM VARIABLES

- **RiAspect** Adjusts image's aspect ration.
- **RiBackG** Changes the image's background color.
- **RiEdge** Outlines edges.
- **RiGamut** Specifies number of colors.
- **RiGrey** Imports as a grey scale image.
- **RiThresh** Controls brightness threshold.

TIPS

- The PCX format was devised by Z-Soft for their PC Paintbrush graphics program.

- **PcxIn** is limited to displaying a maximum of 256 colors.

- Exploding an imported PCX block doubles the drawing file size, since each run of same-color pixels is defined as a solid.

- Turn off system variable **GripBlock** (set to 0) to avoid highlighting all the solid objects making up the block.

PEdit

Edits a 2D polyline, 3D polyline, or 3D mesh — depending on which object is picked (*short for Polyline EDIT*).

Command	Alias	Side Menu	Pull-down	Tablet
pedit	...	[MODIFY]	[Modify]	W 19
		[Pedit:]	[Edit Polyline]	

For 2D polylines:

```
Command: pedit
Select polyline: [pick a 2D polyline]
Close/Join/Width/Edit vertex/Fit/Spline/Decurve/Ltype gen
   /Undo/eXit <X>: e
Next/Previous/Break/Insert/Move/Regen/Straighten/Tangent
   /Width/eXit <N>: b
Next/Previous/Go/eXit <N>:
```

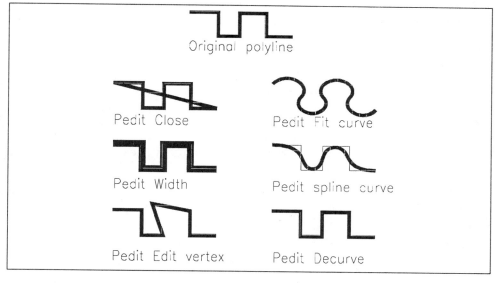

Original polyline

Pedit Close

Pedit Fit curve

Pedit Width

Pedit spline curve

Pedit Edit vertex

Pedit Decurve

COMMAND OPTIONS

Close   Closes an open polyline by joining the two endpoints with a single segment.

Decurve   Reverses the effects of a Fit-curve or Spline-curve operation.

Edit vertex   Edits individual vertices and segments (*see figure, overleaf*):

  Break   Removes a segment or break the polyline at a vertex.

  <Next>   Moves the x-marker to the next vertex.

  Previous   Moves the x-marker to the previous vertex.

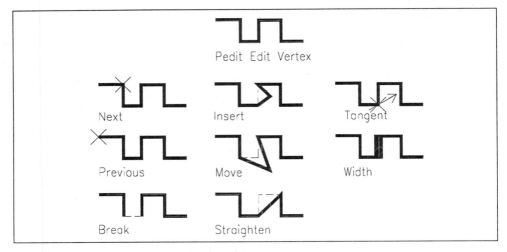

Pedit Edit Vertex

Next   Insert   Tangent

Previous   Move   Width

Break   Straighten

Go	Performs the break.
eXit	Exits the Break sub-submenu.
Insert	Inserts another vertex.
Move	Relocates a vertex.
Next	Moves the x-marker to the next vertex.
Previous	Moves the x-marker to the previous vertex.
Regen	Regenerates the screen to show effect of **PEdit** commands.
Straighten	Draws a straight segment between two vertices:
\<Next\>	Moves the x-marker to the next vertex.
Previous	Moves the x-marker to the previous vertex.
Go	Performs the straightening.
eXit	Exits the Straighten sub-submenu.
Tangent	Shows tangent to current vertex.
Width	Changes the width of a segment.
\<eXit\>	Exist the Edit-vertex submenu.
Fit	Fist a curve to the tangent points of each vertex.
Ltype gen	Specifies linetype generation style.
Join	Adds other polylines to the current polyline.
Open	Opens a closed polyline by removing the last segment.
Spline	Fits a splined curve along the polyline.
Undo	Undoes the most-recent **PEdit** operation.
Width	Changes the width of the entire polyline.
\<eXit\>	Exits the **PEdit** command.

For 3D polylines:

```
Command: pedit
Select polyline: [pick a 3D polyline]
Close/Edit vertex/Spline curve/Decurve/Undo/eXit <X>: E
Next/Previous/Break/Insert/Move/Regen/Straighten/eXit <N>:
```

COMMAND OPTIONS

Close   Closes an open polyline.

Decurve   Reverses the effects of a Fit-curve or Spline-curve operation.

Edit vertex Edits individual vertices and segments:

  Break   Removes a segment or breaks the polyline at a vertex.

    <Next>   Moves the x-marker to the next vertex.

    Previous   Moves the x-marker to the previous vertex.

    Go   Performs the break.

    eXit   Exits the Break sub-submenu.

  Insert   Inserts another vertex.

  Move   Relocates a vertex.

  <Next>   Moves the x-marker to the next vertex.

  Previous   Moves the x-marker to the previous vertex.

  Regen   Regenerates the screen to show effect of **PEdit** commands.

  Straighten Draws a straight segment between two vertices:

    <Next>   Moves the x-marker to the next vertex.

    Previous   Move the x-marker to the previous vertex.

    Go   Performs the straightening.

    eXit   Exits the Straighten sub-submenu.

  eXit   Exits the Edit-vertex submenu.

Open   Removes the last segment of a closed polyline.

Spline curve Fits a splined curve along the polyline.

Undo   Undoes the most-recent **PEdit** operation.

<eXit>   Exits the **PEdit** command.

For 3D meshes:

```
Command: pedit
Select polyline: [pick a 3D mesh]
Edit vertex/Smooth surface/Desmooth/Mclose/Nclose/Undo
   /eXit<X>: E
Vertex (0,0). Next/Previous/Left/Right/Up/Down/Move/REgen
   /eXit <N>:
```

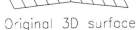

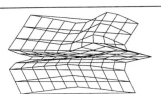

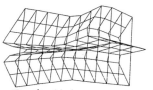

Original 3D surface   Pedit Mclose

Pedit Smooth surface   Pedit Nclose

COMMAND OPTIONS

Desmooth   Reverses the effect of the Smooth surface options.

Edit vertex   Edits individual vertices with the following submenu:

Down	Moves x-marker down the mesh by one vertex.
Left	Moves x-marker left along the mesh by one vertex.
Move	Relocates the vertex to a new position.
<Next>	Moves x-marker along the mesh to the next vertex.
Previous	Moves x-marker along the mesh to the previous vertex.
REgen	Regenerates the drawing to show the effects of **PEdit**.
Right	Moves x-marker right along the mesh by one vertex.
Up	Moves x-marker up the mesh by one vertex.
eXit	Exits the Edit-vertex submenu.

Mclose	Closes the mesh in the m-direction.
Mopen	Opens the mesh in the m-direction.
Nclose	Closes the mesh in the n-direction.
Nopen	Opens the mesh in the n-direction.
Smooth surface	Smoothes the mesh with a B-spline.
Undo	Undoes the most recent **PEdit** operation.
<eXit>	Exits the **PEdit** command.

RELATED AUTOCAD COMMANDS

- **Break**   Breaks a 2D polyline at any position.
- **Chamfer** Chamfers all vertices of a 2D polyline.
- **EdgeSurf** Draws a 3D mesh.
- **Fillet**   Fillets all vertices of a 2D polyline.
- **PLine**   Draws a 2D polyline.
- **RevSurf** Draws a 3D surface of revolution mesh.
- **RuleSurf** Draws a 3D ruled surface mesh.
- **TabSurf** Draws a 3D tabulated surface mesh.
- **3D**   Draws 3D surface objects.
- **3dPoly**   Draws a 3D polyline.

RELATED SYSTEM VARIABLES

- **Splframe** Determines visibility of a polyline spline frame.
- **SplineSegs** Number of lines used to draw a splined polyline.
- **SplineType** Determines B-spline smoothing for 2D and 3D polylines.
- **SurfType** Determines the smoothing using the **Smooth surface** option.

TIP

- During vertex editing, button #2 (*left button on a two-button mouse*) moves the x-marker to the next vertex.

PFace

Draws multi-sided 3D meshes; meant for use by AutoLISP, ADS, and ARx programs (*short for Poly FACE*).

Command	Alias	Side Menu	Pull-down	Tablet
pface	. . .	[DRAW 2]	. . .	. . .
		[SURFACES]		
		[Pface:]		

```
Command: pface
Vertex 1: [pick]
Vertex 2: [pick]
Face 1, vertex 1: 1
Face 1, vertex 2: 2
Face 2, vertex 1: 1
Face 2, vertex 2: 2
```

COMMAND OPTIONS
None

RELATED AUTOCAD COMMAND
■ **3dFace**   Draws three- and four-sided 3D meshes.

RELATED SYSTEM VARIABLE
■ **PFaceVmax** Maximum number of vertices per polyface.

TIP
■ Maximum number of vertices in the m- and n-direction:
  ■ 256 vertices, when entered from the keyboard.
  ■ 32,767 vertices, when entered from a DXF file or created by programming.

Plan

Displays the plan view of the WCS or the UCS.

Command	Alias	Side Menu	Pull-down	Tablet
plan	...	[VIEW]	[View]	M5
		[Plan:]	[3D Viewpoint Presets]	
			[Plan View]	

```
Command: plan
<Current UCS>/Ucs/World: W
Regenerating drawing.
```

Example non-plan view:

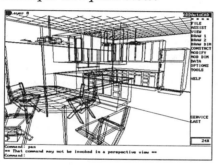

After using the Plan command:

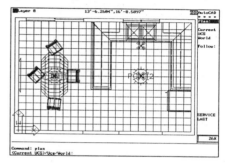

COMMAND OPTIONS

<Current UCS> Shows the plan view of the current UCS.
Ucs   Shows the plan view of a named UCS.
World   Shows the plan view of the WCS.

RELATED AUTOCAD COMMANDS

- **UCS**   Creates new UCS views.
- **VPoint**   Changes the viewpoint of 3D drawings.

RELATED SYSTEM VARIABLE

- **UcsFollow** Automatic plan view display for UCS or WCS.

TIPS

- Typing **VPoint 0,0,0** is an alternative command to the **Plan** command.

- The **Plan** command turns off perspective mode and clipping planes.

- **Plan** does not work in paper space.

- The **Plan** command is an excellent method for turning off perspective mode.

PLine

Draws a complex 2D line made of straight and curved sections of constant and variable width; treated as a single object (*short for Poly LINE*).

Command	Alias	Side Menu	Pull-down	Tablet
pline	pl	[DRAW 1]	[Draw]	K 10
		[Pline:]	[Polyline]	

```
Command: pline
From point: [pick]
Current line-width is 0.0
Arc/Close/Halfwidth/Length/Undo/Width/<Endpoint of line>:
```

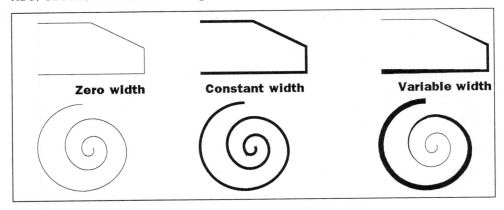

Zero width   Constant width   Variable width

COMMAND OPTIONS

Arc	Displays the submenu for drawing arcs:
Angle	Indicates the included angle of the arc.
CEnter	Indicates the arc's center point.
CLose	Uses an arc to close a polyline.
Direction	Indicates the arc's starting direction.
Halfwidth	Indicates the halfwidth of the arc.
Line	Switches back to the menu for drawing lines.
Radius	Indicates the arc's radius.
Second pt	For drawing a three-point arc.
Undo	Erases the last drawn arc segment.
Width	Indicates the width of the arc.
<Endpoint of arc>	
	Indicates the arc's endpoint.
Close	Closes the polyline with a line segment.
Halfwidth	Indicates the halfwidth of the polyline.

Length	Draws the polyline tangent to the last segment.
Undo	Erases the last-drawn segment.
Width	Indicates the width of the polyline.

\<Endpoint of line\>:
Indicates the polyline's endpoint.

RELATED AUTOCAD COMMANDS

- **Boundary** Draws a polyline boundary.
- **Donut** Draws solid-filled circles as polyline arcs.
- **Ellipse** Draws ellipses as polyline arcs when PEllipse = 1.
- **Explode** Reduces a polyline to lines and arcs with zero width.
- **Fillet** Fillets polyline vertices with a radius.
- **PEdit** Edits the polyline's vertices, widths, and smoothness.
- **Polygon** Draws polygons as polylines of up to 1,024 sides.
- **Rectang** Draws a rectangle out of a polyline.
- **Sketch** Draws polyline sketches, when **SkPoly** = 1.
- **Xplode** Explodes a group of polylines into line and arcs of zero width.
- **3dPoly** Draws 3D polylines.

RELATED SYSTEM VARIABLES

- **PlineGen** Style of linetype generation:
  - **0** Vertex to vertex (*Default*).
  - **1** End to end.
- **PlineWid** Current width of polyline.

TIPS

■ Use the **Boundary** command to automatically outline a region; then use the **List** command to find its area.

■ If you cannot see a linetype on a polyline, change system variable **PlineGen** to 1; this regenerates the linetype from one end of the polyline to the other.

■ If the angle between a joined polyline and polyarc is less than 28 degrees, the transition is chamfered; at greater than 28 degrees, the transition is not chamfered.

■ Use the object snap mode **INTersection** to snap to the vertices of a polyline.

Plot

Creates a copy of the drawing on a vector, raster, or PostScript plotter or printer via the serial or parallel ports; or plots to file on disk.

Command	Alias	Side Menu	Pull-down	Tablet
plot	...	[FILE]	[File]	W 24
		[Print:]	[Print]	

Command: **plot**
Displays dialogue box.

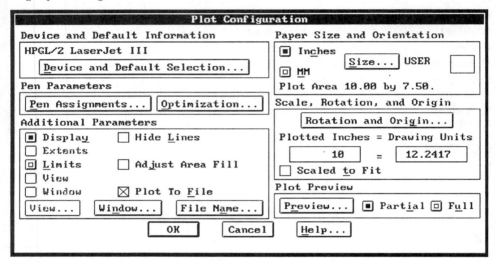

COMMAND OPTIONS

Device and default selection

Selects and configures output devices; displays dialogue box:

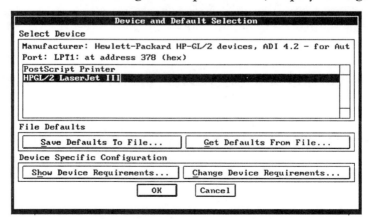

Feature legend

Displays data depending on device's capabilities:

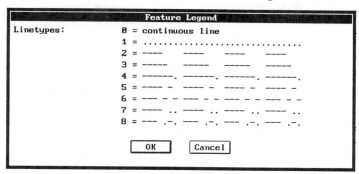

Pen assignments

Assigns pen numbers; displays a dialogue box:

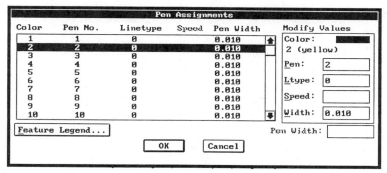

Optimization

Selects pen motion optimization; displays a dialogue box:

Display	Plots current display.
Extents	Plots drawing extents.
Limits	Plots drawing limits.
View	Plots named view; displays dialogue box when the drawing contains saved views:

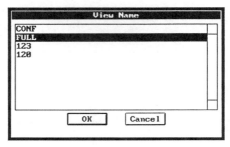

Window	Plot windowed area; displays a dialogue box:

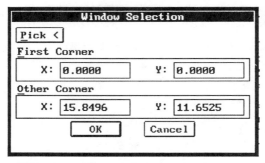

Hide lines	Removes hidden lines.
Adjust area fill	
	Adjusts pen motion for filled areas.
Plot to File	Plots drawing to file.
Size	Specifies size of plot; displays a dialogue box:

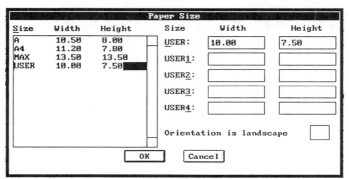

| **Inches** | Plots in inches. |
| **Mm** | Plots in millimeters. |

Rotation and origin
Specifies plot origin and rotation; displays a dialogue box:

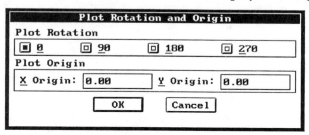

Scaled to fit
Scales plot to fit printable area of paper size.

| **Preview** | Previews the plot. |
| **Partial** | Quick plot preview; displays dialogue box: |

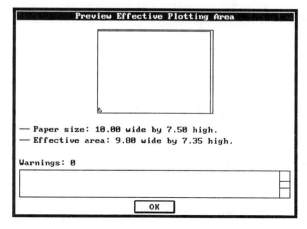

Full Full plot preview; displays in a viewport:

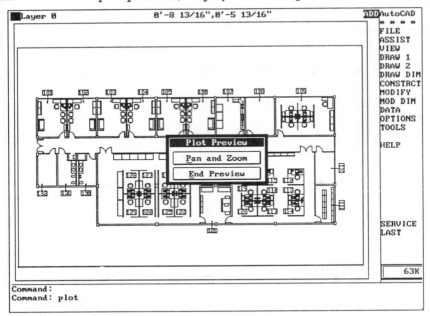

```
Command:
Command: plot
```

RELATED AUTOCAD COMMANDS
- **Config** Selects one or more plotter devices.
- **HpMPlot** Plots combined raster and vector to HPGL/2 devices.
- **PsOut** Saves a drawing in EPS format.

RELATED SYSTEM VARIABLES
- **CmdDia** Determines the **Plot** command's interface:
  - **0** Command-line interface (*compatible with script files*).
  - **1** Dialogue box interface.
- **PlotId** Currently selected plotter number.
- **Plotter** Currently selected plotter name.

RELATED DOS VARIABLE
- **AcadPlCmd** Plot spooler support.

RELATED FILES
- ***.PCP** Plotter configuration parameter files.
- ***.PLT** Plot files created with the **Plot** command.

TIPS

■ As of Release 12, the **Plot** command replaces the **PrPlot** command.

■ As of Release 13, the 'freeplot' feature (starting AutoCAD with the **-p** parameter to plot without using a network license) is no longer available.

■ Plot parameters are stored in PCP files.

■ Don't assume that more levels of optimization produce faster plots. In particular, the elimination of overlapping vectors can dramatically slow down the plotting process.

Point

Draws a 3D point.

Command	Alias	Side Menu	Pull-down	Tablet
point	...	[DRAW 2] [Point:]	[Draw] [Point]	O 10

Command: **point**
Point: [pick]

0	1	2	3	4
32	33	34	35	36
64	65	66	67	68
96	97	98	99	100

COMMAND OPTIONS

None

RELATED AUTOCAD COMMANDS

■ **DdPType** Displays dialogue box for selecting PsMode and PdSize.
■ **Point**   Draws a point.

RELATED SYSTEM VARIABLES

■ **PdMode** Determines the look of a point (*see figure above*).
■ **PdSize**   Determines the size of a point:
　　　　　0 Point is 5% of height of **ScreenSize** system variable.
　　　　　1 No display.
　　　　-10 Ten percent of viewport size.
　　　　10 Ten pixels in size.

TIPS

■ The size and shape of the point is determined by **PdSize** and **PdMode**; changing these values changes the look and size of all points in the drawing with the next regeneration.

■ Entering only the x,y-coordinates places the point at a z-coordinate of the current elevation; setting **Thickness** to a value draws the point as a line in 3D space.

■ Prefix the coordinate with * (*asterisk*) to place a point in the WCS, rather than the current UCS.

■ Use the object snap mode **NODe** to snap to a point.

Polygon

Draws a 2D polygon of between three to 1,024 sides.

Command	Alias	Side Menu	Pull-down	Tablet
polygon	...	[DRAW 1]	[Draw]	N 9
		[Polygon:]	[Polygon]	

```
Command: polygon
Number of sides <4>:
Edge/<Center of polygon>: [pick]
Inscribed in circle/Circumscribed about circle (I/C): I
Radius of circle: [pick]
```

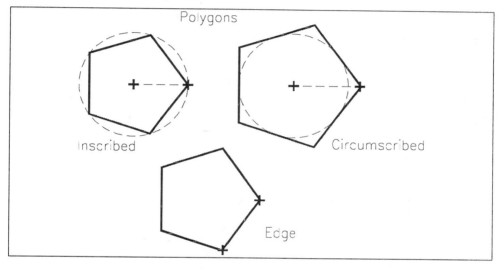

COMMAND OPTIONS

<Center of polygon>

    Indicates the center point of the polygon; then:

 C   Fits the polygon outside of a circle.

 I   Fits the polygon inside a circle.

Edge   Draws the polygon based on the length of one edge.

RELATED AUTOCAD COMMANDS

- **Donut** Draws solid-filled circles with a polyline.
- **Ellipse** Draws ellipsis with a polyline, when **PEllipse** = 1.
- **PEdit**   Edits polylines, include polygons.
- **PLine**   Draws polylines and polyline arcs.
- **Rectang** Draws a rectangle from a polyline.

RELATED SYSTEM VARIABLE

■ **PolySides** Most recently specified number of sides; default is 4.

TIPS

■ Polygons are drawn from polylines; use the **PEdit** command to change the polygon, such as the width of the polyline.

■ The pick point determines the location of polygon's first vertex; polygons are drawn counter-clockwise.

■ Use the system variable **PolySides** to preset the default number of polygon sides.

■ Use the **Snap** command to precisely place the polygon.

■ Use object snap mode **INTersection** to snap to the polygon's vertices.

Preferences

Lets you set a couple of user preferences.

Command	Alias	Side Menu	Pull-down	Tablet
preferences ...	...		[Options]	...
			[Preferences]	

Command: preferences

Displays dialogue box.

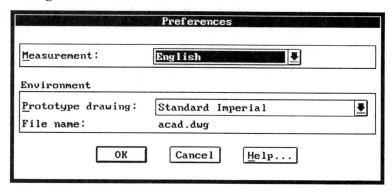

COMMAND OPTIONS

Measurement Selects 'English' or metric units.

Prototype drawing
> Selects from 'Imperial' or metric prototypes.

File name Names the prototype drawing.

RELATED FILES

- ■ ***.DWG** Prototype drawing files in \Acad13\Common\Support subdirectory.
- ■ **Acad.Ini** Stores settings from Preferences command in \Acad13\Dos subdirectory

PsDrag

Controls the appearance of the PostScript image during the **PsIn**
command (*short for PostScript DRAG; an external command in
AcadPs.Exp*).

Command	Alias	Side Menu	Pull-down	Tablet
psdrag	...	[FILE]	[File]	...
		[IMPORT]	[Import]	
		[PsDrag:]	[PostScript]	
			[Display]	

Command: **psdrag**
PSIN drag mode <0>:

PsDrag set to 0:   **PsDrag set to 1:**

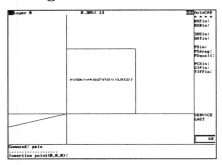 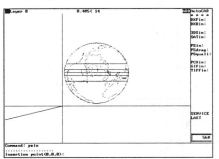

COMMAND OPTIONS

0   Turns **PsDrag** off.
1   Turns **PsDrag** on.

RELATED AUTOCAD COMMAND

■ **PsIn**   Imports a PostScript file.

RELATED SYSTEM VARIABLE

■ **PsQuality** Display options for PostScript files:
            75 Display filled at 75dpi (*Default*)
              0 Display bounding box and filename; no image.
        -75 Display image outline at 75dpi; no fill.

TIP

■ The **PsDrag** command is automatically set to 0 when system variable
PsQuality is set to 0 since both variables cause PostScript images to display
just their bounding box.

PsFill

Fills a 2D polyline outline with a raster PostScript pattern (*short for PostScript FILL; an external command in AcadPs.Exp*).

Command	Alias	Side Menu	Pull-down	Tablet
psfill	...	...	[Draw]	...
			[Hatch]	
			[PostScript Fill]	

```
Command: psfill
Select polyline: [pick]
PostScript pattern (. = none) <.>/?
```

COMMAND OPTIONS

.   (*Period*) Selects no fill pattern.
?   List available fill patterns.
*   Don't outline pattern with polyline.

RELATED AUTOCAD COMMAND

■ **BHatch**   Fills an area with a vector harch pattern.

RELATED SYSTEM VARIABLE

■ **PsQuality** Display options for PostScript files:
    75 Display filled at 75dpi (*Default*)
     0 Display bounding box and filename; no image.
   -75 Display image outline at 75dpi; no fill.

RELATED FILE

Acad.Psf   PostScript fill definition file in \Acad13\Common\Support.

TIP

■ The following PostScript fill patterns are defined in file Acad.Psf (*pattern name is followed by parameters and default values*):

Grayscale   Grayscale = 50

RGBcolor   Red = 50
                               Green = 50
                               Blue = 50

A llogo
Frequency = 1.0
Separation = 25
Linewidth = 0
ForegroundGray = 100
BackgroundGray = 0

 Lineargray
Levels = 256
Cycles = 1
Angle = 0.0
ForegroundGray = 100
BackgroundGray = 0

 Radialgray
Levels = 256
ForegroundGray = 100
BackgroundGray = 0

 Square
Scale = 1.0
Separation = 25
LineWidth = 1
ForegroundGray = 100
BackgroundGray = 0

 Waffle
Scale = 1.0
Proportion = 30
LineWidth = 1
UpLeftGray = 100
BotRight Gray = 50
TopGray = 0

 ZigZag
Scale = 1.0
LineWidth = 1
ForegroundGray = 100
BackgroundGray = 0

Stars
Scale = 1.0
LineWidth = 1
ForegroundGray = 100
BackgroundGray = 0

Brick

Scale = 1.0
LineWidth = 1
BrickGray1 = 100
BrickGray2 = 50
BackGroundGray = 0

 Specks

Scale = 1.0
ForegroundGray = 100
BackgroundGray = 0

Psin

Imports an EPS (encapsulated PostScript) file into the drawing (*short for PostScript INput; an external command in AcadPs.Exp*).

Command	Alias	Side Menu	Pull-down	Tablet
psin	. . .	[FILE]	[File]	. . .
		[IMPORT]	[Import]	
		[PSquali:]	[PostScript]	
			[Import]	

Command: **psin**
Select filename from dialogue box.
Insertion point <0,0,0>: **[pick]**
Scale factor:

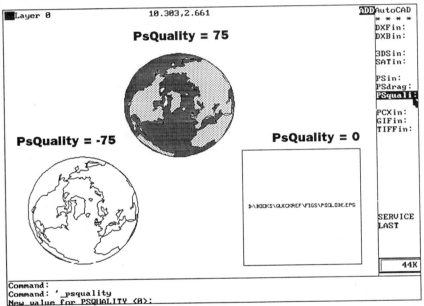

COMMAND OPTIONS
None

RELATED AUTOCAD COMMANDS
- **PsDrag**   Toggles display of bounding box during placement.
- **GifIn**   Imports a GIF raster file.
- **PcxIn**   Imports a PCX raster file.
- **PsOut**   Exports an EPS file.
- **TiffIn**   Imports a TIFF raster file.

RELATED SYSTEM VARIABLE

■ **PsQuality** Display options for placing an EPS file (*see figure*):

    75 Display filled at 75dpi (*Default*)

      0 Display bounding box and filename: no image.

    -75 Display image outline at 75dpi: no fill.

RELATED FILES

Found in \Acad13\Common\Support subdirectory:

■ **Acad.Psf**   PostScript fill definition.

■ **AcadPsc.Ps** *An empty file.*

■ **AcadPsd.Ps** Provides dummy 'statusdict', 'serverdict', and other LaserWriter operators.

■ **AcadPsf.Ps** Font initialization for GhostScript.

■ **AcadPsi.Ps** Ghostscript master initialization file.

■ **AcadPss.Ps** GhostScript symbol font encoding vector.

TIPS

■ AutoCAD uses an in-house modified version of GhostScript, a freeware PostScript clone.

■ The 'acadpsversion' operator returns local version number:

    `2.2-ACADPS:Q001-JW1`

for AcadPs.Exp.

■ The Acad.Psf file defines all fonts included with:
  ■ Adobe Type Manager for Windows.
  ■ Adobe Plus Pack.
  ■ Adobe Font Pack 1.
  ■ Linguist PostScript fonts distributed with AutoCAD.

■ **PsIn** places the PostScript as an anonymous block '*U' in the drawing.

■ When the EPS block is first placed in the drawing, it is of unit size.

PsOut

Exports the current drawing as an encapsulated PostScript file (*an external command in Acadps.Exp*).

Command	Alias	Side Menu	Pull-down	Tablet
psout	. . .	[FILE]	[File]	W 25
		[Export]	[Export]	
		[PSout:]	[PostScript]	
			[Export]	

Command: **psout**
Specify filename in dialogue box.
What to export--Display, Extents, Limits, View or Windows <D>:
Include a screen preview image in the file?(None/EPSI/TIFF)<None>:
Screen preview image size (128x128 is standard)? (128/256/512)<128>:
Enter the Size or Width, Height (in Inches) <>:
Effective plotting area: *ww* by *hh* high

COMMAND OPTIONS
None

RELATED AUTOCAD COMMANDS
- **Plot**   Exports dawing in a variety of formats, including raster EPS.
- **PsIn**   Imports EPS files.

RELATED SYSTEM VARIABLE
- **PsProlog** Specifies the PostScript prologue information.

RELATED FILES
- ***.EPS**   Extension of file produced by PsOut.
- **Acad.Psf**   PostScript fill definition file found in \Acad13\Common\Support.

TIPS
- The 'screen preview image' is only used for screen display purposes since graphics software generally cannot display PostScript graphic files.

- Although Autodesk recommends using the smallest screen preview image size (128 x 128), even the largest preview image (512 x 512) has a minimal effect on file size and screen display time.

- The screen preview image size has no effect on the quality of the Post-Script output.

- If you're not sure which screen preview format to use, select TIFF.

PSpace

Switches from model space to paper space (*short for Paper SPACE*).

Command	Alias	Side Menu	Pull-down	Tablet
pspace	ps	[VIEW]	[View]	V 13
		[Pspace:]	[Paper Space]	

Command: **pspace**

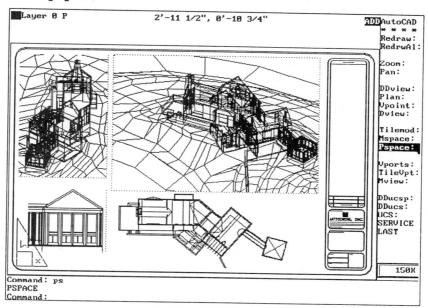

COMMAND OPTIONS
None

RELATED AUTOCAD COMMANDS
- **MSpace**   Switches from paper space to model space.
- **MView**   Creates viewports in paper space.
- **MvSetup** Creates paper space setup for a new drawing.
- **UcsIcon**   Toggles display of paper space icon.
- **Zoom**   The **XP** option scales paper space relative to model space.

RELATED SYSTEM VARIABLES
- **MaxActVp** Maximum number of viewports displaying an image.
- **TileMode** Must equal 0 for paper space to work.
- **PsLtScale** Linetype scale relative to paper space.

TIPS

■ Use paper space to lay out multiple views of a single drawing.

■ Paper space is known as 'drawing composition' in other CAD packages.

■ When a drawing is in paper space, AutoCAD displays 'P' on the status line and the paper space icon:

QUICK START: Enabling Paper Space.

Entering paper space for the first time can be a mystifying experience, since your drawing literally disappears. Here are the steps to take:

1. Turn Tilemode off:
   Command: **tilemode 0**

2. Enter paper space:
   Command: **pspace**

3. Although the drawing area goes blank, don't worry: your drawing has not been erased. To see your drawing, you need to create at least one viewport:
   Command **mview fit**
   ...and your drawing reappears!

4. Now switch back to model space:
   Command: **mspace**

5. Use the **Zoom** and **Pan** command to make the drawing smaller or larger within the paper space viewport.

6. Switch back to paper space with **PS**. Create a few more viewports by picking points with the **MView** command. Try overlapping a couple of viewports. Switch back to model space with **MS** and set different zoom levels for each viewport.

7. Switch back to paper space with **PS**. Now use the **Move** and **Stretch** commands to change the position and size of the paper space viewports. Draw a title border around all the viewports.

8. Some other paper space-related commands to experiment with are:
VpLayer, Zoom XP, PsLtScale, MvSetup, and **HpMPlot.**

Purge

Removes unused named objects from the drawing: blocks, dimension styles, layers, linetypes, shapes, text styles, application id tables, and multiline styles.

Command	Alias	Side Menu	Pull-down	Tablet
purge	. . .	[DATA]	[Data]	. . .
		[Purge:]	[Purge]	

Command: **purge**
Purge unused Blocks/Dimstyles/LAyers/LTypes/SHapes/STyles
    /APpids/Mlinestyles/All: **A**

Sample response:
No unreferenced blocks found.
Purge layer DOORWINS? <N> **y**
Purge layer TEXT? <N> **y**
Purge linetype CENTER? <N> **y**
Purge linetype CENTER2? <N> **y**
No unreferenced text styles found.
No unreferenced shape files found.
No unreferenced dimension styles found.

COMMAND OPTIONS

Blocks   Purges named but unused blocks.
Dimstyles Purges unused dimension styles.
LAyers   Purges unused layers.
LTypes   Purges unused linetypes.
SHapes   Purges unused shape files.
STyles   Purges unused text styles.
APpids   Purges unused application id table of ADS and AutoLISP apps.
Mlinestyles Purges unused multiline styles.
All   Purges drawing of all eight named objects, if necessary.

RELATED AUTOCAD COMMANDS

■ **End**   Two **End** commands in a row can remove spurious information from a drawing.
■ **WBlock** Writes the current drawing to disk (with the * option) and removes spurious information from the drawing.

TIPS

■ As of Release 13, **Purge** can be used at any time; it no longer must be used as the first command used after a drawing is loaded.

■ It may be necessary to use the **Purge** command several times; follow each purge with the **End** command, then **Open** the drawing and **Purge** again. Repeat until **Purge** reports nothing to purge.

QSave

Saves the current drawing without requesting a filename (*short for Quick SAVE*).

Command	Alias	Side Menu	Pull-down	Tablet
qsave	...	[FILE]	[File]	T 24
		[Save:]	[Save]	

Command: **qsave**

COMMAND OPTIONS
None

RELATED AUTOCAD COMMANDS
- **End**   Saves the drawing, without requesting a filename, and ends AutoCAD.
- **Save**   Saves drawing, after requesting the filename.
- **SaveAs**   Saves the drawing with a different filename.

RELATED SYSTEM VARIABLES
- **DbMode**   Indicates whether the drawing has changed since it was loaded.
- **DwgName**   Current drawing filename (*Default: "UNNAMED"*).
- **DwgTitled** Status of drawing's filename:
    - **0** Name is "UNNAMED".
    - **1** Name is other than UNNAMED.
- **DwgWrite**   Drawing's read-write status:
    - **0** Read-only.
    - **1** Read-write.

TIPS
- When the drawing is unnamed, the **QSave** command requests a file name.

- When the drawing file, its subdirectory, or drive (such as a CD-ROM drive) are marked 'read-only,' use the **SaveAs** command to save the drawing to another filename, subdir, or drive.

QText

Displays a line of text as a rectangular box (*short for Quick TEXT*).

Command	Alias	Side Menu	Pull-down	Tablet
qtext	...	[OPTIONS]	[Options]	Y 22
		[DISPLAY]	[Display]	
		[Qtext:]	[Text Frame Only]	

Command: **qtext**
ON/OFF <Off>: **on**

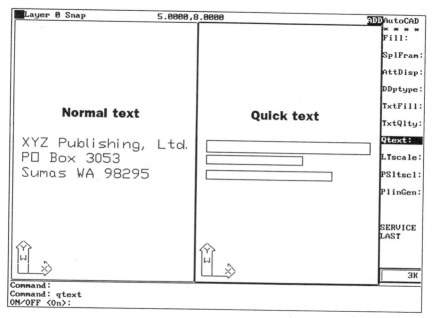

COMMAND OPTIONS

ON   Turns quick text on, after the next **Regen** command.
OFF   Turns quick text off, after the next **Regen** command.

RELATED AUTOCAD COMMANDS

- **DdRModes** Toggles **QText** via a dialogue box.
- **Regen**   Regenerates the screen; makes quick text take effect.

RELATED SYSTEM VARIABLE

- **QTextMode** Holds the current state of quick text mode.

TIPS

- To reduce the redraw and regen time of text, use **QText** to turn lines of text into rectangles, which redraw faster.

■ The length of a **QText** box does not necessarily match the actual length of the text.

■ Turning on **QText** does not affect text during plotting; qtext blocks are plotted as normal text.

■ To find invisible text, such as a line of text made only of spaces, turn on **QText**, thaw all layers, and **Zoom** to extents; the invisible text shows up as rectangles.

Quit

Exits AutoCAD without saving changes to the drawing, from the most recent **Save** or **End** command.

Command	Alias	Side Menu	Pull-down	Tablet
quit	exit	[FILE]	[File]	X 24
		[Exit:]	[Exit]	

Command: **quit**

Displays dialogue box.

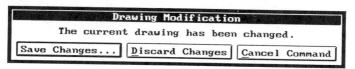

COMMAND OPTIONS

Save changes Saves changes made to drawing before leaving AutoCAD.
Discard changes
Does not save the changes; drawing reverts to its original state.
Cancel command
Does not quit AutoCAD; does not save changes.

RELATED AUTOCAD COMMANDS

- **End** Saves the drawing and exits AutoCAD.
- **SaveAs** Saves the drawing by another name or to another subdirectory or drive.

RELATED SYSTEM VARIABLES

- **DbMod** Indicates whether the drawing has changed since it was loaded.

RELATED FILES

- ***.DWG** AutoCAD drawing files.
- ***.BAK** Backup file.
- ***.BK**n Additional backup files, such as BK0, BK1, BK2, etc.

TIPS

- You can make changes to a drawing, yet preserve its original format: first, use the **SaveAs** command to save the drwaing by another name; then, use the **Quit** command to preserve the drawing in its original state.

- Even if you accidently save over a drawing, you can recover the previous version: first, use the DOS **Erase** or **Rename** command to rename the DWG file; then, use the DOS **Rename** command to rename the backup BAK file to DWG.

Ray

Creates a semi-infinite construction line.

Command	Alias	Side Menu	Pull-down	Tablet
ray	...	[DRAW 1]	[Draw]	L 9
		[Ray:]	[Ray]	

```
Command: ray
From point: [pick]
Through point: [pick]
```

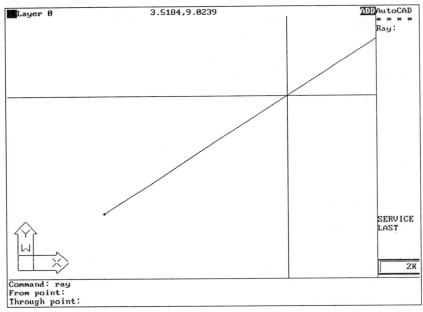

COMMAND OPTIONS

None

RELATED AUTOCAD COMMANDS

- **DdModify** Modifies a ray.
- **Line** Draws a line.
- **XLine** Creates an infinite construction line.

TIPS

■ The 'ray' object is semi-inifinite in length: you specify the starting point and direction; AutoCAD draws from the start point to "infinity."

■ A ray is a 'construction line' that displays but does not plot.

■ The ray has all properties of a line: it can have color, layer, linetype, be used as a cutting edge, etc.

RConfig

Configures output devices for the Render module (*short for Render CONFIG; an external command in Render.Arx*).

Command	Alias	Side Menu	Pull-down	Tablet
rconfig	...	[TOOLS]	[Options]	...
		[RENDER]	[Render Configure]	
		[Config:]		

Command: **rconfig**

COMMAND OPTIONS

1	Shows current **Render** configuration.
2	Configures rendering output device.
3	Configures **Render** window.
<0>	Exits to AutoCAD.

RELATED AUTOCAD COMMANDS

- **Config**   Configures input and output devices for AutoCAD.
- **DlxConfig** Selects graphics board for **Render**.
- **HpMPlot** Plots one rendered viewport with wireframe viewports to HPGL/2 devices.
- **Render**   Performs the rendering.
- **RPref**   Specifies rendering preferences.

RELATED DOS VARIABLES

*It is not necessary to set any of these variables before using **Render**, unless a Targa board is used:*
- **AveFaceDir** Points to working directory to store faces and triangles produced during rendering.
- **AveMaps** Points to subdirectory containing texture maps.
- **RenderCfg** Points to the location of the Render.Cfg configuration file.
- **RdPAdi** Points to the location of the protected-mode ADI rendering display driver file.
- **RhPAdi** Points to the location of the protected-mode ADI rendering hardcopy driver file.
- **Targa**   Specifies memory and i/o address for Targa graphics board.
- **TargaSet** Specifies Targa model number and graphic board options.

RELATED FILES

- **Render.Cfg** The configuration file for Render in \Acad13\Dos subdir.
- **Rc*.Exp** *and* **Rd*.Exp**
  Rendering display drivers in \Acad13\Dos\Drv subdirectory.
- **Rh*.Exp** Rendering hardcopy drivers in \Acad13\Dos\Drv.
- **AdiRend.Exp**
  'Magic' all-purpose rendering display driver name.

- **AdiRndHc.Exp**
  'Magic' all-purpose rendering hardcopy driver name.

TIPS

- All graphics boards trade off higher resolution for fewer colors. For renderings, a larger number of colors is more important than a higher resolution. As a suitable tradeoff, select 256 colors and the highest associated resolution.

- **Render** supports the following hardcopy output devices:
  - Canon Bubblejet (*driver file: RhpCanBj.Exp*).
  - HPGL/2 devices (*driver file: RhpRtl.Exp*).

- HPGL/2 devices specifically supported by the RhpRtl.Exp driver:
  - HP DesignJet 200, 600, 650C.
  - HP PaintJet XL300.
  - HP 7600 Color and Monochrome electrostatic plotters.
  - HP LaserJet III and 4.

- **Render** supports these specialized graphics board:
  - IBM 8514/A and XGA (*Driver file: Rc85Xga.Exp*).
  - Targa 12, 24, 32 and Truevision (*Driver file: RdpTarga.Exp*).
  - Targa + (*Driver file: RcpTargp.Exp*).
  - Super VGA (*Driver file: RcpSVadi.Exp*).
  - VESA-compliant VGA (*Driver file: RcpVesa2.Exp*).

- To use the VESA-compliant rendering driver, your computer must first load the graphic board's own VESA driver.

- In addition, almost all graphics boards can perform rendering via the 'Accelerated Display Driver;' use the **Config** command to select a board.

- Use the **AveFaceDir** variable to point to a RAM drive to help speed up complex renderings.

QUICK START: Setting up Render for the first time.

1. (*Optional*) Create a DOS batch file for the **Render** environment variables.

2. Start AutoCAD and use the **Config** command to select the graphics board, resolution, and color depth for performing renderings.

2. With the **RConfig** command, select hardcopy output device, if any.

3. (Optional) Use the **HpConfig** command to configure AutoCAD for mixed wireframe/rendering output on an HPGL/2-compatible device.

4. With the **RPref** command, specify rendering options.

5. The **SaveImg** command lets you output renderings to a file on disk.

Recover

Recovers a damaged drawing without user intervention.

Command	Alias	Side Menu	Pull-down	Tablet
recover	...	[FILE]	[File]	...
		[MANAGE]	[Management]	
		[Recover:]	[Recover]	

Command: **recover**

Sample output:

```
Drawing recovery.
Drawing recovery log.
Scanning for sentinels    99% done
Scanning completed.
Validating objects in the handle table.
Valid objects 1452    Invalid objects 0
Validating objects completed.
Used contingency data.
Salvaged database from drawing.
41       Blocks audited
Pass 1 956      objects audited
Pass 2 956      objects audited
Pass 3 1400     objects audited
Total errors found 0 fixed 0
Regenerating drawing.
```

COMMAND OPTIONS
None

RELATED AUTOCAD COMMAND
■ **Audit**   Checks a drawing for integrity.

TIPS
■ The **Open** command automatically invokes the **Recover** command if AutoCAD detects that the drawing is damaged.

■ **Recover** does not ask permission to repair damaged parts of the drawing file; use the **Audit** command if you want to control the repair process.

■ The **Quit** command discards changes made by the **Recover** command.

■ If the **Recover** and **Audit** commands don't fix the problem, try using the **DxfOut** and **DxfIn** commands.

Rectang

Draws a rectangle out of a polyline.

Command	Alias	Side Menu	Pull-down	Tablet
rectang	...	[DRAW 1]	[Draw]	...
		[Rectang:]	[Polygon]	
			[Rectangle]	

Command: **rectangle**
First corner: **[pick]**
Other corner: **[pick]**

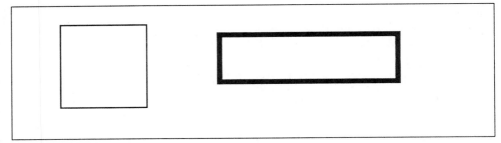

COMMAND OPTIONS
None

RELATED AUTOCAD COMMANDS
- **Donut**   Draws solid-filled circles with a polyline.
- **Ellipse**   Draws ellipsis with a polyline, when **PEllipse** = 1.
- **PEdit**   Edits polylines, including rectangles.
- **PLine**   Draws polylines and polyline arcs.
- **Polygon** Draws a polygon (3 to 1,024 sides) from a polyline.

TIPS
- Rectangles are drawn from polylines; use the **PEdit** command to change the rectangle, such as the width of the polyline.

- The pick point determines the location of the rectangle's first vertex; rectangles are drawn counter-clockwise.

- Use the **Snap** command and object snap modes to precisely place the rectangle.

- Use object snap mode **INTersection** to snap to the rectangle's vertices.

Redefine

Restores the meaning of an AutoCAD command after being disabled by the **Undefine** command.

Command	Alias	Side Menu	Pull-down	Tablet
redefine	...	...	...	...

Command: redefine
Command name:

COMMAND OPTIONS
None

RELATED AUTOCAD COMMANDS
- *All commands* All AutoCAD commands can be redefined.
- **Undefine** Disables the meaning of an AutoCAD command.

TIPS
- Prefix any command with a . (*period*) to temporarily redefine the undefinition, as in:
  Command: .line

- Prefix any command with an _ (*underscore*) to make an English-language command work in any lingual version of AutoCAD, as in:
  Command: _line

Redo

Reverses the effect of the most recent **Undo** and U command.

Command	Alias	Side Menu	Pull-down	Tablet
redo	. . .	[ASSIST]	[Assist]	U 9-10
	'	[Redo:]	[Redo]	

Command: **redo**

COMMAND OPTIONS
None

RELATED AUTOCAD COMMAND
- **Undo** Undoes the most recent series of AutoCAD commands.

RELATED SYSTEM VARIABLE
- **UndoCtl** Determines the state of the **Undo** command.

TIP
- The **Redo** command is limited to undoing a single undo, while the **Undo** and **U** commands undo operations all the way back to the beginning of the editing session.

'Redraw

Ver. 1.0

Redraws the current viewport to clean up the screen.

Command	Alias	Side Menu	Pull-down	Tablet
'redraw	r	[VIEW]	[View]	L11-P11
		[Redraw:]	[Redraw View]	

Command: redraw

Before redraw:

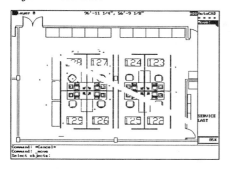

After redraw:

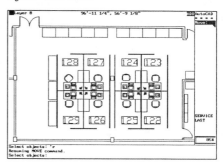

COMMAND OPTION

[Esc]   Cancels the redraw.

RELATED AUTOCAD COMMANDS

- ■ **RedrawAll** Redraws all viewports.
- ■ **Regen** Regenerates the current viewport.
- ■ **RegenMin** A **Dlx** command that zooms in the furthest without causing a regen.
- ■ **Zoom** The **Vmax** option zooms the furthest out without causing a regeneration.

RELATED SYSTEM VARIABLE

- ■ **SortEnts** Controls the order of redrawing objects:
  - 0 Sorted by order in the drawing database.
  - 1 Sorted for object selection.
  - 2 Sorted for object snap.
  - 4 Sorted for redraw.
  - 8 Sorted for creating slides.
  - 16 Sorted for regenerations.
  - 32 Sorted for plotting.
  - 64 Sorted for PostScript plotting.

TIPS

■ Use **Redraw** to clean up the screen after a lot of editing.

■ Some commands automatically redraw the screen when they are done.

■ **Redraw** does not affect objects on frozen layers.

■ Use the **RedrawAll** command to redraw all viewports.

■ For the fastest redraws, configure AutoCAD with the 'Accelerated Display Driver.' To help conserve memory, select the 16-bit display list rather than the 32-bit display list.

'RedrawAll

Redraws all viewports to clean up the screen.

Command	Alias	Side Menu	Pull-down	Tablet
'redrawall	...	[VIEW]	[View]	Q11-R11
		[RedrwAl:]	[Redraw All]	

Command: redrawall

COMMAND OPTION
[Esc]   Cancels the redraw.

RELATED AUTOCAD COMMANDS
- **Redraw**   Redraws only the current viewport.
- **RegenAll** Regenerates all viewports.

RELATED SYSTEM VARIABLE
- **SortEnts** Controls the order of redrawing objects.

TIPS
- **RedrawAll** does not affect objects on frozen layers.

- Use the **Redraw** command to redraw a single viewport.

Regen

Regenerates the current viewport to update the drawing.

Command	Alias	Side Menu	Pull-down	Tablet
regen	...	...	...	J 11

```
Command: regen
Regenerating drawing.
```

COMMAND OPTION

[Esc]   Cancels the regeneration.

RELATED AUTOCAD COMMANDS

■ **Redraw**   Quickly cleans up the current viewport.
■ **RegenAll** Regenerates all viewports.
■ **RegenAuto** Checks with you before doing most regenerations.
■ **ViewRes** Controls whether zooms and pans are regens or redraws.

RELATED SYSTEM VARIABLE

■ **RegenMode** Current setting of **RegenAuto**:
> 0 Off.
> 1 On (*Default*).

TIPS

■ Some commands automatically force a regeneration of the screen; other commands queue the regen.

■ To save on regeneration time:
  ■ Freeze layers you are not working with.
  ■ Use **QText** to turn text into rectangles.
  ■ Place hatching last on its own layer.

■ Use the **RegenAll** command to regenerate all viewports.

RegenAll

Rel. 10

Regenerates all viewports.

Command	Alias	Side Menu	Pull-down	Tablet
regenall	...	...	...	K 11

Command: **regenall**
Regenerating drawing.

COMMAND OPTION
[Esc]   Cancels the regeneration process.

RELATED AUTOCAD COMMANDS
- **RedrawAll** Redraws all viewports.
- **Regen** Regenerates the current viewport.
- **RegenAuto** Checks with you before doing most regenerations.
- **ViewRes** Controls whether zooms and pans are regens or redraws.

RELATED SYSTEM VARIABLE
- **RegenMode** Current setting of **RegenAuto**.

TIPS
- **RegenAll** does not regenerate objects on frozen layers.
- Use the **Regen** command to regenerate a single viewport.

'RegenAuto

AutoCAD asks you before performing a regeneration, when turned off (*short for REGENeration AUTOmatic*).

Command	Alias	Side Menu	Pull-down	Tablet
'regenauto	...	...	...	...

```
Command: regenauto
ON/OFF <On>: off
```

Example:
```
Command: regen
About to regen, proceed? <Y>:
```

COMMAND OPTIONS
OFF   Turns on "About to regen, proceed?" message.
ON   Turns off "About to regen, proceed?" message.

RELATED AUTOCAD COMMAND
■ **Regen**   Forces a regeneration in the current viewport.

RELATED SYSTEM VARIABLES
■ **Expert**   Suppresses the "About to regen, proceed?" message when value is greater than 0.
■ **RegenMode** Current setting of **RegenAuto** command.

TIPS
■ If a regeneration is caused by a transparent command, AutoCAD delays it with the message, "Regen queued."

■ Release 12 reduces the number of regenerations by expanding the virtual screen from 16 bits to 32 bits.

Region

Creates a 2D region from closed objects (*formerly the* **Solidify** *command; an external command in Acis.Dll*).

Command	Alias	Side Menu	Pull-down	Tablet
region	. . .	[CONSTRCT]	[Construct]	J 8
		[Region:]	[Region]	

```
Command: region
Select objects: [pick]
Select objects: [Enter]
1 loop extracted.
1 region created.
```

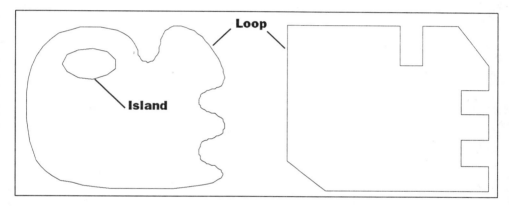

COMMAND OPTIONS
None

RELATED AUTOCAD COMMANDS
All.

RELATED SYSTEM VARIABLE.
- **DelObj**   Toggles whether objects are deleted during the **Region** conversion.

TIPS
- The **Region** command converts:
  - Closed line sets.
  - Closed 2D and planar 3D polylines.
  - Closed curves.

- The **Region** command rejects open objects, intersections, and self-intersecting curves.

- Splined and curve-fitted polylines are not converted into spline objects.

- The resulting region is unpredictable when more than two curves share an endpoint.

- Polylines with width loose their width when converted to a region.

DEFINITIONS

Curve
- An object made of circles, ellipses, splines, and joined circular and elliptical arcs.

Island
- A closed shape fully within (not touching or intersecting) another closed shape.

Loop
- A closed shape made of closed polylines, closed lines, and curves.

Region
- A 2D closed area defined as an ACIS object.

Reinit

Reinitializes the digitizer, display, plotter and input-output ports, and reloads the Acad.Pgp file (*short for REINITialize*).

Command	Alias	Side Menu	Pull-down	Tablet
reinit	...	[TOOLS]	[Tools]	...
		[Reinit:]	[Reinitialize]	

Command: **reinit**

Displays dialogue box.

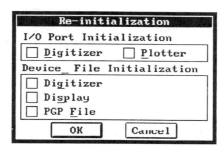

COMMAND OPTIONS

Digitizer   Reinitializes port connected to digitizer.
Plotter   Reinitializes port connected to plotter.
Digitizer   Reinitializes digitizer driver.
Display   Reinitializes display driver.
Pgp File   Reloads **Acad.Pgp** file.

RELATED AUTOCAD COMMAND

■ **Menu**   Reloads menu file.

RELATED SYSTEM VARIABLE

■ **Re-init**   Reinitializes via system variable settings.

RELATED FILES

■ **Acad.Pgp** The program parameters file in \Acad13\Common\Support subdir.
■ ***.EXP**   Device drivers in \Acad13\Dos\Drv subdirectory.

TIPS

■ Use the **Reinit** command after editing the Acad.Pgp via the **Shell** command.

■ AutoCAD allows you to connect both the digitizer and the plotter to the same port since you don't need the digitizer during plotting; use the **Reinit** command to reinitialize the digitizer after plotting.

■ AutoCAD reinitializes all ports and reloads the **Acad.Pgp** file each time another drawing is loaded.

Rename

Allows you to change the names of blocks, dimension styles, layer, linetypes, text styles, UCS names, views, and viewports.

Command	Alias	Side Menu	Pull-down	Tablet
rename	...	...	...	...

```
Command: rename
Block/Dimstyle/LAyer/LType/Style/Ucs/VIew/VPort:
```

Example:
```
Command: rename
Block/Dimstyle/LAyer/LType/Style/Ucs/VIew/VPort: B
Old block name: diode-20
New block name: diode-02
```

COMMAND OPTIONS

Block	Changes the name of a block.
Dimstyle	Changes the name of a dimension style.
LAyer	Changes the name of a layer.
LType	Changes the name of a linetype.
Style	Changes the name of a text style.
Ucs	Changes the name of a UCS configuration.
VIew	Changes the name of a view configuration.
VPort	Changes the name of a viewport configuration.

RELATED AUTOCAD COMMANDS

- **DdLModes** Changes layer names via a dialogue box.
- **DdRename** Displays dialogue box for renaming.
- **DdUcs** Changes UCS configuration names via a dialogue box.
- **Files** Changes the names of files on disk.

RELATED SYSTEM VARIABLES

- **CeLayer** Name of current layer.
- **CeLtype** Name of current linetype.
- **DimStyle** Name of current dimension style.
- **InsName** Name of current block.
- **TextStyle** Name of current text style.
- **UcsName** Name of current UCS view.

Render

Creates a rendering of 3D objects (*an external command in Render.Arx*).

Command	Alias	Side Menu	Pull-down	Tablet
render	...	[TOOLS]	[Tools]	L 1
		[RENDER]	[Render]	
		[Render:]	[Render]	

```
Command: render
Using current view.
Default scene selected. | / - \
```

Displays dialogue box.

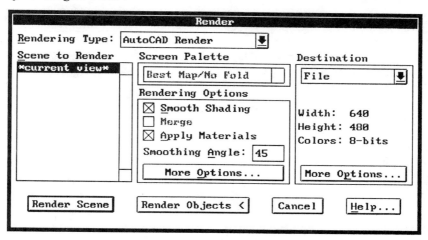

COMMAND OPTIONS

Rendering Type
> Selects from AutoCAD Render, AutoVision, and third-party renderers, if loaded into system.

Scene to Render
> Selects scene name, defined by the **Scene** command.

Screen Palette Selects palette for 256-color graphics boards; not required for 16-bit or better graphics boards.

Smooth Shading
> Toggles smooth or faceted shading.

Merge Combine smultiple images.

Apply Materials
> Applies texture mapping defined by the **RMat** command.

Smoothing Angle
> Sets the threshold angle at which **Render** smooths facets.

More Options Additional rendering options:

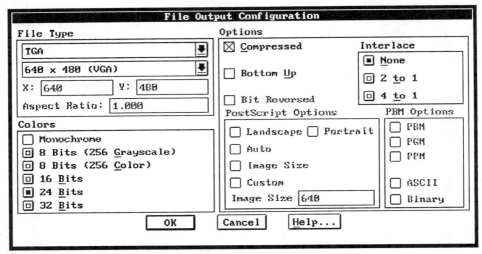

Destination Output rendering to viewport, window, or file.
More Options Additional output options:

Render Scene Render entire drawing.
Render Objects
> Render selected objects; unselected objects disappear.

RELATED AUTOCAD COMMANDS

- *All rendering-related commands.*
- **DView** Creates perspective view.
- **Hide** Removes hidden lines from wireframe view.
- **Shade** Creates simple shadings of 3D objects.

TIPS

■ If you do not place a light or define a scene, **Render** uses the current view and places a single light at your eye.

■ If you do not select a light or scene, **Render** renders all objects using all lights and the current view.

- To run a quick check rendering, use the **Render Objects** option.

- When outputting to a file, you have the following file format options: GIF, X11, PBM, BMP, TGA, PCX, Sun, FITS, PostScript, TIFF, Fax Group III, and IFF.

QUICK START: Your first rendering.

- *Basic rendering:*

1. Create a 3D drawing or select a 3D sample drawing, such as Linkrods.Dwg in \Acad13\Common\Sample.

2. Use the **Config** and **RConfig** commands to configure display and hardcopy rendering devices.

3. Enter the **Render** command and wait a few seconds.

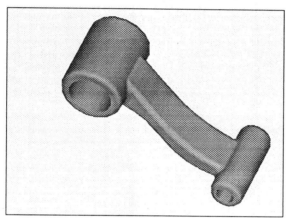

- *Advanced Rendering:*

1. (*Optional*) Use **Config** and **RConfig**; load a 3D drawing.

2. Use **MatLib** to load material definitions (texture mapping) into drawing.

3. With the **RMat** command, assign materials to colors, layers, and objects.

4. Use the **Light** command to place and aim lights: point, spot, and distant lights.

5. The **Scene** command collects lights and a viewpoint into a named object.

6. Render the named scene with the **Render** command.

7. Use the **SaveImg** command to save the rendering to a TIFF, Targa, or GIF file on disk.

8. View the save rendering file with the **Replay** command.

9. (*Optional*) Export the rendering to 3D Studio with the **3dsOut** command.

'RenderUnload

Unloads **Render** to free up memory for AutoCAD (*an external command in Render.Arx*).

Command	Alias	Side Menu	Pull-down	Tablet
'renderunload	. . .		. . .	. . .
. . .				

Command: **renderunload**
AutoCAD Render has been unloaded from memory.

COMMAND OPTIONS
None

RELATED AUTOCAD COMMANDS
All rendering commands

TIP
■ **RenderUnload** frees memory by removing the **Render** code from system RAM; all **Render** commands are still immediately available since any rendering command automatically reloads the **Render** module.

RendScr

Redisplays the most-recent rendering (*short for RENDder SCReen; an external command in Render.Arx*).

Command	Alias	Side Menu	Pull-down	Tablet
rendscr	. . .	. . .	. . .	. . .

Command: **rendscr**

COMMAND OPTIONS
None

Replay

Displays a GIF, TIFF, or Targa file as a bitmap (*an external command in Render.Arx*).

Command	Alias	Side Menu	Pull-down	Tablet
replay	. . .	[TOOLS]	[Tools]	. . .
		[Replay:]	[Image]	
			[View]	

Command: **replay**

Displays dialogue box.

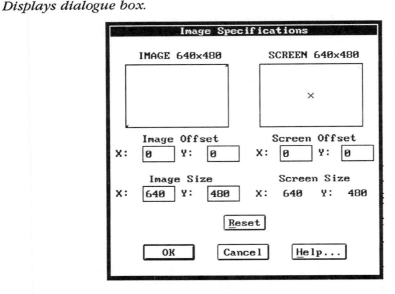

COMMAND OPTIONS

Image   Selects displayed area by clicking on image tile.
Image Offset Reports the x,y-coordinates of the image's lower-left corner.
Image Size   Reports size of image in pixels.
Screen   Fills entire viewport with image.
Screen Offset Reports he x,y-coordinates of the image's lower-left corner.
Reset   Restores values.

RELATED AUTOCAD COMMANDS

- **SaveImg** Saves a rendering as a GIF, TIFF, or Targa raster file.
- **GifIn** Imports a GIF file as a vector file.
- **PcxIn** Imports a PCX file as a vector file.
- **TiffIn** Import a TIFF file as a vector file.

RELATED FILES

- ***.GIF**   Any GIF file.
- ***.TIF**   Any RGBA TIFF file, up to 32-bits in color depth.
- ***.TGA**   Any RGBA Targa v2.0 file, up to 32-bits in color depth.

In subdirectory \Autovis\Maps of the CD-ROM distribution disc:
- ***.TGA**   140 Targa-format images.

'Resume

Resumes a script file after pausing it by pressing the [**Backspace**] key.

Command	Alias	Side Menu	Pull-down	Tablet
'resume	. . .	. . .	. . .	. . .

Command: **resume**

COMMAND OPTIONS
[**Backspace**] Pauses the script file.
[**Esc**]   Stop the script file.

RELATED AUTOCAD COMMANDS
■ **RScript**   Reruns the current script file.
■ **Script**   Loads and runs a script file.

RELATED SYSTEM VARIABLES
■ *None*

Revolve

Creates a 3D solid object by revolving a closed object about an axis
*(formerly the **SolRev** command; an external command in Acis.Dll).*

Command	Alias	Side Menu	Pull-down	Tablet
revolve	...	[DRAW 2]	[Draw]	L 8
		[SOLIDS]	[Solids]	
		[Revolve:]	[Revolve]	

```
Command: revolve
Select objects: [pick]
Select objects: [Enter]
Axis of revolution - Object/X/Y/<Start point of axis>: [pick]
Angle of revolution <full circle>: [Enter]
```

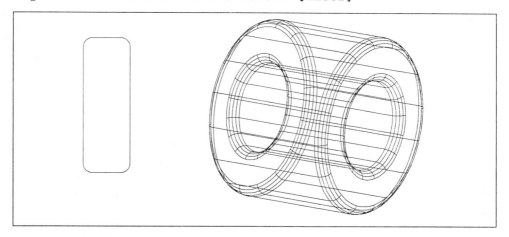

COMMAND OPTIONS

Object   Selects the object that determines axis of revolution.
<Start point>   Indicates the axis of revolution.
X   Uses positive x-axis as axis of revolution.
Y   Uses positive y-axis as axis of revolution.

RELATED AUTOCAD COMMANDS

- **Extrude** Extrudes a 2D object into a 3D solid model.
- **Rotate**   Rotates open and closed objects, forming a 3D surface.

TIPS

- **Revolve** works with just one object at a time.

- **Revolve** works with one of these objects:
  - Closed polylines.
  - Circles, ellipses, donuts, and polygons.
  - Closed splines and regions.

- **Revolve** will not work with:
  - Open objects.
  - Crossing or self-intersecting polylines.

RevSurf

Generates a 3D surface of revolution defined by a path curve and an axis (*short for REVolved SURFace*).

Command	Alias	Side Menu	Pull-down	Tablet
revsurf	...	[DRAW 2]	[Draw]	N 8
		[SURFACES]	[Surfaces]	
		[Revsurf:]	[Revolved Surface]	

```
Command: revsurf
Select path curve: [pick]
Select axis of revolution: [pick]
Start angle <0>: [Enter]
Included angle (+=ccw, -=cw) <Full circle>: [Enter]
```

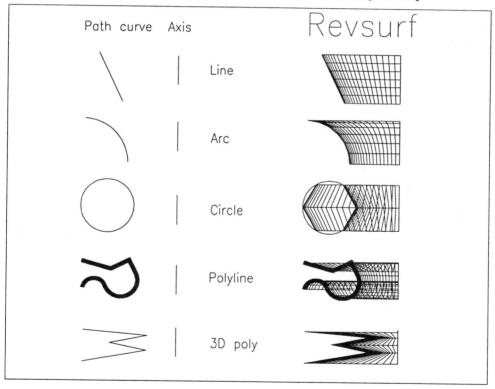

COMMAND OPTIONS

<Full circle> Revolves object through 360 degrees.

Included angle Specifies angle of revolution.

RELATED AUTOCAD COMMANDS

- **EdgeSurf** Creates a 3D surface bounded by four edges.
- **PEdit** Edits revolved surfaces.
- **Revolve** Revolves a 2D closed object into a 3D solid.
- **RuleSurf** Creates a 3D ruled surface.
- **TabSurf** Creates a 3D tabulated surface.

RELATED SYSTEM VARIABLES

- **SurfTab1** Mesh density in M-direction.
- **SurfTab2** Mesh density in N-direction.

TIPS

- Unlike the **Revolve** command, **RevSurf** works with open and closed objects.

- If a multi-segment polyline is the axis of revolution, the rotation axis is defined as the vector pointing from the first vertex to the last vertex, ignoring the location of intermediate vertices.

DEFINITIONS

Axis of Revolution
- The axis about which the object is rotated.
- Defines the m-direction; stored in system variable **SurfTab1**.

Path Curve
- The object being revolved.
- Defines the n-direction; stored in system variable **SurfTab2**.

RMat

Applies material definitions (texture maps) to colors, layers, and objects; used by the **Render** command (*short for Render MATerials; an external command in Render.Arx*).

Command	Alias	Side Menu	Pull-down	Tablet
rmat	. . .	[TOOLS]	[Tools]	. . .
		[RENDER]	[Render]	
		[Mater'l:]	[Materials]	

Command: **rmat**

Displays dialogue box.

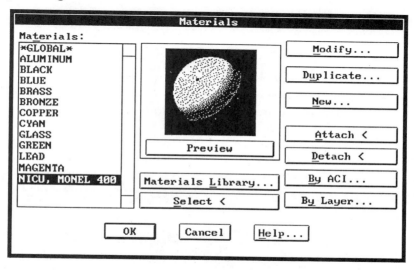

COMMAND OPTIONS

Materials   Lists names of materials loaded into drawing, by the **MatLib** command.

Preview   Previews the material mapped to a sphere.

Materials Library

    Displays the **MatLib** dialogue box.

Select   Selects the objects to which to attach the material definition.

Modify   Edits a material definition; displays dialogue box:

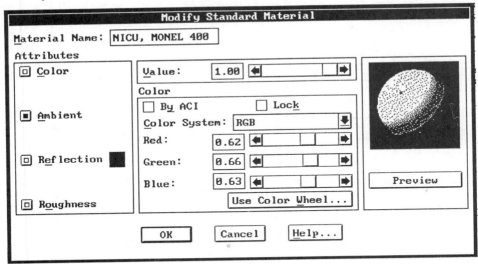

Duplicate   Duplicates a material definition so that you can edit it.
New   Creates a new material definition.
Attach   Selects the objects to attach the material definition.
Detach   Selects the objects to detach a material definition.
By ACI   Attaches material to ACI number; displays dialogue box:

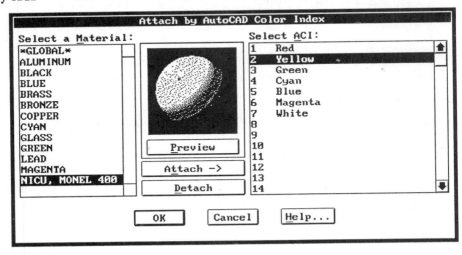

By Layer   Attaches material to layer name.

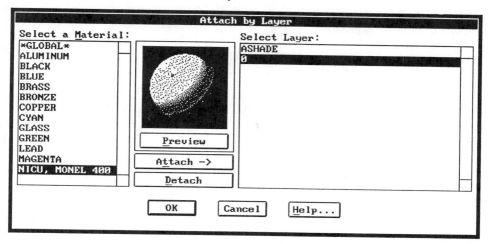

RELATED AUTOCAD COMMANDS
- **MatLib**   Loads material definitions into drawing.
- **Render**   Render drawing using material definitions.

TIPS
■ The **By ACI** option lets you attach a material definition to all objects of one color.

■ The **By Layer** option lets you attach a material definition to all objects on one layer.

■ One set of material definitions is in file \Acad13\Common\Support\ Render.Mli. A more extensive set is in \Autovis\Av_supt\Autovis\Mli on the CD-ROM distribution disc.

DEFINITIONS
ACI
■ AutoCAD Color Index, the formal name for Autodesk's unique color numbering system (see **Layer** command for list).

GLOBAL
■ The default material definition in all drawings:
- Color   = ACI #18, a shade of grey.
- Ambient   = 0.10
- Reflection = 0.20
- Roughness = 0.50

HLS
■ The Hue-Lightness-Saturation method of defining colors.

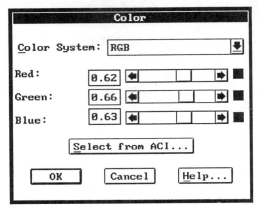

RGB
■ The Red-Green-Blue method of defining colors.

Material Definition
■ Defines a rendered surface texture by four parameters: color, ambient light, reflection, and roughness.

Rotate

Rotates objects about a base point.

Command	Alias	Side Menu	Pull-down	Tablet
rotate	...	[MODIFY]	[Modify]	W13
		[Rotate:]	[Rotate]	

```
Command: rotate
Select objects: [pick]
Select objects: [Enter]
Base point: [pick]
<Rotation angle>/Reference: R
Reference angle <0>:
New angle:
```

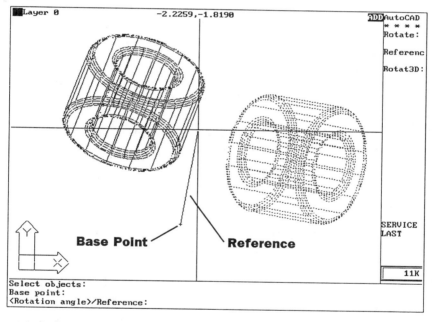

COMMAND OPTIONS

<Rotation angle>

Specifies the angle of rotation.

Reference Indicates a starting reference angle and an ending reference angle.

RELATED AUTOCAD COMMAND

■ **Change** Rotates text objects.

Rotate3D

Rotates objects about an axis in 3D space (*an external command in Geom3d.Exp*).

Command	Alias	Side Menu	Pull-down	Tablet
rotate3d	. . .	[MODIFY]	. . .	. . .
		[Rotate:]		
		[Rotat3D:]		

Command: **rotate3d**
Select objects: **[pick]**
Select objects: **[Enter]**
Axis by Object/Last/View/Xaxis/Yaxis/Zaxis/<2 points>:
<Rotation angle>/Reference: **R**
Reference angle <0>:
New angle:

COMMAND OPTIONS

Object   Selects object to specify rotation axis.
Last   Selects last-picked axis.
View   Currents view direction is the rotation axis.
Xaxis/Yaxis/Zaxis
               Uses the a-, y- or z-axis as the rotation axis.
<2 points> stwo points on rotation axis.

RELATED AUTOCAD COMMANDS
- **Mirror3d** Mirrors objects in 3D space.
- **Rotate**   Rotates objects in 2D space.

RELATED SYSTEM VARIABLES
- *None*

RPref

Specify options for the **Render** command (*short for Render PREFerences; an external command in Render.Arx*).

Command	Alias	Screen menu	Pull-down	Tablet
rpref	. . .	[TOOLS]	[Tools]	0 1
		[RENDER]	[Render]	
		[Prefs:]	[Preferences]	

Command: **rpref**

Displays dialogue box.

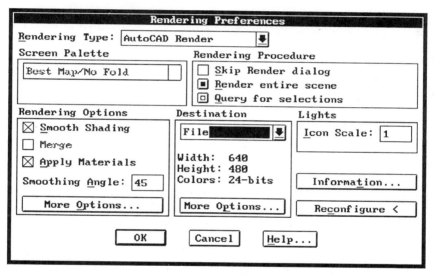

COMMAND OPTIONS

Rendering Type

Selects the AutoCAD Render, AutoVision, and third-party renderers, if loaded into system.

Screen Palette

Selects the palette for 256-color graphics boards; not required for 16-bit or better graphics boards.

Smooth Shading

Toggles smooth or faceted shading.

Merge   Combines multiple images.

Apply Materials

Applies texture mapping defined by the **RMat** command.

Smoothing Angle
Sets the threshold angle at which **Render** smooths facets.
More Options Lists additional render options.
Skip Render Dialog
Creates rendering without displaying **Render**'s dialogue box.
Render entire screen
Renders all objects in scene.
Query for selections
Selects objects to render.
Destination   Outputs rendering to viewport, window, or file.
More Options Lists additional output options.
Lights Icon Scale
Specifies the size of light blocks relative to current scale factor.
Information   Starts **Stats** command.
Reconfigure   Starts RConfig command.

RELATED AUTOCAD COMMANDS

■ *All rendering-related commands*

'RScript

Repeats the script file (*short for Repeat SCRIPT*).

Command	Alias	Side Menu	Pull-down	Tablet
'rscript	. . .	. . .	. . .	. . .

Command: **rscript**

COMMAND OPTIONS
None

RELATED AUTOCAD COMMANDS
- **Resume** Resumes a script file after being interrupted.
- **Script** Loads and runs a script file.

RuleSurf

Draws a 3D ruled surface between two objects (*short for RULEd SURFace*).

Command	Alias	Side Menu	Pull-down	Tablet
rulesurf	...	[DRAW 2]	[Draw]	...
		[SURFACES]	[Surfaces]	
		[Rulsurf:]	[Ruled Surface]	

```
Command: rulesurf
Select first defining curve: [pick]
Select second defining curve: [pick]
```

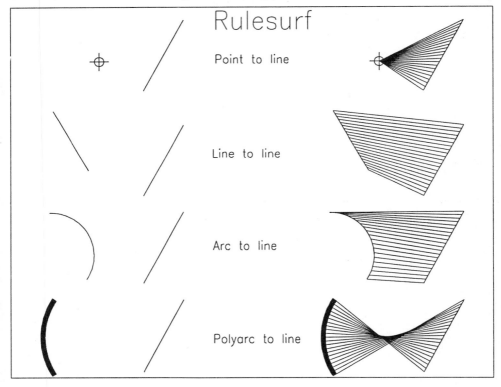

COMMAND OPTIONS
None

RELATED AUTOCAD COMMANDS

- **Edgesurf** Draws a 3D surface bounded by four edges.
- **Revsurf** Draws a 3D surface of revolution.
- **Tabsurf** Draws a 3D tabulated surface.
- **3D** Draws primitive 3D objects.

RELATED SYSTEM VARIABLE

- **Surftab1** Determines the number of rules drawn.

TIPS

- The **RuleSurf** command uses these objects as the boundary curve:
  - Point, line, arc, or circle.
  - Polyline or 3D polyline.

- If one boundary is closed, then the other boundary must also be closed; the exception is using a point as a boundary.

- The **RuleSurf** command begins drawing its mesh as follows:
  - **Open objects:** from the object's endpoint closest to your pick point.
  - **Circles:** from the zero-degree quadrant.
  - **Closed polylines:** the last vertex.

- Since **RuleSurf** draws its mesh with a circle in the opposite direction from a closed polylines, use a donut in place of the circle.

Save

Saves the drawing to disk, after always prompting for a filename.

Command	Alias	Side Menu	Pull-down	Tablet
save	. . .	. . .	. . .	. . .

Command: **save**

Displays dialogue box.

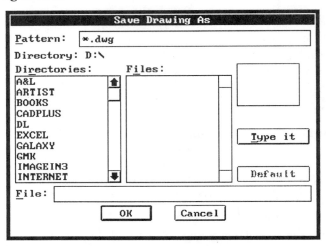

COMMAND OPTIONS
None

RELATED AUTOCAD COMMANDS
- **End**   Saves the drawing and exits AutoCAD.
- **Quit**   Exits AutoCAD without saving the drawing.
- **SaveAs**   Saves the drawing by a different name.
- **SaveAsR12** Saves drawing in Release 12 format.

RELATED SYSTEM VARIABLES
- **DbMod**   Indicates whether the drawing was modified during the current editing session.
- **DwgName**   Name of the drawing; 'UNNAMED' when unnamed.

TIPS
■ The **Save** command always displays the **Save Drawing** dialogue box, unlike other software applications. To avoid the dialogue box, use the **QSave** command.

■ When the drawing is unnamed, the **Save** command mimics the **SaveAs** command and displays the **Save Drawing As** dialogue box.

SaveAs

Saves the current drawing to disk as a Release 13-format DWG drawing file; when you save the drawing with a different filename, the drawing takes on the new name.

Command	Alias	Side Menu	Pull-down	Tablet
saveas	. . .	[FILE]	[File]	T 25
		[SaveAs:]	[Save As]	

Command: **saveas**

Displays dialogue box.

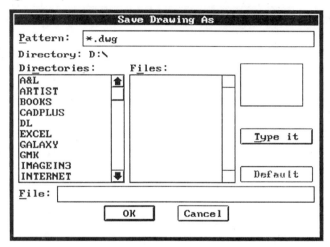

COMMAND OPTIONS

None

RELATED AUTOCAD COMMANDS

- **End**   Saves the drawing and exits AutoCAD.
- **Quit**   Exits AutoCAD without saving the drawing.
- **Save**   Saves the drawing with the current name.
- **SaveAsR12** Saves drawing in Release 12-format DWG.

RELATED SYSTEM VARIABLES

- **DbMod**   Indicates whether the drawing was modified during the current editing session.
- **DwgName**   Name of the drawing; 'UNNAMED' when unnamed.

SaveAsR12

Saves the current drawing to disk as a Release 12-format DWG drawing file.

Command	Alias	Side Menu	Pull-down	Tablet
saveas	...	[FILE]	[File]	...
		[EXPORT]	[Export]	
		[SaveR12:]	[Release 12 DWG]	

Command: **saveasr12**

Example output:

```
Save as release 12 drawing log.
Writing drawing header.
Writing objects database.
Changed XLINE to release 12 objects.  2 found.
Changed TOLERANCE to release 12 objects.  5 found.
Changed SPLINE to release 12 objects.  16 found.
Changed REGION to release 12 objects.  1 found.
Changed RAY to release 12 objects.  2 found.
Changed MLINE to release 12 objects.  19 found.
Changed 3DSOLID to release 12 objects.  2 found.
Changed LEADER to release 12 objects.  1 found.
Changed ELLIPSE to release 12 objects.  1 found.
Writing layer table.
Writing text font and shape table.
Writing linetype table.
Writing view table.
Writing coordinate system table.
Writing viewport table.
Writing registered application table.
Writing dimension style table.
Writing viewport object table.
Writing block definition table.
```

COMMAND OPTIONS
None

RELATED AUTOCAD COMMANDS
- **Quit**   Exits AutoCAD without saving the drawing.
- **Save**   Saves the drawing with the current name in Release 13-format.
- **SaveAs**   Saves drawing by another name in Release 13-format.

RELATED SYSTEM VARIABLES
- **DwgName**   Name of the drawing; 'UNNAMED' when unnamed.
- **HpBound**   Draws boundary as a polyline boundary (*R12-compatible*).
- **PEllipse** Draws ellipsis as a polyarc (*R12-compatible*).

TIPS

- The **SaveAsR12** command translates the Release 13 drawing to a DWG file compatible with Release 12 by:
    - Converting R13-specific objects to R12 equivalents.
    - Stripping out objects that cannot be translated into R12.

- These R13 objects are converted (*this list is more accurate than Autodesk's documentation*):
    - Ellipse: polyarc.
    - Multiline: parallel polylines, arcs, filled arcs, and filled polygons.
    - Spline: splined polyline.
    - Ray and Xline: converted to lines, cut off at the drawing extents.
    - Hatch pattern: associativity is dropped.
    - Dimension: remains as an associative dimension with text intact.
    - Leader: leader line beomes a polyline; arrowhead becomes a solid; MText becomes text.
    - Tolerance: polylines and text (tolerance symbols are gibberish)
    - MText: paragraph text becomes lines of text.
    - Text styles that contain TrueType fonts are converted to the TXT font.
    - Bodies, 3D solids, and 2D regions: loose collection of polylines and arcs. To convert these objects to 3D polyfaces, use the **3dsOut** command, re-import with the **3dsIn** command, and then use the **SaveAsR12** command.

- These R13 objects are deleted (*this list is more accurate than Autodesk's documentation*):
    - Text formatting codes specific to MText.
    - Shapes in linetypes and the global linetype scale in CeLtScale.
    - Rays and Xlines outside of the drawing extents.
    - User-defined objects.
    - Groups and multiline styles.
    - OLE objects (from Windows version).
    - Xref overlays and ASE link information.
    - Preview BMP image.
    - Render's material assignments.
    - Dictionary group codes, ADE lock bit, and object visibility flag.
    - All R13-specific system variables.

■ Exert some control over SaveAsR12 with the **Explode** and **Xplode** commands, which convert complex objects (such as multilines and 3D solids) into polylines, arcs, and other simpler objects.

■ During conversion, the **SaveAsR12** command displays a list of changed and deleted objects (called 'the drawing log'); unfortunately, AutoCAD doesn't save the log to disk, unless you first type the **LogFileOn** command to capture the text screen to the Acad.Log file.

■ There is *no* equivalent 'SaveAsR12DXF' command for creating Release 12-compatible DXF files; the **DxfIx** utility provided with earlier releases of AutoCAD does not work.

SaveImg

Saves a rendered image as a GIF, TIFF, or Targa file on disk (*an external command in Render.Arx*).

Command	Alias	Side Menu	Pull-down	Tablet
saveimg	. . .	[TOOLS]	[Tools]	. . .
		[SaveImg:]	[Image]	
			[Save]	

Command: **saveimg**

Displays dialogue box.

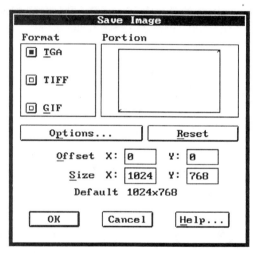

COMMAND OPTIONS

Portion	Selects the portion of image to be saved.
Format	Selects TGA (Targa), TIFF, or GIF format.
Reset	Resets values to their original settings.
Offset	Specifies offset distance in pixels: 0,0 is lower-left corner.
Size	Specifies upper-right distance in pixels.
Options	Selects options for TGA and TIFF output.

Dialogue box for TIFF format options:

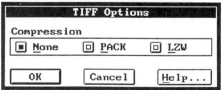

Dialogue box for TGA format options:

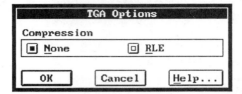

RELATED AUTOCAD COMMANDS

- **SaveImage** Saves a thumbnail image of the drawing to BMP file.
- **<Prt Scr>** Saves entire screen to Vibscrn.Bmp file,when configured with the 'Accelerated Display Driver'.

Scale

Changes the size of selected objects, to make them smaller or larger.

Command	Alias	Side Menu	Pull-down	Tablet
scale	. . .	[MODIFY]	[Modify]	W 12
		[Scale:]	[Scale]	

```
Command: scale
Select objects: [pick]
Select objects: [Enter]
Base point: [pick]
<Scale factor>/Reference: r
Reference length <1>:
```

```
Select objects:
Base point:
<Scale factor>/Reference:
```

COMMAND OPTIONS

Reference Supplies a reference value.

<Scale factor> Indicate scale factor, which applies equally in the x-, y- and z-
directions.

RELATED AUTOCAD COMMANDS

■ **Insert**   Allows a block to be scaled independently in the x-, y-, and z-
directions.

■ **Plot**   Allows a drawing to be plotted at any scale.

Scene

Collects lights and a viewpoint into a named scene (*an external command in Render.Arx*).

Command	Alias	Side Menu	Pull-down	Tablet
scene	...	[TOOLS]	[Tools]	L 2
		[RENDER]	[Render]	
		[Scene:]	[Scenes]	

Command: **scene**

Displays dialogue box.

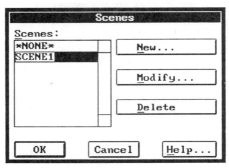

COMMAND OPTIONS

New   Creates a new named scene; displays a dialogue box.
Modify   Changes an existing scene definition; displays a dialogue box.

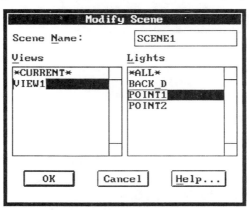

Scene name Enters a name for the scene.
Views   Selects a named view.
Lights   Select one or more lights.
Delete   Deletes scene from drawing; displays a dialogue box.

RELATED AUTOCAD COMMANDS

■ **Light**   Places lights in the drawing for **Scene** command.
■ **Render**   Uses scenes to create renderings.
■ **View**   Creates named views for the **Scene** command.

TIPS

■ Before you can use the **Scene** command, you need to create at least one named view (with the **View** command) or place at least one light (with the Light command). Otherwise, there is no need to use the **Scene** command.

■ If you select no lights for a scene, **Render** uses ambient light.

■ Scene parameters are stored as attribute definitions in a block.

'Script

Runs an ASCII file containing a sequence of AutoCAD instructions to automatically execute a series of commands.

Command	Alias	Side Menu	Pull-down	Tablet
'script	...	[TOOLS]	[Tools]	...
		[Script:]	[Run Script]	

```
Command: script
Script file <>:
```

COMMAND OPTIONS
[Backspace] Interrupts the script.
[Esc] Stops the script.
~ Displays the file dialogue box.

RELATED AUTOCAD COMMANDS
- **Delay** Pauses, in milliseconds, before executing the next command.
- **Resume** Resumes a script after a script has been interrupted.
- **RScript** Repeats a script file.

TIPS
- Since the **Script** command is a transparent command, it can be used during another command.

- Prefix the **VSlide** command to preload it into memory; this results in a faster slide show:
```
*vslide
```

- AutoCAD can start with a script file on the command line:
```
C:\ acad13 dwgname scrname
```

Since the script filename must follow the drawing filename, use a dummy drawing filename, such as 'X'.

- You can make a script file more flexible (pause for user input, branch with conditionals, and so on) by inserting AutoLISP functions.

QUICK START: Writing a script file.
1. A script file consists of the exact keystrokes you type for a command. The script file must be plain ASCII text, so write the script file using a text editor, rather than a word processor.

2. Here is an example script that places a door symbol in the drawing:
```
; Inserts DOOR2436 symbol at x,y = (76,100)
; x-scale = 0.5, y-scale = 1.0, rotation = 90 degrees
insert door2436 76,100 0.5 1.0 90
```

3. In the script, these characters have special meaning:
-     *(Space or end-of-line)* Equivalent to pressing the spacebar or **[Enter]** key.
- ;   *(Semi-colon)* Include a comment in the script file.
- *   *(Asterisk)* Prefix the **VSlide** command to preload its SLD file.

4. Save script file with any 8-character file name and the .SCR extension. For this example, use 'InsDoor.Scr'.

5. Return to AutoCAD and run the script with the **Script** command:
```
Command: script
Script file: insdoor.scr
Command: insert
Block name (or ?): door2436
Insertion point: 76,100
X scale factor <1>/Corner/XYZ: 0.5
Y scale factor (default = X):1.0
Rotation angle <0>:90
```

6. Rerun the script with the **RScript** command.

Section

Creates a 2D region object from the insersection of a plane and a 3D solid (*formerly the **SolSect** command; an external command in Acis.Dll*).

Command	Alias	Side Menu	Pull-down	Tablet
section	...	[DRAW 2]	[Draw]	Y 16
		[SOLIDS]	[Solids]	
		[Section:]	[Section]	

```
Command: section
Select objects: [pick]
Select objects: [Enter]
Section plane by Object/Zaxis/View/XY/YZ/ZX/<3 points>:
```

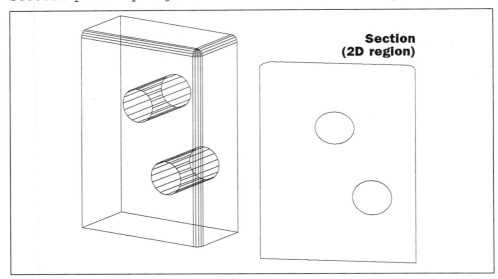

Section
(2D region)

COMMAND OPTIONS

Object　　Aligns section plane with one of these objects:
- Circle or ellipse.
- Arc or elliptical arc.
- 2D spline or 2D polyline.

Zaxis　　　Specifies the normal (z-axis) to the section plane.
View　　　Uses the current view plane as the section plane.
XY　　　　Uses the x,y-plane of the current view.
YZ　　　　Uses the y,z-plane of the current view.
ZX　　　　Uses the z,x-plane of the current view.
<3 points>　Picks three points to specify the section plane.

RELATED AUTOCAD COMMANDS

■ Slice   Cuts a slice out of a solid model.

TIPS

■ Section blocks are placed on the current layer, not the object's layer.

■ Regions are ignored.

■ One cutting plane is required for each selected solid.

■ The **Last** option was removed from Release 13.

Select

Creates a selection set of objects before executing a command.

Command	Alias	Side Menu	Pull-down	Tablet
select	...	[ASSIST]	[Assist]	U14–U22
		[SERVICE]	[Select Objects]	

Command: **select**
Select objects: **[pick]**

COMMAND OPTIONS

A	Continues to add objects after using the **R** option (*short for Add*).
AU	Switches from **[pick]** to **C** or **W** mode, depending whether an object is found at the initial pick point (*short for AUtomatic*).
ALL	Selects all objects in the drawing.
BOX	Goes into **C** or **W** mode, depending on how the cursor moves.
C	Selects objects inside and crossing the selection box (*short for Crossing*).
CP	Selects all objects inside and crossing the selection polygon.
F	Selects all objects crossing a polyline (*short for Fence*).
G	Selects objects contained in a named group (*short for Group; new to Release 13*).
L	Selects the last-drawn object still visible on the screen (*short for Last*).
M	Makes multiple selections before AutoCAD scans the drawing; saves time in a large drawing (*short for Multiple*).
P	Selects the previously selected objects (*short for Previous*).
R	Remove objects from the selection set (*short for Remove*).
SI	Select only a single set of objects before terminating **Select** command (*short for SIngle*).
U	Removes the most-recently added selected objects (*short for Undo*).
W	Selects all objects inside the selection box (*short for Window*).
WP	Selects an objects inside the selection polygon.
[pick]	Selects a single object.
[Enter]	Exits the **Select** command.
[Esc]	Aborts the **Select** command.

RELATED AUTOCAD COMMAND

- **Filter**   Specifies objects that are added to the selection set.

RELATED SYSTEM VARIABLES

- **PickAdd**   Controls how objects are added to a selection set.
- **PickAuto**   Controls automatic windowing at the Select Objects: prompt.
- **PickDrag**   Controls method of creating a selection box.
- **PickFirst**   Controls command-object selection order.

'SetVar

Lists the settings of system variables; allows you to change variables that are not read-only (*short for SET VARiable*).

Command	Alias	Side Menu	Pull-down	Tablet
'setvar	...	[OPTIONS]	...	...
		[Sys Var:]		

```
Command: setvar
Variable name or ?:
```

Example:
```
Command: setvar
Variable name or ?: visretain
New value for VISRETAIN <0>: 1
```

COMMAND OPTIONS

Variable name Indicates the system variable name you want to access.

?   Lists the names and settings of system variables.

TIPS

■ See Appendix A for the complete list of all system variables found in AutoCAD Release 13.

■ Almost all system variables can be set without using the **SetVar** command. For example,
```
Command: visretain
New value for VISRETAIN <0>: 1
```

■ More than 30 system variables are not listed by the **SetVar** command. These system variables are used by third-party programmers, by Autodesk for debugging, or are obsolete:
  - ■ _LInfo, _PkSer, and _Server.
  - ■ AuxStat, AxisMode, and AxisUnit.
  - ■ DbgIInstall.
  - ■ EntExts, EntMods, and ErrNo.
  - ■ Flatland and Force_Paging.
  - ■ GlobCheck.
  - ■ LazyLoad.
  - ■ MaxObjMem and MacroTrace.
  - ■ NodeName.
  - ■ PHandle.
  - ■ QaFlags.
  - ■ Re-Init.
  - ■ UserI1 through UserI5, UserR1 through UserR5, and UserS1 through UserS5.

Shade

Performs 16- and 256-color shaded renderings, and quick hidden-line removal of 3D drawings.

Command	Alias	Side Menu	Pull-down	Tablet
shade	...	[TOOLS]	[Tools]	O 2
		[SHADE]	[Shade]	
		[Shade]		N 2

```
Command: shade
Regenerating drawing.
Shading 50% done.
Shading complete.
```

ShadEdge = 0

ShadEdge = 1

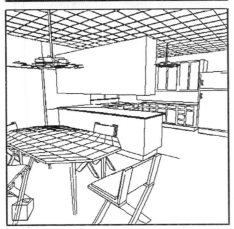

ShadEdge = 2

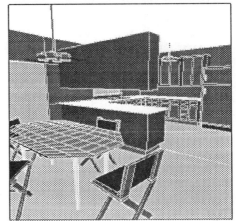

ShadEdge = 3

COMMAND OPTIONS

None

RELATED AUTOCAD COMMANDS

- **DView**   Does hidden-line removal of perspective views.
- **Hide**   Does true hidden-line removal of 3D drawings.
- **MSlide**   Saves a rendered view as an SLD-format slide file.
- **MView**   Does a hidden-line view of individual viewports during plots and prints.
- **Plot**   Does a hidden-line view during plotting.
- **Render**   Performs a more realistic rendering.

RELATED SYSTEM VARIABLES

- **ShadEdge**   Determines the style of shading:

    0 256-color shading.

    1 256-color shading with outlined polygons.

    2 Hidden-line removal.

    3 16-color shading (*Default*).

- **ShadeDif** Determines the shading contrast (*Default=70*).

TIPS

- As an alternative to the **Shade** command, the **Render** module does high-quality renderings of 3D drawings but takes longer to complete the rendering.

- The smaller the viewport, the faster the rendering.

Shape

Inserts a predefined shape in the current drawing; shapes are more compact than blocks but are more difficult to create.

Command	Alias	Side Menu	Pull-down	Tablet
shape	. . .	. . .	[Draw] [Insert] [Shape]	. . .

```
Command: shape
Shape name (or ?):
Starting point: [pick]
Height <>:
Rotation angle <0>:
```

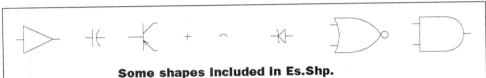

Some shapes included in Es.Shp.

COMMAND OPTIONS

Shape name   Indicates the name of the shape to insert.
?   Lists the names of currently loaded shapes.

RELATED AUTOCAD COMMANDS

- **Load**   Loads an SHX-format shape file into the drawing.
- **Insert**   Inserts a block into the drawing.
- **Style**   Loads SHX font files into the drawing.

RELATED SYSTEM VARIABLE

- **ShpName** Current SHP filename.

TIPS

- Shapes are defined by SHP files, which must first be compiled into SHX files before they can be loaded by the **Load** command.

- Compile an SHP file into an SHX file with the **Compile** command.

- AutoCAD comes with three SHX shape files, located in the \Acad13\Common\Sample subdirectory:
  - **Es.Shx**   Electronic component shapes (*see figure above*).
  - **Pc.Shx**   Printed circuit board shapes.
  - **St.Shx**   Surface texture shapes for mechanical parts drawings.

Shell

Temporarily exit AutoCAD to the DOS operating system (*an external command defined in Acad.Pgp*).

Command	Alias	Side Menu	Pull-down	Tablet
shell	sh	...	[Tools] [External Commands] [Shell]	Y24 - 25

```
Command: shell
OS Command:
```

COMMAND OPTIONS

[Enter]	Stay in DOS for more than one command.
Exit	Return to AutoCAD from DOS.

RELATED COMMANDS

- **End**   Exit AutoCAD back to DOS

The following commands are defined by Acad.Pgp:

- **Catalog**   Equivalent to the DOS command **DIR /W**.
- **Del**   Executes the DOS command **DEL**.
- **Dir**   Executes the DOS command **DIR**.
- **Edit**   Executes the DOS program **EDIT**.
- **Type**   Executes the DOS command **TYPE**.

RELATED FILE

- **Acad.Pgp** The external command definition file, in subdirectory \Acad13\Common\Support.

QUICK START: Adding a command to the Acad.Pgp file.

1. Load the Acad.Pgp file into a text editor.

2. The PGP file uses this format to add a command:
   ```
   CommandName,[DOS request],MemoryReserve,[*]Prompt,ReturnCode
   ```

Meaning of the format:
- **CommandName:** The name you type at AutoCAD's Command prompt.
- **DOS Request:** The command AutoCAD feeds to DOS.
- **MemoryReserve:** Always 0, held over from old versions of AutoCAD.
- **Prompt:** A phrase to prompt user action.
- ***Prompt:** User's response to prompt may contain spaces.
- **ReturnCode: 0** Return to AutoCAD's text sreen.
-              **1** Loads **$Cmd.Dxb** file into drawing upon return.
-              **2** Loads **$Cmd.Dxb** as a block into the drawing.
-              **4** Returns to AutoCAD's previous screen mode, usually the graphics screen.

For our example, we may want to add easy access to the WordPerfect word processor. Add this line anywhere in the Acad.Pgp file:

```
WP, WP, 0, File to edit: ,4
```

3. Save the file and return to AutoCAD.

4. Use the **ReInit** command to reload the Acad.Pgp file.

5. Enter **WP** at the Command: prompt:

```
Command: wp
```

6. AutoCAD shells out to DOS and prompts you:

```
File to edit:
```

Enter the name of a text file; AutoCAD launches WordPerfect with the file.

7. To return to AutoCAD, you must exit WordPerfect.

ShowMat

Lists the material attached to an object *(short for SHOW MATerial; an undocumented command in Render.Arx)*.

Command	Alias	Side Menu	Pull-down	Tablet
showmat	...	...	...	...

Command: **showmat**
Select object: **[pick]**

Example output:
Material BRONZE is explicitly attached to the object.

COMMAND OPTIONS
None

RELATED AUTOCAD COMMANDS
- **MatLib**   Loads material definitions into the drawing.
- **RMat**   Attaches materials to objects, colors, and layers.

Sketch

Allows freehand drawing as lines or polylines.

Command	Alias	Side Menu	Pull-down	Tablet
sketch	..	[DRAW 1]	[Draw]	. . .
		[Sketch:]	[Sketch]	

```
Command: sketch
Record increment <0.1000>: [Enter]
Sketch.  Pen eXit Quit Record Erase Connect .
```

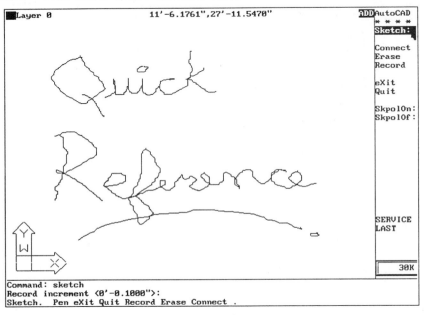

COMMAND OPTIONS

Commands can be invoked by digitizer buttons:

Connect   Connects to the last drawing segment (*Button #6*).

Erase   Erases temporary segments as the cursor moves over them (*Button #6*).

eXit   Records the temporary segments and exit the **Sketch** command (*Button #3*).

Pen   Lifts and lowers the pen (*Pick button, #0*).

Quit   Discards temporary segments and exit the **Sketch** command (*Button #4*).

Record   Records the temporary segments as permanent (*Button #2*).

.   (*Period*) Connects the last segment to the current point (*Button #1*).

RELATED AUTOCAD COMMANDS

- **Line**   Draws line segments.
- **PLine**   Draws polyline and polyline arc segments.

RELATED SYSTEM VARIABLES

- **SketchInc**   The current recording increment for **Sketch**.
- **SkPoly**   Controls the type of sketches recorded:
  - **0**   Records sketches as lines.
  - **1**   Record sketches as polylines.

TIPS

- During the **Sketch** command, the definitions of the pointing device's buttons change to:

Button Number	Meaning	Equivalent Keystroke
0	Raise and lower the *pen*	P
1	Draw line to current *point*	.
2	*R*ecord sketch	R
3	Record sketch and e*X*it	X
4	Discard sketch and *Q*uit	Q
5	*E*rase sketch	E
6	*C*onnect to last-drawn segment	C

- Only the first three (or two) button-commands are available on three- (or two-) button mice.

- Pull-down menus are unavailable during the **Sketch** command.

Slice

Cuts a 3D solid with a plane, creating two 3D solids (*formerly the SolCut command; an external command in Acis.Dll*).

Command	Alias	Side Menu	Pull-down	Tablet
solcut	...	[DRAW 2]	[Draw]	Y17
		[SOLIDS]	[Solids]	
		[Slice:]	[Slice]	

Command: **slice**
Select objects: **[pick]**
Select objects: **[Enter]**
Slicing plane by Object/Zaxis/View/XY/YZ/ZX/<3 points>:
Both sides/<Point on desired side of the plane>:

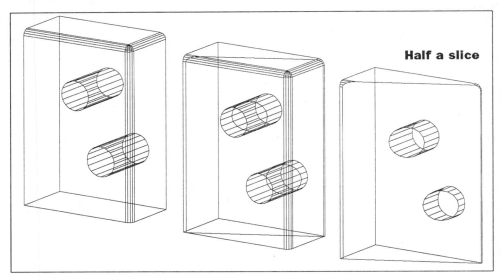

Half a slice

COMMAND OPTIONS

Object	Aligns cutting plane with a circle, ellipse, arc, elliptical arc, 2D spline, or 2D polyline.
View	Aligns cutting plane with viewing plane.
XY	Aligns cutting plane with x,y-plane of current UCS.
YZ	Aligns cutting plane with y,x-plane of current UCS.
Zaxis	Aligns cutting plane with two normal points.
ZX	Aligns cutting plane with z,x-plane of current UCS.
<3 points>	Aligns cutting plane with three points.

Both sides   Retains both halves of cut solid model.
<Point on desired side of the plane>
            Retains either half of cut solid model.

'Snap

Sets the drawing resolution, grid origin, isometric mode, and angle.

Command	Ctrl Key	Side Menu	Pull-down	Tablet
'snap	[Ctrl]+B	[ASSIST]	[Assist]	V 21
		[Snap:]	[Snap]	
	[F9]			

```
Command: snap
Snap spacing or ON/OFF/Aspect/Rotate/Style <1.0000>:
```

COMMAND OPTIONS

Aspect   Sets separate x- and y-increments.
OFF   Turns snap off.
ON   Turns snap on.
Rotate   Rotates the crosshairs for snap and grid.
Snap spacing Sets the snap increment.
Style   Switches between standard and isometric style.

RELATED AUTOCAD COMMANDS

- **DdRModes** Sets snap values via a dialogue box.
- **Grid**   Turns on the grid.
- **Isoplane** Switches to a different isometric drawing plane.

RELATED SYSTEM VARIABLES

- **SnapAng** Current angle of the snap rotation.
- **SnapBase** Base point of the snap rotation.
- **SnapIsopair** Current isometric plane setting.
- **SnapMode** Determines whether snap is on.
- **SnapStyl** Determines style of snap.
- **SnapUnit** The current snap increment in x- and y-directions.

TIP

- The **Snap** command controls aspects the following commands:
  - Rotation angle of the grid and ortho modes.
  - Turning isometric mode on and off.
  - Grid aspect ration.

Solid

Draws solid filled triangles and quadrilaterals; does *not* create a 3D ACIS solid.

Command	Alias	Side Menu	Pull-down	Tablet
solid	...	[DRAW 1]	[Draw]	...
		[Solid:]	[Polygon]	
			[Solid]	

```
Command: solid
First point: [pick]
Second point: [pick]
Third point: [pick]
Fourth point: [pick]
```

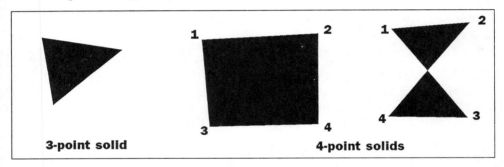

3-point solid   **4-point solids**

COMMAND OPTIONS
None

RELATED AUTOCAD COMMANDS
- **Fill**   Turns object fill off and on.
- **Trace**   Draws lines with width.
- **PLine**   Draws polylines and polyline arcs with width.

RELATED SYSTEM VARIABLE
- **FillMode** Determines whether solids are displayed filled or outlined.

TIP
- The pick order for drawing a solid is counter-intuitive; see figure above for the pick order to create a rectangle and a bowtie.

'Spell

Checks the spelling of text in the drawing (*an external command in AcSpell.Dll*).

Command	Alias	Side Menu	Pull-down	Tablet
'spell	...	[TOOLS]	[Tools]	T 4
		[Spell:]	[Spelling]	

```
Command: spell
Select objects:
```

If incorrect text is found, displays dialogue box:

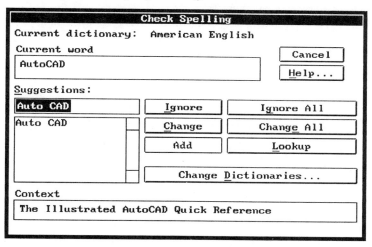

COMMAND OPTIONS

Ignore	Ignores the spelling and go on to next word.
Ignore all	Ignores all words with this spelling.
Change	Changes to suggested spelling.
Change all	Changes all words with this spelling.
Add	Adds word to user dictionary.
Lookup	Checks spelling of work in Suggestions box.

Change dictionaries
Selects a different dictionary.

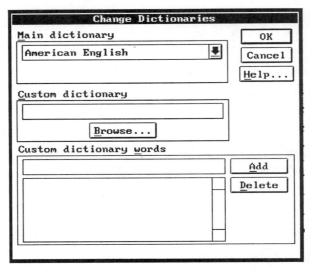

RELATED AUTOCAD COMMAND
- **DdEdit**   Edits text.

RELATED SYSTEM VARIABLES
- **DctMain** Name of main spelling dictionary.
- **DctCust** Name of custom spelling dictionary.

RELATED FILES
- **Enu.Dct** Dictionary word file in \Acad13\Common\Support.
- ***.Cus**   Custom dictionary files.

TIP
- When **Spell** is complete, it displays the following dialogue box:

Sphere

Draws a 3D sphere as a solid model *(formerly the SolSphere command; an external command in Acis.Dll)*..

Command	Alias	Side Menu	Pull-down	Tablet
sphere	. . .	[DRAW 2]	[Draw]	K 7
		[SOLIDS]	[Solids]	
		[Sphere:]	[Sphere]	

```
Command: sphere
Center of sphere <0,0,0>: [pick]
Diameter/<Radius> of sphere: [pick]
```

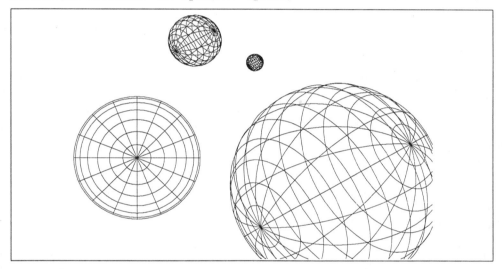

COMMAND OPTIONS

Center of sphere
    Locates the center point of the sphere.
Diameter Specifies diameter of the sphere.
Radius Specifies radius of the sphere.

RELATED AUTOCAD COMMANDS

- **Box**   Draws solid boxes.
- **Cone**   Draws solid cones.
- **Cylinder** Draws solid cylinders.
- **Torus**   Draws solid tori.
- **Wedge**   Draws solid wedges.
- **3D**   Draws a surface meshed sphere.

The Illustrated AutoCAD Quick Reference ■ **377**

Spline

Draws NURBS (non-uniform rational Bezier spline) curves (*an external command in Acis.Dll*).

Command	Alias	Side Menu	Pull-down	Tablet
spline	...	[DRAW 1]	[Draw]	K 4
		[Spline:]	[Spline]	

```
Command: spline
Object/<First point>: [pick]
Enter point: [pick]
Close/Fit tolerance/<Enter point>: [pick]
Close/Fit tolerance/<Enter point>: [Enter]
Enter start tangent: [pick]
Enter end tangent: [pick]
```

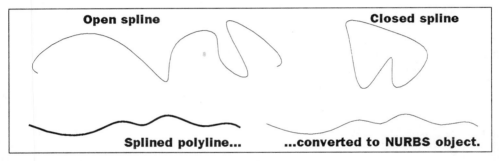

Open spline   **Closed spline**

Splined polyline...   **...converted to NURBS object.**

COMMAND OPTIONS

Close   Closes spline at the start point.
Fit   Changes spline tolerance; 0 = curve passes through fit points.
Object   Converts 2D and 3D splined polylines into a NURBS spline.

RELATED AUTOCAD COMMANDS

- **PLine**   Draws splined polyline.
- **SplinEdit**   Edits a NURBS spline.

RELATED SYSTEM VARIABLE

- **DelObj**   Toggles whether the original polyline is deleted with the **Object** option.

TIP

- A polyline with width looses its width when converted to a NURBS spline.

SplinEdit

Edits a NURBS spline (*an external command in Acis.Dll*).

Command	Alias	Side Menu	Pull-down	Tablet
splinedit	...	[MODIFY]	[Modify]	W 18
		[SplinEd:]	[Edit Spline]	

```
Command: splinedit
Select spline: [pick]
Fit data/Close/Move vertex/Refine/rEverse/Undo/eXit <X>: F
Add/Close/Delete/Move/Purge/Tangents/toLerance/eXit <X>:
```

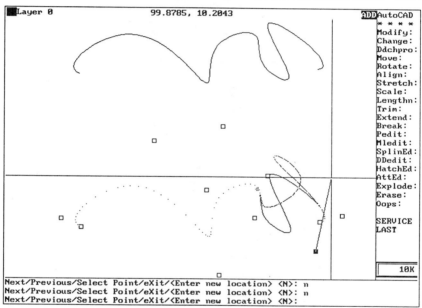

COMMAND OPTIONS

Fit data	Edits the spline's fit points:
Add	Adds fit points.
Close	Closes the spline, if open.
Delete	Removes fit points.
Move	Moves fit points.
Open	Opens the spline, if closed.
Purge	Removes fit point data from drawing.
Tangents	Edits the start and end tangents.
toLerance	Refits spline with new tolerance value.
<eXit>	Exits suboptions.
Close	Close the spline, if open.

Move vertex Moves a control vertex.
Open   Opens the spline, if closed.
Refine   Adds a control point, change the spline's order or weight.
rEverse   Reverses the spline's direction.
Undo   Undoes the most-recent edit change.
<eXit>   Exits the **SplinEdit** command.

RELATED AUTOCAD COMMANDS

- **PEdit**   Edits a splined polyline.
- **Spline**   Draws a NURBS spline.

TIPS

- The spline loses its fit data when you use the following **SplinEdit** command options:
  - **Refine.**
  - **Fit Purge.**
  - **Fit Tolerance** followed by **Fit Move.**
  - **Fit Tolerance** followed by **Fit Open** or **Fit Close**.

- The maximum order for a spline is 26; once the order has been elevated, it cannot be reduced.

- The larger the 'weight,' the closer the spline is to the control point.

Stats

Lists statistics of the most-recent rendering (*short for STATisticS; an external command in Render.Arx*).

Command	Alias	Side Menu	Pull-down	Tablet
stats	...	[TOOLS]	[Tools]	...
		[RENDER]	[Render]	
		[Stats:]	[Statistics]	

Command: **stats**

Displays dialogue box.

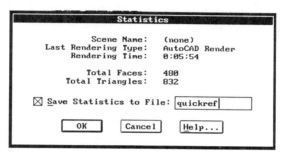

COMMAND OPTION
Save Statistics to File
>   Saves rendering statistics to file.

RELATED AUTOCAD COMMAND
■ **Render**   Creates renderings.

DEFINITIONS
Scene name
■ Name of the currently selected scene.
■ When no scene is current, displays '(none)'.

Last rendering type
■ Name of currently selected renderer.
■ Default is AutoCAD Render.

Rendering time
■ Time required to create most-recent rendering.
■ Reported in HH:MM:SS (hours, minutes, seconds) format.

Total faces
■ Number of faces processed in most-recent rendering.
■ A single 3D object consists of many faces.

Total triangles
■ Number of triangles processed in most-recent rendering.
■ A rectangular face is typically divided into two triangles.

'Status

Displays information about the current drawing and environment.

Command	Alias	Side Menu	Pull-down	Tablet
'status	...	[DATA]	[Data]	...
		[STATUS:]	[Status]	

Command: **status**

Example output for the Acad.Dwg prototype drawing:

```
 30 objects in C:\ACAD13\COMMON\SUPPORT\ACAD
 Model space limits are X:    0.0000   Y:     0.0000    (Off)
                        X:   12.0000   Y:     9.0000
 Model space uses       *Nothing*
Display shows       X:     0.0000  Y:     0.0000
                    X:    15.8496  Y:    11.6525
Insertion base is   X:     0.0000  Y:     0.0000 Z:  0.0000
Snap resolution is  X:     1.0000  Y:     1.0000
Grid spacing is     X:     0.0000  Y:     0.0000

Current space:      Model space
Current layer:      0
Current color:      BYLAYER -- 7 (white)
Current linetype:   BYLAYER -- CONTINUOUS
Current elevation:   0.0000  thickness:     0.0000
Fill on  Grid off  Ortho off  Qtext off  Snap off  Tablet off
Object snap modes:      None
Free disk: 34316288 bytes
Virtual memory allocated to program: 17544 KB
Amount of program in physical memory/Total (virtual) program size: 36%
Total conventional memory: 8 KB      Total extended memory: 6512 KB
Swap file size: 4504 KB
Page faults: 1691    Swap writes: 633     Swap reclaims: 435
```

COMMAND OPTION

[F1]   Returns to the graphics screen.

RELATED AUTOCAD COMMANDS

- **DbList**   Lists information about all objects in the drawing.
- **List**   Lists information about selected objects.
- **Stats**   Lists information of the most-recent rendering.

DEFINITIONS

Model space limits, Paper space limits
- The x,y-coordinates stored in the **LimMin** and **LimMax** system variables.
- 'Off' indicates limits checking is turned off (sysatem variable **LimCheck**).

Model space uses, Paper space uses
- The x,y-coordinates of the lower-left and upper-right extents of objects in the drawing.
- 'Over' indicates drawing extents exceeds the drawing limits.

Display shows
- The x,y-coordinates of the lower-left and upper-right corners of the current display.

Insertion base is
- The x,y,z-coordinates stored in system variable **InsBase**.

Snap resolution is, Grid spacing is
- The snap and grid settings, as stored in the **SnapUnit** and **GridUnit** system variables.

Current space
- Indicates whether model or paper space is current.

Current layer, Current color, Current linetype, Current elevation, Thickness
- The current values for the layer name, color, linetype name, elevation, and thickness, as stored in system variables **CeLayer**, **CeColor**, **CeLType**, **Elevation**, and **Thickness**.

Fill, Grid, Ortho, Qtext, Snap, Tablet
- The current settings for the fill, grid, ortho, qtext, snap, and tablet modes, as stored in the system variables **FillMode**, **GridMode**, **OrthoMode**, **QTextMode**, **SnapMode**, and **TabMode**.

Object snap modes
- The currently set object modes, as stored in system variable **OsMode**.

Free disk (dwg + temp = C)
- Amount of free disk space on the drive storing AutoCAD's temporary files, as pointed to by system variable **TempPrefix**.

Free physical memory
- Amount of free RAM.

Free swap file space
- Amount of free space in AutoCAD's swap file on disk.

StlOut

Exports 3D solids and bodies in binary or ASCII SLA format (*short for STereoLithography OUTput; formerly the SolStlOut command; an external command in Acis.Dll*).

Command	Alias	Side Menu	Pull-down	Tablet
stlout	...	[FILE]	[File]	...
		[EXPORT]	[Export]	
		[STLout:]	[Stereolithography]	

```
Command: stlout
Select a single solid for STL output.
Select objects: [pick]
Create binary STL file? <Y>:
```

Example of a small portion of an STL file in ASCII format:

```
solid AutoCAD
    facet normal -7.020345e-016 -9.807852e-001 1.950903e-001
       outer loop
          vertex 1.0000000e+001 1.1903397e+001 1.9011325e+001
          vertex 1.0000000e+001 1.2095498e+001 1.9977082e+001
          vertex 1.2726627e-001 1.2095498e+001 1.9977082e+001
       endloop
     endfacet
   ...
endsolid AutoCAD
```

COMMAND OPTIONS

Y   Creates a binary-format SLA file.
N   Creates a ASCII-format SLA file.

RELATED AUTOCAD COMMANDS

■ *All solid modeling commands.*
■ **AcisOut**   Exports 3D solid models to an ASCII SAT format ACIS file.
■ **AmeConvert**
              Converts AME v2.x solid models into ACIS models.

RELATED SYSTEM VARIABLE

■ **FaceTRes** Determines the resolution of triangulating solid models.

RELATED FILE

■ *.STL   SLA-compatible file with STL extension.

TIPS

■ The solid model must lie in the positive x,y,z-octant of the WCS.

■ The **STLout** command exports a single 3D ACIS solid; it does not export ACIS regions or any other AutoCAD object.

DEFINITIONS

STL

■ Stereolithography data file, which consists of a faceted representation of the ACIS model.

SLA

■ StereoLithography Apparatus.

ACIS

■ 'Alan, Charles, Ian, Spatial' is the solid modeling engine used by AutoCAD Release 13 and licensed from Spatial Technologies.

Stretch

Stretches objects to lengthen, shorten or distort them.

Command	Alias	Side Menu	Pull-down	Tablet
stretch	...	[MODIFY]	[Modify]	X 17
		[Stretch:]	[Stretch]	

```
Command: stretch
Select objects: c
First corner: [pick]
Other corner: [pick]
Select objects: [Enter]
Base point: [pick]
New point: [pick]
```

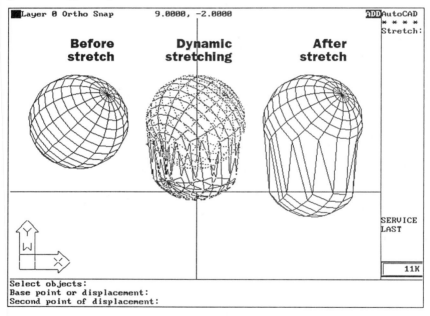

COMMAND OPTIONS
None

RELATED AUTOCAD COMMANDS
- **Change**   Changes the size of lines, circles, text, blocks, and arcs.
- **Scale**   Increases or decreases the size of any object.

TIPS

■ The effect of the **Stretch** command is not always obvious; be prepared to use the **Undo** command.

■ The first time you select objects for the **Stretch** command, you must use **Crossing** object selection.

■ Objects entirely within the selection window are moved, rather than stretched.

■ The **Stretch** command will not move a hatch pattern unless the hatch's origin is included in the selection set.

■ Use the **Stretch** command to automatically update associative dimensions by including the dimension's endpoint in the selection set.

'Style

Creates and modifies text styles based on a font file.

Command	Alias	Side Menu	Pull-down	Tablet
'style	. . .	[DATA]	[Data]	U 4
		[Style:]	[Text Style]	

```
Command: style
Text style name (or ?) <STANDARD>:
Font file <ROMANS>:
 Height <0.0000>: [Enter]
 Width factor <1.00>: [Enter]
Obliquing angle <0>: [Enter]
Backwards? <N> [Enter]
Upside-down? <N> [Enter]
Vertical? <N> [Enter]
STANDARD is now the current text style.
```

COMMAND OPTIONS
None

RELATED AUTOCAD COMMANDS
- **Change**   Changes the style assigned to selected text.
- **Compile**   Compiles SHP and PFB source files into SHX font files.
- **DText**   Places text using current style; allows change of style.
- **MText**   Places paragraph text.
- **Purge**   Removes unused text style definitions.
- **Rename**   Renames a text style name.
- **Text**   Enters text using current style; allows change of style.

RELATED SYSTEM VARIABLES
- **TextFill** Toggles fill of PostScript and TrueType fonts:
  - **0**   Fill turned off (*Default*)
  - **1**   Fill turned on.
- **TextQlty** Sets the quality (resolution) of PostScript and TrueType fonts:
  - **0**   Minimum.
  - **50**   Default value.
  - **100** Maximum.
- **TextStyle** The current text style.
- **TextSize** The current text height.

RELATED FILES
Font files are found in subdirectory \Acad13\Common\Support:

TIPS ·

■ AutoCAD Release 12 added support for PostScript fonts; Release 13 added support for TrueType fonts.

■ AutoCAD's SHX fonts display the faster than TrueType fonts, which display faster than PostScript fonts.

■ The **TextFill** and **TextQlty** system variables greatly affect the speed of text display in a drawing. Here are the results from timing a drawing containing all fonts supplied with Release 13. The default settings is the baseline (= 1):

   ■ Default settings (TextFill = 0, TextQlty = 50, QText = 0): **1.0**
   ■ Raise text quality to 100: **0.70** (*70% as fast as the default settings, or about 1.4 times slower*).
   ■ Lower text quality to 0: **2.0** (*Twice as fast as the default settings*).
   ■ Turn text fill on: **0.34** (*Three times as slow as the default settings*).
   ■ Turn quick text on: **8.7** (*Nearly nine times faster than the default settings*).

■ Source files need no longer be compiled (with the **Compile** command) into SHX files before being loaded into the drawing.

■ As of Release 12, the **Style** command compiles on the fly.

■ TrueType fonts cannot be compiled with the **Compile** command.

PostScript fonts:

cibt.pfb	ABC abc 123 !@#
cobt.pfb	ABC abc 123 !@#
eur.pfb	ABC abc 123 !@#
euro.pfb	ABC abc 123 !@#
par.pfb	ABC abc 123 !@#
rom.pfb	ABC abc 123 !@#
romb.pfb	ABC abc 123 !@#
romi.pfb	ABC abc 123 !@#
sas.pfb	ABC abc 123 !@#
sasb.pfb	ABC abc 123 !@#
sasbo.pfb	ABC abc 123 !@#
saso.pfb	ABC abc 123 !@#
te.pfb	ABC ABC 123 !@#
teb.pfb	ABC ABC 123 !@#
tel.pfb	ABC ABC 123 !@#

Vector SHX fonts:

complex.shx ABC abc 123 !@#
gothice.shx 𝕬𝕭𝕮 𝖆𝖇𝖗 123 !@#
gothicg.shx 𝖀𝕭𝕮 abc 123 !@#
gothici.shx 𝕳𝕭𝕼 𝖆𝖇𝖗 123 !@#
greekc.shx ??? ??? 123 !@#
greeks.shx ??? ??? 123 !@#
isocp.shx ABC abc 123 !@#
isocp2.shx ABC abc 123 !@#
isocp3.shx ABC abc 123 !@#
isoct.shx A B C a b c 1 2 3 ! @ #
isoct2.shx A B C a b c 1 2 3 ! @ #
isoct3.shx A B C a b c 1 2 3 ! @ #
italic.shx *ABC abc 123 !@#*
italicc.shx *ABC abc 123 !@#*
italict.shx *ABC abc 123 !@#*
monotxt.shx ABC abc 123 !@#
romanc.shx ABC abc 123 !@#
romand.shx **ABC abc 123 !@#**
romans.shx ABC abc 123 !@#
romant.shx ABC abc 123 !@#
scriptc.shx 𝒜ℬ𝒞 abc 123 !@#
scripts.shx 𝒜ℬ𝒞 abc 123 !@#
simplex.shx ABC abc 123 !@#
syastro.shx ☉♀♀ ✶'' 123 !@#
symap.shx ⌀△ ⚐⚒☖ 123 !@#
symath.shx ℵ'| ←↓∂ 123 !@#
symeteo.shx ⚊ |\ 123 !@#
symusic.shx ♩♪ ♩♪ 123 !@#
txt.shx ABC abc 123 !@#

TrueType fonts:

bgothl.ttf	ABC ABC 123 !@#
bgothm.ttf	ABC ABC 123 !@#
compi.ttf	±°′ ©℗© ○○▫□
comsc.ttf	ABC abc 123 !@#
dutch.ttf	ABC abc 123 !@#
dutchb.ttf	ABC abc 123 !@#
dutchbi.ttf	ABC abc 123 !@#
dutcheb.ttf	ABC abc 123 !@#
dutchi.ttf	ABC abc 123 !@#
monos.ttf	ABC abc 123 !@#
monosb.ttf	ABC abc 123 !@#
monosbi.ttf	ABC abc 123 !@#
monosi.ttf	ABC abc 123 !@#
swiss.ttf	ABC abc 123 !@#
swissb.tff	ABC abc 123 !@#
swissbi.ttf	ABC abc 123 !@#
swissbo.ttf	ABC abc 123 !@#
swissc.ttf	ABC abc 123 !@#
swisscb.ttf	ABC abc 123 !@#
swisscbi.ttf	ABC abc 123 !@#
swisscbo.ttf	ABC abc 123 !@#
swissci.ttf	ABC abc 123 !@#
swissck.ttf	ABC abc 123 !@#
swisscki.ttf	ABC abc 123 !@#
swisscl.ttf	ABC abc 123 !@#
swisscli.ttf	ABC abc 123 !@#
swisse.ttf	ABC abc 123 !@#
swisseb.ttf	ABC abc 123 !@#
swissek.ttf	ABC abc 123 !@#
swissel.ttf	ABC abc 123 !@#
swissi.ttf	ABC abc 123 !@#
stylu.ttf	ABC abc 123 !@#
swissk.ttf	ABC abc 123 !@#
swisski.ttf	ABC abc 123 !@#
swissko.ttf	ABC abc 123 !@#
swissl.ttf	ABC abc 123 !@#
swissli.ttf	ABC abc 123 !@#
umath.ttf	ABΨ αβψ + − × /
vinet.ttf	ABC abc 123 !@#

■ The effect of the **TextQlty** system variable on the display of PostScript and TrueType fonts:

TextQlty set to 0 (low):

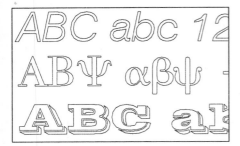

TextQlty set to 100 (high):

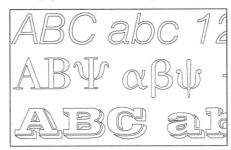

■ The effect of the **TextFill** system variable on the display of PostScript and TrueType fonts:

TextFill set to 0 (off):

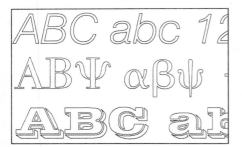

TextFill set to 1 (on):

Subtract

Removes the volume of one 3D model or 2D region from another
(formerly the SolSub command; an external command in Acis.Dll).

Command	Alias	Side Menu	Pull-down	Tablet
subtract	...	[DRAW 2]	[Construct]	Y 14
		[SOLIDS]	[Subtract]	
		[Subtrac:]		

```
Command: subtract
Select objects: [pick]
Select objects: [Enter]
1 solid selected.
Objects to subtract from them..
Select objects: [pick]
Select objects: [Enter]
1 solid selected.
```

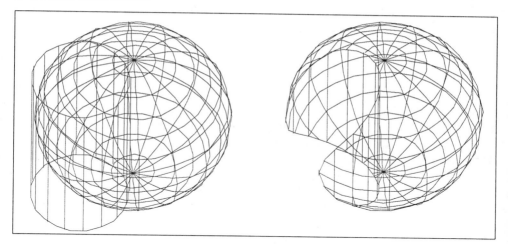

COMMAND OPTIONS
None

RELATED ACIS COMMAND
- **Intersect** Removes all but the intersection of two solid volumes.
- **Union** Joins two solids together

Tablet

Configures, calibrates, and toggles the digitizing tablet for menus and pointing area.

Command	Ctrl+	Side Menu	Function Key	Tablet
tablet	T	[Settings]	[F10]	S 19-22
		[next]		
		[TABLET:]		
				X 25

Command: **tablet**
Options (ON/OFF/CAL/CFG):

COMMAND OPTIONS

CAL	Calibrates the coordinates for the tablet.
CFG	Configures the menu areas on the tablet.
OFF	Turns off the tablet's digitizing mode.
ON	Turns on the tablet's digitizing mode.

RELATED SYSTEM VARIABLE

■ **TabMode** Toggles use of the tablet:
> **0** Tablet mode disabled.
> **1** Tablet mode enabled.

RELATED FILES

■ **Acad.Mnu** Menu source code that defines functions of tablet menu areas, in \Acad13\Dos\Support.

■ **Mc.Exe** Menu compiler; semi-automates the creation of a tablet menu file; in \Acad13\Common\Sample.

■ **Tablet.Dwg** AutoCAD drawing of the printed template overlay; in the \Acad13\Common\Sample.

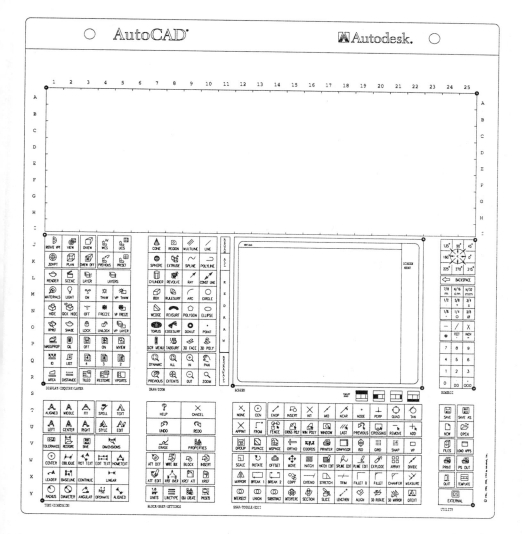

TIPS

■ Since version 2.5, AutoCAD includes a tablet overlay in the package.

■ To customize or change the size of the AutoCAD tablet overlay, edit the Tablet.Dwg file, then plot it out to fit your digitizer.

■ The **Tablet** command does not work if a digitizing tablet has not been configured with the **Config** command.

- AutoCAD supports up to four independent menu areas; macros are specified by the ***TABLET1 through ***TABLET4 sections of the Acad.Mnu menu file.

- Menu areas may be skewed but corners must form a right angle.

DEFINITIONS

Affine transformation:
- 3 pick points.
- Sets an arbitrary linear 2D transformation with independent x,y-scaling and skewing.

Orthagonal transformation:
- 2 pick points.
- Sets the translation; scaling and rotation angle remain uniform.

Outcome of fit:
- A report on the results of the 3 transformation types (affine, orthagonal, projective).
- AutoCAD reports 5 types of outcomes:
  - **Exact**   Enough points to transform data.
  - **Success**   More than enough points to transform data.
  - **Impossible** Not enough points to transform data.
  - **Failure**   Too many colinear and coincident points.
  - **Cancelled** Fitting cancelled during projective transform.

Projective transformation
- 4 pick points.
- Maps a perspective projection from one plane to another plane.
- A limited form of 'rubber sheeting': straight lines remain straight but not necessarily parallel.

Residual
- Largest: where mapping is least accurate.
- Second largest: second-least accurate.

RMS error
- Root mean square error
- Smaller is better: measures closeness of fit.

Standard deviation
- Measures standard deviation of residuals.
- Near zero: residual at each point is roughly the same.

TabSurf

Draws a tabulated surface as a 3D mesh; defined by a path curve, and a direction vector (*short for TABulated SURFace*).

Command	Alias	Side Menu	Pull-down	Tablet
tabsurf	...	[DRAW 2]	[Draw]	P 8
		[SURFACES]	[Surfaces]	
		[Tabsurf:]	[Tabulated Surface]	

Command: **tabsurf**
Select path curve: **[pick]**
Select direction vector: **[pick]**

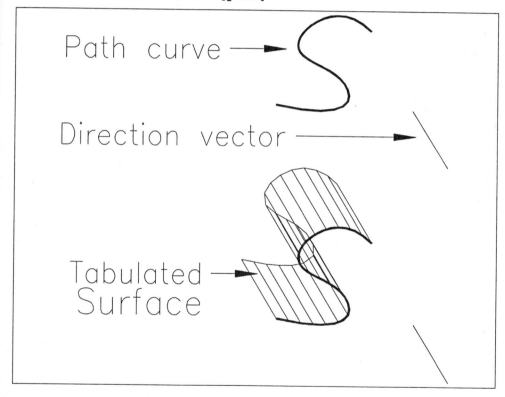

Path curve ➝ S

Direction vector ➝ \

Tabulated ➝ Surface

COMMAND OPTIONS
None

RELATED AUTOCAD COMMANDS

- **Edge** Changes the visibility of 3D face edges.
- **Explode** Reduces a tabulated surface into 3D faces.
- **PEdit** Edits a 3D mesh, such as tabulated surfaces.
- **EdgeSurf** Draws a 3D mesh surface between boundaries.
- **RevSurf** Draws a revolved 3D mesh surface around an axis.
- **RuleSurf** Draws 3D mesh surface between open or closed boundaries.
- **3D** Creates 3D objects out of surface meshes.

RELATED SYSTEM VARIABLE

- **SurfTab1** Defines the number of tabulations drawn by **TabSurf** in the n-direction.

TIPS

- The path curve can be open or closed:
    - Line, 2D polyline, and 3D polyline.
    - Arc, circle, and ellipse.

- The direction vector defines the direction and length of extrusion.

- The number of m-direction tabulations is always 2 and lies along direction vector.

- The number of n-direction tabulations is determined by system variable **SurfTab1** (*default* = 6) along curves only.

Text

Places one line of text in the drawing.

Command	Alias	Side Menu	Pull-down	Tablet
text	...	...	[Draw]	...
			[Text]	
			[Single-Line Text]	

```
Command: text
Justify/Style/<Start point>: j
Align/Fit/Center/Middle/Right/TL/TC/TR/ML/MC/MR/BL/BC/BR: r
Height <0.2000>: [Enter]
Rotation angle <0>: [Enter]
Text:
```

COMMAND OPTIONS

[Enter]	Continess text one line below previously-placed text line.
Justify	Displays the justification submenu:
Align	Aligns the text between two points with adjusted text height.
Fit	Fits the text between two points with fixed text height.
Center	Centesr the text along the baseline.
Middle	Centers the text horizontally and vertically.
Right	Right-justifies the text.
TL	Top-left justification.
TC	Top-center justification.
TR	Top-right justification.
ML	Middle-left justification.
MC	Middle-center justification.
MR	Middle-right justification.
BL	Bottom-left justification.
BC	Bottom-center justification.
BR	Bottom-right justification.
<Start point>	Left-justifies the text.
Style	Displays the style submenu:
Style name	Indicates a different style name.
?	Lists the currently loaded styles.

RELATED AUTOCAD COMMANDS

- **Change** — Changes the text height, rotation, style and content.
- **DText** — Places new text to the drawing interactively.
- **MText** — Places paragraph text.
- **Style** — Creates new text styles.

RELATED SYSTEM VARIABLES

■ **TextSize** The current height of text.

■ **TextStyle** The current style.

TIPS

■ By default, text is placed left-justified.

■ The location of the 12 standard text justification modes:

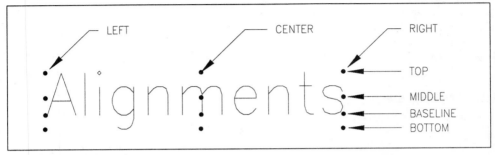

■ Use a width factor of 0.85 to squeeze in 15% more text, yet maintain readability.

■ See the **Style** command for a list of text fonts included with Release 13.

'TextScr

Switches from the graphics screen to the text screen in single-screen systems (*short for TEXT SCReen*).

Command	Alias	Side Menu	Function Key	Tablet
'textscr	...	...	[F1]	...

Command: textscr

```
Send F1 | Text Screen                                              Go Text
Output Inches=Drawing Units or Fit or ? <Fit>:

Standard values for output size
Size      Width      Height
A          8.00       10.50
B         10.00       16.00
C         16.00       21.00
D         21.00       33.00
E         33.00       43.00
F         28.00       40.00
G         11.00       90.00
H         28.00      143.00
J         34.00      176.00
K         40.00      143.00
A4         7.80       11.20
A3        10.70       15.60
A2        15.60       22.40
A1        22.40       32.20
A0        32.20       45.90
USER       5.00        7.00

Enter the Size or Width,Height (in Inches) <USER>:
Effective plotting area:  5.00 wide by 5.44 high
13100 objects
Command:
```

COMMAND OPTIONS

Send F1   Returns to graphics screen.
Go Text   Switches to AutoCAD's text screen.

RELATED AUTOCAD COMMANDS

■ **DlxText**   Displays text screen in a window when AutoCAD is configured with 'Accelerated Display Driver.'
■ **GraphScr** Switches from text screen to graphics screen.

RELATED SYSTEM VARIABLE

■ **ScreenMode** Reports whether screen is in text or graphics mode.
　　　　　　　0 Text screen.
　　　　　　　1 Graphics screen.
　　　　　　　2 Dual screen displaying both text and graphics.

TIP

■ **TextScr** does not work with dual-screen systems.

'Tiffin

Imports TIF raster files into the drawing as a block (*an external file in Raster.Exp*).

Command	Alias	Side Menu	Pull-down	Tablet
'tifin	...	[FILE]	[File]	...
		[IMPORT]	[Import]	
		[TIFFin:]	[Raster]	
			[TIFF]	

```
Command: tifin
TIFF file name:
Insertion point <0,0,0>:
Scale factor:
```

COMMAND OPTIONS
None

RELATED AUTOCAD COMMANDS
- **PsIn**   Imports EPS files.
- **GifIn**   Imports GIF raster files.
- **PcxIn**   Imports PCX raster files.
- **Replay**   Displays GIF, TIFF, and TGA files as raster images.

RELATED SYSTEM VARIABLES
- **RiAspect** Adjusts image's aspect ration.
- **RiBackG** Changes the image's background color.
- **RiEdge**   Outlines edges.
- **RiGamut** Specifeis number of colors.
- **RiGrey**   Imports as a grey scale image.
- **RiThresh** Controls brightness threshold.

TIPS
- The TIFF format (*short for tagged image file format*) was invented by Aldus and Microsoft for desktop publishing software.

- **TiffIn** is limited to displaying a maximum of 256 colors.

- Exploding an imported TIFF block doubles the drawing file size.

- Each run of similarly-colored pixels is defined as a solid.

- Turn off system variable **GripBlock** (*set it to 0*) to avoid highlighting all the solid objects making up the block.

'Time

Display timely information about the current drawing.

Command	Alias	Side Menu	Pull-down	Tablet
'time	...	[DATA]	[Data]	...
		[TIME:]	[Time]	

```
Command: time
Current time:              15 Sep 1996 at 14:12:44.250
Times for the drawing:
Created:                   15 Sep 1956 at 14:06:55.580
Last updated:              10 Feb 1995 at 12:30:08.930
Total editing time:        10957 days 00:05:48.670
Elapsed timer (on):        0 days 00:05:48.670
Next automatic save in:    0 days 00:04:32:120
Display/ON/OFF/Reset:
```

COMMAND OPTIONS

Display	Displays the current time information.
OFF	Turns the user timer off.
ON	Turns the user timer on.
Reset	Resets the user timer.
[F1]	Return to graphics screen.

RELATED AUTOCAD COMMAND

■ **Status**   Displays information about the current drawing and environment.

RELATED SYSTEM VARIABLES

■ **CDate**   The current date and time.
■ **Date**   The current date and time in Julian format.
■ **TdCreate**   Date and time the drawing was created.
■ **TdInDwg**   The time the drawing spent in AutoCAD.
■ **TdUpdate**   The last date and time the drawing was changed.
■ **TdUsrTimer** The current user timer setting.
■ **SaveTime**   The automatic drawing save interval.

TIP

■ The times displayed by the **Time** command are only accurate when the computer's clock is accurate; unfortunately, the clock in most personal computers strays by many minutes per week.

Tolerance

Places geometric tolerancing symbols and text.

Command	Alias	Side Menu	Pull-down	Tablet
tolerance	...	[DRAW DIM]	[Draw]	V 1
		[Toleran:]	[Dimensioning]	
			[Tolerance]	

```
Command: tolerance
[select collection of tolerance symbols]
Enter tolerance location: [pick]
```

Displays dialogue box.

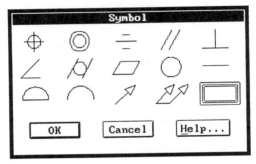

Select a tolerance symbol:
   Location symbols:

⊕   Position.

◎   Concentricity and coaxiality.

⹀   Symmetry.

   Orientation symbols:

//   Parallelism.

⟂   Perpendicularity.

∠   Angularity.

   Form symbols:

⌭   Cylindricity.

▱   Flatness.

○   Circularity and roundness.

■ Straightness.

Profile symbols:

⌒ Profile of the surface.

⌒ Profile of the line.

⟋ Circular runout.

⟋⟋ Total runout.

After selecting a symbol, the following dialogue box appears:

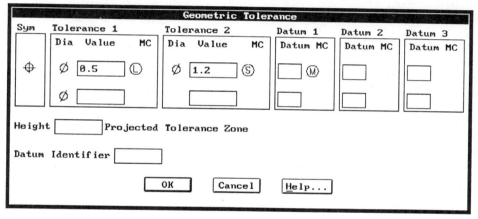

COMMAND OPTIONS

Sym Insert geometric characteristic symbol.
Tolerance Insert first tolerance value.
  Dia Places optional ⌀ (*diameter*) symbol.
  Value Places tolerance value.
  MC Places material condition: modifies tolerance symbol; displays dialogue box:

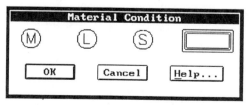

Material condition symbols:

(M) Maximum material condition.

(L) Least material condition.

(S) Regardless of feature size.

Datum   Insert datum reference.
Height   Insert projected tolerance zone value.
Projected Tolerance Zone
               Places projected tolerance zone symbol.
Datum Identifier
               Creates datum identifier symbol, such as —A—

RELATED FILES

In \Acad13\Common\Support:
- **Gdt.Shp**   Tolerance symbol definition source file.
- **Gdt.Shx**   Compiled tolerance symbol file.

DEFINITIONS

Datum:
- A theoretically-exact geometric reference.
- Establishes the tolerance zone for the feature.
- These objects can be used as a datum:
  - Point, line, and plane.
  - Cylinder, and other geometry.

Material condition:
- These symbols modify the geometric characteristics and tolerance values.
- Modifiers for features that vary in size.

Projected tolerance zone:
- Specifies the height of the fixed perpendicular part's extended portion.
- Changes the tolerance to positional tolerance.

Tolerance:
- Indicates amount of varience from perfect form.

Torus

Draws a 3D torus as a solid model (*formerly the SolTorus command; an external command in Acis.Dll*).

Command	Alias	Side Menu	Pull-down	Tablet
torus	...	[DRAW 2]	[Draw]	0 7
		[SOLIDS]	[Solids]	
		[Torus:]	[Torus]	

```
Command: torus
Center of torus <0,0,0>: [pick]
Diameter/<Radius> of torus: [pick]
Diameter/<Radius> of tube: [pick]
```

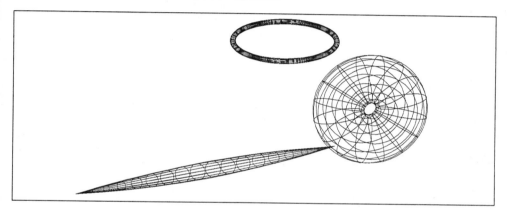

COMMAND OPTIONS

Diameter   Indicates the diameter of the torus and the tube.
<Radius>   Indicates the radius of the torus and the tube.

RELATED AUTOCAD COMMANDS

- **Ai_Torus** Creates a torus made from 3D polyfaces.
- **Box**   Draws solid boxes.
- **Cone**   Draws solid cones.
- **Cylinder** Draws solid cylinders.
- **Sphere**   Draws solid spheres.
- **Wedge**   Draws solid wedges.

TIPS

- **Torus** allows self-intersecting tori.

- A negative torus radius creates the football shape.

- When the torus radius is negative, the tube radius must be a larger positive number; for example, with a torus radius of -1.99, the tube radius must be greater than +1.99.

Trace

Draws lines with width.

Command	Alias	Side Menu	Pull-down	Tablet
trace	. . .	[DRAW 2]	. . .	. . .
		[Trace:]		

```
Command: trace
Trace width <0.0500>: [Enter]
From point: [pick]
To point: [pick]
To point: [Enter]
```

COMMAND OPTION
[Enter]   Exits the **Trace** command.

RELATED AUTOCAD COMMANDS
- **Line**   Draws lines with zero width.
- **MLine**   Draws up to 16 parallel lines.
- **PLine**   Draws polylines and polyline arcs with varying width.

RELATED SYSTEM VARIABLES
- **FillMode** Toggles display of fill or outline traces (*Default = 1, on*).
- **TraceWid** The current width of the trace (*Default = 0.05 units*).

TIPS
- Traces are drawn along the centerline of the pick points.

- Display of a trace segment is delayed by one pick point.

- During drawing of traces, you cannot backup since an **Undo** option is missing; if you require this feature, draw wide lines with the **PLine** command, setting the **Width** option.

- There is no option for controlling joints (always beveled) or endcapping (always square); if you require these features, draw wide lines with the **MLine** command, setting the solid fill, endcap, and joint options with the **MlStyle** command.

'TreeStat

Displays the status of the drawing's spatial index, including the number and depth of nodes.

Command	Alias	Side Menu	Pull-down	Tablet
'treestat	...	...	...	...

Command: **treestat**

Sample output for Acad.Dwg:

```
Model-space branch
-------------------
Oct-tree, depth limit = 30
Subtree containing objects with defined extents:
     Nodes: 1    Objects: 0
     Average objects per node: 0.00
     Average node depth: 5.00
     Nodes with population 0: 1
Total nodes: 4    Total objects: 0


Paper-space branch
-------------------
Quad-tree, depth limit = 20
Subtree containing objects with defined extents:
     Nodes: 1    Objects: 0
     Average objects per node: 0.00
     Average node depth: 5.00
     Nodes with population 0: 1
Total nodes: 4    Total objects: 0
```

COMMAND OPTIONS
None

RELATED SYSTEM VARIABLES

- **TreeDepth** Size of the tree-structured spatial index in *xxyy* format:
  - **xx** Number of model space nodes (*Default = 30*).
  - **yy** Number of paper space nodes (*Default = 20*).
  - **-xx** 2D drawing.
  - **+xx** 3D drawing (*Default*).
  - **3020** Default value of **TreeDepth**.
- **TreeMax** Maximum number of nodes (*Default = 10,000,000*).

TIPS

■ Better performance occurs with fewer objects per oct-tree node.

■ When redraws and object selection seem slow, increase the value of system variable **TreeDepth**.

■ Each node consumes 80 bytes of memory.

DEFINITIONS

Oct tree:
■ The model space branch of the spatial index.
■ Objects are either 2D or 3D.
■ 'Oct' comes from the eight volumes in x,y,z-coordinate system of 3D space.

Quad tree:
■ The paper space branch of the spatial index.
■ All objects are two-dimensional.
■ 'Quad' comes from the four areas in the x,y-coordinate system of 2D space.

Spatial index
■ Objects indexed by oct-region to record their position in 3D space.
■ Has a tree structure with two primary branches: oct tree and quad tree.
■ Objects are attached to 'nodes'; each node is a branch on the 'tree.'

Trim

Ver. 2.5

Trims lines, arcs, circles, and 2D polylines back to a real or projected cutting line or view.

Command	Alias	Side Menu	Pull-down	Tablet
trim	...	[MODIFY]	[Modify]	X 18
		[Trim:]	[Trim]	

```
Command: trim
Select cutting edges: (Projmode=UCS, Edgemode=No extend)
Select objects: [pick]
Select objects: [Enter]
<Select object to trim>/Project/Edge/Undo: [pick]
```

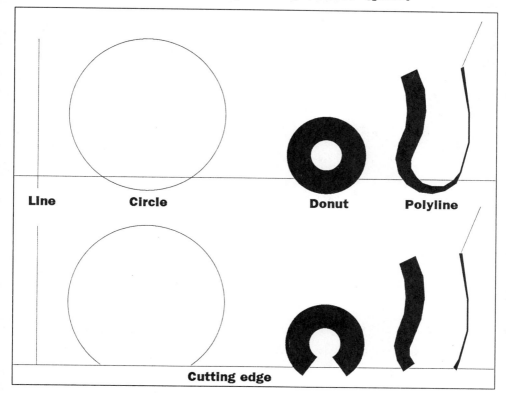

Line   Circle   Donut   Polyline

Cutting edge

COMMAND OPTIONS

Select object to trim

Picks the objects at the trim end.

Edge   Selects type of trim (*new to Release 13*):
  Extend   Extends cutting edge to trim object.
  No extend   Only trims at actual cutting edge (*Release 12 compatible*).
Project   Selects trim projection mode (*new to Release 13*):
  None   Uses only objects as cutting edge (*Release 12 compatible*).
  Ucs   Trims at x,y-plane of current UCS.
  View   Trims at current view plane.
Undo   Untrims the last trim action.

RELATED AUTOCAD COMMANDS

- **Change**   Changes the size of lines, arcs, and circles.
- **Extend**   Lengthens lines, arcs, and polylines.
- **Lengthen** Lengthens open objects.
- **PEdit**   Changes polylines.
- **Stretch**   Lengthens or shortens lines, arcs, and polylines.

Undoes the most recent AutoCAD command (*short for Undo*).

Command	Alias	Side Menu	Pull-down	Tablet
u	. . .	[ASSIST]	[Assist]	U 7-8
		[U:]	[Undo]	

Command: **u**

COMMAND OPTIONS
None

RELATED AUTOCAD COMMANDS
- **Oops**   Unereses the most-recently erased object.
- **Quit**   Exits the drawing, undoing all changes.
- **Redo**   Redoes the most-recent undo.
- **Undo**   Allows more sophisticated control over undo.

RELATED SYSTEM VARIABLE
- **UndoCtl** Determines the state of undo control.

TIPS
- The **U** command is convenient for stepping back through the design process, undoing one command at a time.

- The **U** command is the same as the **Undo 1** command; for greater control over the undo process, use the **Undo** command.

- The **Redo** command redoes the most-recent undo only.

- The **Quit** command restores the drawing to its original state.

- Since the undo mechanism creates a mirror drawing file on disk, disable the **Undo** command with system variable **UndoCtl** (set it to 0) when your computer is low on disk space.

- Commands that involve writing to file and plotting are not undone by the **U** and **Undo** commands.

Ucs

Defines a new coordinate plane (*short for User Coordinate System*).

Command	Alias	Side Menu	Pull-down	Tablet
UCS	. . .	[VIEW:]	[View]	J 4-5
		[UCS:]	[Set UCS]	

```
Command: ucs
Origin/ZAxis/3point/OBject/View/X/Y/Z/Prev/Restore/Save/Del/
    ?/<World>:
```

COMMAND OPTIONS

Del	Deletes the name of a saved UCS.
OBject	Aligns UCS with a picked object.
Origin	Moves the UCS to a new origin point.
Prev	Restores the previous UCS orientation.
Restore	Restore a named UCS.
Save	Saves the current UCS by name.
View	Aligns the UCS with the current view.
<World>	Aligns the UCS with the WCS.
X	Rotates the UCS about the x-axis.
Y	Rotates the UCS about the y-axis.
Z	Rotates the UCS about the z-axis.
ZAxis	Aligns the UCS with a new origin and z-axis.
3point	Aligns the UCS with a point on the positive x-axis and positive x,y-plane.
?	Lists the names of saved UCS orientations.

RELATED AUTOCAD COMMANDS

- **DdUcs**   Modifies the UCS via a dialogue box.
- **UcsIcon**   Controls the visibility of the UCS icon.
- **Plan**   Change the view to the plan view of the current UCS.

RELATED SYSTEM VARIABLES

- **UcsFollow**   Automatically show plan view in new UCS.
- **UcsIcon**   Determines visibility and location of UCS icon.
- **UcsOrg**   WCS coordinates of UCS icon.
- **UcsXdir**   X-direction of current UCS.
- **UcsYdir**   Y-direction of current UCS.
- **WorldUcs**   Correlation of WCS and UCS.

TIPS

- Use the **UCS** command to draw entities at odd angles in 3D space.

- Although you can create a UCS in paper space, you cannot use 3D viewing commands.

- A UCS can be aligned with these objects:
    - Point, line, trace, 2D polyline, and solid.
    - Arc and circle.
    - Text, shape, dimension, and attribute definition.
    - 3D face and block reference.

- A UCS will not align with these objects:
    - Mline, ray, xline, and 3D polyline.
    - Spline and ellipse.
    - Leader and viewport.
    - 3D solid, 3D mesh, and region.

DEFINITIONS

UCS:

- User-defined 2D coordinate system oriented in 3D space.
- Sets a working plane, orients 2D objects, defines the extrusion direction, and the axis of rotation.
- Sometimes known as the ACS or auxiliary coordinate system.

WCS:

- World coordinate system.
- The default 3D x,y,z-coordinate system.

Ucsicon

Controls the location and display of the UCS icon.

Command	Alias	Side Menu	Pull-down	Tablet
ucsicon	...	[OPTIONS]	[Options]	...
		[UCSicon:]	[UCS]	
			[Icon]	

```
Command: ucsicon
ON/OFF/All/Noorigin/ORigin <ON>:
```

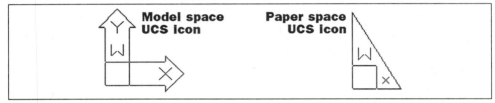

COMMAND OPTIONS

All   Makes **UcsIcon** command's changes apply to all viewports.
Noorigin   Always display UCS icon in lower-left corner.
OFF   soff display of UCS icon.
ON   Turns on display of UCS icon.
ORigin   Displays UCS icon at the current UCS origin.

RELATED AUTOCAD COMMAND

■ **UCS**   Creates and controls user-defined coordinate systems.

RELATED SYSTEM VARIABLE

■ **UcsIcon**   Determines the display and origin of the UCS icon.

Undefine

Makes an AutoCAD command unavailable.

Command	Alias	Side Menu	Pull-down	Tablet
undefine	...	...	...	...

```
Command: undefine
Command name:
```

Example usage:
```
Command: undefine
Command name: line
Command: line
Unknown command.  Type ? for list of commands.
Command: .line
From point:
```

COMMAND OPTION

(*Period*) Precede undefined command with period to temporarily redefine it.

RELATED AUTOCAD COMMAND

■ **Redefine** Redefines an AutoCAD command.

RELATED SYSTEM VARIABLES

■ *None*

TIP

■ In menu macros written with international language versions of AutoCAD, precede command names with an underscore character (_) to automatically translate the name.

Undo

Undo the effect of previous commands.

Command	Alias	Side Menu	Pull-down	Tablet
undo	. . .	. . .	. . .	. . .

```
Command: undo
Auto/Control/BEgin/End/Mark/Back/<number>:
```

COMMAND OPTIONS

Auto	Treats a menu macro as a single command.
Back	Undoes back to the marker.
BEgin	Groups a sequence of operations (*the Group option in R12*).
Control	Limits the options of the **Undo** command.
All	Toggles on full undo.
None	Turns off undo feature.
One	Limits the Undo command to a single undo.
End	Ends the group option.
Mark	Sets a marker.
<number>	Indicates the number of commands to undo.

RELATED AUTOCAD COMMANDS

- **Oops**   Unerases the most-recently erased object.
- **Quit**   Leaves the drawing without saving changes.
- **Redo**   Undoes the most recent undo.
- **U**   Single-step undo.

RELATED SYSTEM VARIABLES

- **UndoCtl**   Indicates the state of Undo:
  - 0 Undo is disabled.
  - 1 Undo is enabled.
  - 2 Single-command undo.
  - 3 Auto-group mode enabled.
  - 4 Group is currently active.
- **UndoMarks** Number of undo marks placed in the **Undo** control stream.

TIP

- Since the undo mechanism creates a mirror drawing file on disk, disable the **Undo** command with system variable **UndoCtl** (set it to 0) when your computer is low on disk space.

Union

Joins to solids and regions together into a single model (*formerly the SolUnion command; an external command in Acis.Dll*).

Command	Alias	Side Menu	Pull-down	Tablet
union	. . .	[DRAW 2]	[Construct]	Y 13
		[SOLIDS]		[Union]
		[Union:]		

```
Command: union
Select objects: [pick]
Select objects: [pick]
```

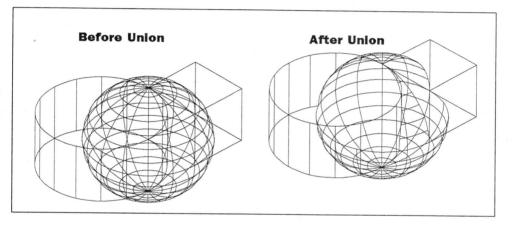

Before Union **After Union**

COMMAND OPTIONS
None

RELATED AUTOCAD COMMANDS
- **Intersect** Creates a solid model from the intersection of two objects.
- **Subtract** Creates a solid model by subtracting one from another.

'Units

Controls the display and format of coordinates and angles.

Command	Alias	Side Menu	Pull-down	Tablet
'units	. . .	. . .	. . .	. . .

Command: **units**

Report formats: (Examples)
  1. Scientific   1.55E+01
  2. Decimal   15.50
  3. Engineering   1'-3.50"
  4. Architectural   1'-3 1/2"
  5. Fractional   15 1/2

With the exception of Engineering and Architectural formats, these formats can be used with any basic unit of measurement. For example, Decimal mode is perfect for metric units as well as decimal English units.

Enter choice, 1 to 5 <2>: **[Enter]**
Number of digits to right of decimal point (0 to 8) <4>:

Systems of angle measure: (Examples)

  1. Decimal degrees   45.0000
  2. Degrees/minutes/seconds   45d0'0"
  3. Grads   50.0000g
  4. Radians   0.7854r
  5. Surveyor's units   N 45d0'0" E

Enter choice, 1 to 5 <1>: **[Enter]**
Number of fractional places for display of angles (0 to 8)
  <0>:

Direction for angle 0:
    East   3 o'clock   =   0
    North   12 o'clock   =   90
    West   9 o'clock   =   180
    South   6 o'clock   =   270
Enter direction for angle 0 <0>: **[Enter]**

Do you want angles measured clockwise? <N> **[Enter]**

COMMAND OPTION
[F1]   Returns to graphics screen.

RELATED AUTOCAD COMMANDS

- **DdUnits** Set units via a dialogue box.
- **MvSetup** Sets up a drawing with multiple viewports.

RELATED SYSTEM VARIABLES

- **AngBase** Direction of zero degrees.
- **AngDir** Direction of angle measurement.
- **AUnits** Units of angles.
- **AuPrec** Displayed precision of angles.
- **LUnits** Units of measurement.
- **LuPrec** Displayed precision of coordinates.
- **UnitMode** Toggles type of display of units.

TIPS

- Since **Units** is a transparent command, you can use it to change units during another command.

- The 'Direction Angle:' prompt lets AutoCAD start angle measurement from any direction.

- AutoCAD accepts the following notation for angle input:
  - **<** Specifies an angle based on current units setting.
  - **<<** Bypasses angle translation set by **Units** command; use 0-angle-is-east direction and decimal degrees.
  - **<<<** Bypasses angle translation; use angle units set by **Units** command, and 0-angle-is-east direction.

- The system variable **UnitMode** forces AutoCAD to display units in the same manner that you enter them.

- Do not use a suffix (such as **r** or **g**) for angles entered as radians or grads; instead, use the **Units** command to set angle measurement to radians and grads.

'View

Ver. 2.0

Saves and displays the view in the current viewport by name.

Command	Alias	Side Menu	Pull-down	Tablet
'view	. . .	. . .	. . .	. . .

```
Command: view
?/Delete/Restore/Save/Window: s
View name to save:
```

COMMAND OPTIONS

Delete   Deletes a named view.
Restore   Restores a named view.
Save   Saves the current view with a name.
Window   Saves a windowed view with a name.
?   List the names of views saved in the current drawing.

RELATED AUTOCAD COMMANDS

- **DdView** Create and displays named views via a dialogue box.
- **Rename** Changes the names of views.

RELATED SYSTEM VARIABLES

- **ViewCtr** The coordinates of the center of the view.
- **ViewSize** The height of the view.

TIPS

- Name views in your drawing to quickly move from one detail to another.

- View names are up to 31 characters long and may not contain spaces.

- The **Plot** command plots named views of a drawing.

- Entities outside of the window created by the **Window** option may be displayed but are not plotted.

- You create separate views in model and paper space; when listing named views (with ?), AutoCAD indicates an "M" or "P" next to the view name.

ViewRes

Controls the roundness of curved entities; determines whether zooms and pans are performed as redraws or regens (*short for VIEW RESolution*).

Command	Alias	Side Menu	Pull-down	Tablet
viewres	. . .	. . .	. . .	. . .

Command: **viewres**
Do you want fast zooms? <Y> **[Enter]**
Enter circle zoom percent (1-20000) <100>: **1000**
Regenerating drawing.

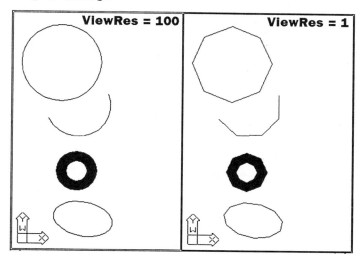

ViewRes = 100   ViewRes = 1

COMMAND OPTIONS

Do you want fast zooms?
> Yes: AutoCAD tries to make every zoom and pan a redraw (faster).
> No: Every zoom and pan causes a regeneration (slower).

Enter circle zoom percent (1-20000)
> Smaller values display faster but make circles look less round (*see figure*).

RELATED AUTOCAD COMMAND

■ **RegenAuto** Determines whether AutoCAD uses redraws or regens.

VIConv

Converts Visual Link data for use by AutoVision (*short for Visual Link CONVert; an external command in Render.Arx*).

Command	Alias	Side Menu	Pull-down	Tablet
vlconv	. . .	. . .	. . .	. . .

Command: **vlconv**

Displays dialogue box.

COMMAND OPTIONS

Overwrite Off (*Default*): AutoVision material assignments are preserved.

           On: Visual Link material assignments overwrite AutoVision's assignments.

TIPS

■ Visual Link data consists of trees, paths, and material assignments.

■ The Visual Link data is still available after conversion.

VpLayer

Controls the visibility of layers in viewports when TileMode is turned off (*short for ViewPort LAYER*).

Command	Alias	Side Menu	Pull-down	Tablet
vplayer	. . .	[DATA]	[DATA]	M5 - O5
		[VPlayer:]	[Viewport Layer Controls]	

```
Command: vplayer
?/Freeze/Thaw/Reset/Newfrz/Vpvisdflt:
Select a viewport: [pick]
```

COMMAND OPTIONS

Freeze	Indicates the names of layers to freeze in this viewport.
Newfrz	Creates new layers which will be frozen in newly-created viewports (*short for NEW FReeZe*).
Reset	Resets the state of layers based on the Vpvisdflt settings.
Thaw	Indicates the names of layers to thaw in this viewport.
Vpvisdflt	Determines which layers will be frozen in a newly-created viewport (*short for ViewPort VISibility DeFauLT*).
?	Lists the layers frozen in the current viewport.

RELATED AUTOCAD COMMANDS

- **DdLModes** Toggles the visibility of layers in viewports via a dialogue box.
- **Layer** Creates and controls layers in all viewports.
- **MView** Creates and joins viewports when tilemode is off.
- **MvSetup** Sets up a drawing with paper space.

RELATED SYSTEM VARIABLE

- **TileMode** Controls whether viewports are tiled or overlapping.

VPoint

Changes the viewpoint of a 3D drawing (*short for ViewPOINT*).

Command	Alias	Side Menu	Pull-down	Tablet
vpoint	...	[VIEW]	[View]	K 1
		[Vpoint:]	[3D Viewpoint]	
			[Tripod]	

```
Command: vpoint
Rotate/<View point> <0.0000,0.0000,1.0000>:
```

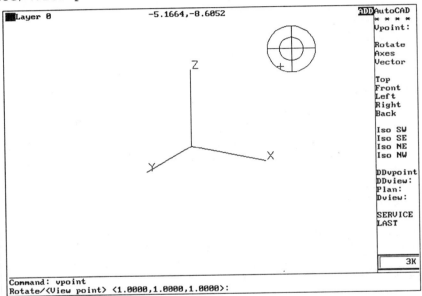

COMMAND OPTIONS

[Enter]	Brings up visual guides (*see figure above*).
Rotate	Indicates the new 3D viewpoint by angle.
<View point>	Indicates the new 3D viewpoint by coordinates.

RELATED AUTOCAD COMMANDS

- **DdVpoint**   Adjusts viewpoint via a dialogue box.
- **DView**   Changes the viewpoint of 3D objects, plus allows perspective mode.

RELATED SYSTEM VARIABLES

- **VpointX, VpointY, VpointZ**
  X-, y-, z-coordinates of current 3D view.
- **WorldView**   Determines whether **VPoint** coordinates are in WCS or UCS.

ViewPorts *or* VPorts

Creates viewports (or windows) of the current drawing: tiled when
TileMode is on; overlapping when **TileMode** is off.

Command	Side Menu	Ctrl+	Pull-down	Tablet
viewports	[ViEW]	V	[View]	R 5
	[Vpoint:]		[Tiled Viewports]	
vports				V 22

Command: **vports**
Save/Restore/Delete/Join/SIngle/?/2/<3>/4:

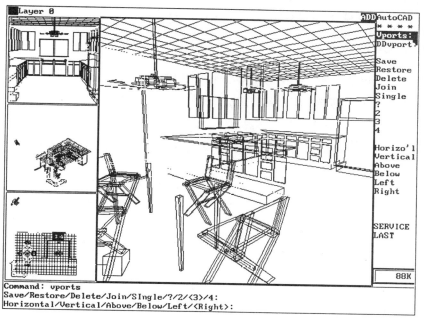

COMMAND OPTIONS

Delete	Deletes a viewport definition.
Join	Joins two viewports together as one.
Restore	Restores a viewport definition.
Save	Save the settings of a viewport by name.
SIngle	Joins all viewports into a single viewport.
2	Splits the current viewport into two:
Horizontal	Creates one viewport over another.
<Vertical>	Creates one viewport beside another.

<3>	Splits the current viewport into three:
Horizontal	Creates three viewports over each other.
Vertical	Creates three viewports beside each other.
Above	Creates two viewports over one viewport.
Below	Creates two viewports below one viewport.
Left	Creates two viewports left of one viewport.
<Right>	Creates two viewports right of one viewport.
4	Splits the current viewport into four.
?	Lists the names of saved viewport configurations.

RELATED AUTOCAD COMMANDS

- **MView** Creates viewports in paper space.
- **RedrawAll** Redraws all viewports.
- **RegenAll** Regenerates all viewports.
- **[Ctrl]+V** Moves focus to the next viewport.

RELATED SYSTEM VARIABLES

- **CvPort** The current viewport.
- **MaxActVp** The maximum number of active viewports.
- **TileMode** Controls whether viewports can be overlapping or tiled.

VSlide

Displays an SLD-format slide file in the current viewport (*short for View SLIDE*).

Command	Alias	Side Menu	Pull-down	Tablet
vslide	...	[TOOLS]	[Tools]	...
		[VSLIDE:]	[Slide]	
			[View]	

Command: **vslide**
Slide file <>:

COMMAND OPTIONS
~   (*Tilde*) Displays the file dialogue box.

RELATED AUTOCAD COMMANDS
- **MSlide**   Creates an SLD-format slide file of the current viewport.
- **Redraw**   Erases the slide from the screen.

RELATED AUTODESK PROGRAM
- **SlideLib.Exe** Creates an SLB-format library file of a group of slide files.

RELATED SYSTEM VARIABLES
- *None*

TIP
- For faster viewing of a series of slides, an asterisk preceeding **VSlide** preloads the slide file, as in:
  Command: ***vslide filename**

WBlock

Writes a block, or part, or all of the drawing to disk (*short for Write BLOCK*).

Command	Alias	Side Menu	Pull-down	Tablet
wblock	...	[FILE]	[File]	W 8
		[EXPORT]	[Export]	
		[Wblock:]	[Block]	

Command: **wblock**
File name:
Block name:

COMMAND OPTIONS

=	(Equals) Block is written to disk using block's name as filename.
*	(Asterisk) Entire drawing is written to disk.
[Enter]	Creates a block on disk of selected objects.
[Space]	Moves selected objects to the specified drawing.

RELATED AUTOCAD COMMAND

■ **Block**   Creates a block of a group of objects.

Wedge

Draws a 3D wedge as a solid model *(formerly the SolWedge command; an external command in Acis.Dll)*.

Command	Alias	Side Menu	Pull-down	Tablet
wedge	...	[DRAW 2]	[Draw]	N 7
		[SOLIDS]	[Solids]	
		[Wedge:]	[Wedge]	

```
Command: wedge
Center/<Corner of wedge> <0,0,0>: [pick]
Cube/Length/<other corner>: [pick]
Height:
```

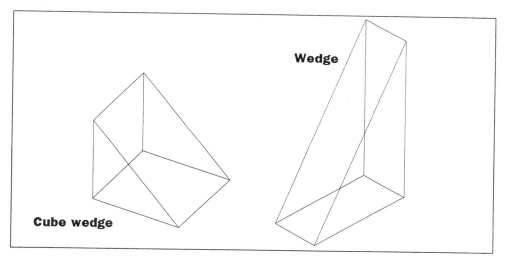

Wedge

Cube wedge

COMMAND OPTIONS

Center	Draws wedge base about a center point.
Corner	Draws wedge base between two pick points.
Cube	Draws a cubic wedge.
Length	Specifies length, width, and height of wedge.

RELATED AUTOCAD COMMANDS

- **Ai_Wedge** Draws wedge as a 3D surface model.
- **Box** Draws solid boxes.
- **Cone** Draws solid cones.
- **Cylinder** Draws solid cylinders.
- **Sphere** Draws solid spheres.
- **Torus** Draws solid tori.

'WhatsNew

Describes many — though not all — new features in Release 13 (*an external command in R13New.Lsp*).

Command	Alias	Side Menu	Pull-down	Tablet
'whatsnew	...	...	[Help]	...
			[What's New in Release 13]	

Command: **whatsnew**

Displays dialogue box.

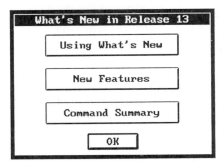

COMMAND OPTIONS

Using What's New
> Help on using the **WhatsNew** dialogue box.

New Features
> A brief summary of a number of new features in Release 13.

Command Summary
> Summary of most new and changed commands in Release 13.

RELATED AUTOCAD COMMANDS

- **Help**   Lists helpful information about AutoCAD commands and system variables.
- **'?**   Provides context-sensitive help during a command.

RELATED FILES

Found in \Acad13\Dos\Support:

- **R13New.Ahp** Help for the **WhatsNew** command.
- **R13New.Dat** Text file for New Features section of **WhatsNew** command.
- **R13New.Dcl** Dialogue box definitions for **WhatsNew** command.
- **R13New.Hdx** Compiled help file.
- **R13New.Lsp** Code for launching the **WhatsNew** command.
- **R13New.Slb** Slide library containing images for **WhatsNew** dialogue boxes.

XBind

Binds portions of an externally-referenced drawing to the current drawing (*short for eXternal BINDing*).

Command	Alias	Side Menu	Pull-down	Tablet
xbind	...	[FILE]	[File]	...
		[Xbind:]	[Bind]	

Command: **xbind**
Block/Dimstyle/LAyer/LType/Style: **b**
Dependent Block name(s):

COMMAND OPTIONS

Block	Binds blocks to current drawing.
Dimstyle	Binds dimension styles to current drawing.
LAyer	Binds layer names to current drawing.
LType	Binds linetype definitions to current drawing.
Style	Binds text styles to current drawing.

RELATED AUTOCAD COMMANDS

- **XRef**   Attaches another drawing the current drawing.
- **XrefClip**   Inserts an externally-referenced block.

RELATED SYSTEM VARIABLES

- *None*

XLine

Places an infinitely-long construction line.

Command	Alias	Side Menu	Pull-down	Tablet
xline	...	[DRAW 1]	[Draw]	L 10
		[Xline:]	[Construction Line]	

```
Command: xline
Hor/Ver/Ang/Bisect/Offset/<From point>: [pick]
Through point: [pick]
```

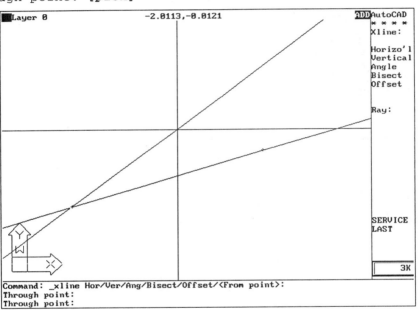

COMMAND OPTIONS

Ang	Places the construction line at an angle.
Bisect	Bisects an angle with the construction line.
<From point>	Places the construction line through a point.
Hor	Places a horizontal construction line.
Offset	Places the construction line parallel to another object.
Ver	Places a vertical construction line.

RELATED AUTOCAD COMMANDS

- **DdModify** Modifies characteristics of the xline and ray objects.
- **Ray** Places a semi-infinite construction line.

TIP

- The ray and xline construction lines do not plot.

'Xplode

Reduces complex objects to their primitive constituent parts; provides greater user control than the **Explode** command (*short for eXplode; an external command in Xplode.Lsp*).

Command	Alias	Side Menu	Pull-down	Tablet
'xplode	xp	. . .	. . .	W 20

```
Command: xplode
Select objects: [pick]
Select objects: [Enter]
Xplode Individually/<Globally>: [Enter]
All/Color/LAyer/LType/Inherit from parent block/<Explode>:
```

COMMAND OPTIONS

Individually	Explodes one object at a time.
Globally	Applies explode to all selected objects.
All	Prompts for changes *after* exploding.
Color	Specifies color after explosion.
LAyer	Specifies layer after explosion.
LType	Specifies lineytpe after explosion.
Inherit	Sets color, linetype, and layer to that of the original block.
<Explode>	Mimics the **Explode** command.

RELATED AUTOCAD COMMANDS

- **Explode** Original **Explode** command.
- **U** Undoes the effects of the **Xplode** command.

TIPS

- **Color** option:
  - **BYLAYER** Exploded objects inherit color from the original object's layer.
  - **BYBLOCK** Exploded objects inherit color from the original object.

- **LAyer** option:
  - By default, exploded objects inherit the current layer, not the original's layer.

- **LType** option:
  - **BYLAYER** Exploded objects inherit linetype from the original object's layer.
  - **BYBLOCK** Exploded objects inherit linetype from the original object.

Xref

Attaches a drawing to the current drawing (*short for eXternal REFerence*).

Command	Alias	Side Menu	Pull-down	Tablet
xref	...	[FILE]	[File]	P 8-10
		[Xref:]	[External Reference]	

Command: **xref**
?/Bind/Detach/Path/Reload/Overlay/<Attach>:

COMMAND OPTIONS

<Attach>	Attaches another drawing to the current drawing.
Bind	Makes the externally-referenced drawing part of the current drawing.
Detach	Removes the externally-referenced drawing.
Overlay	Overlays the externally-referenced drawing (*new to R13*).
Path	Respecifies the path to the externally-referenced drawing.
Reload	Updates the externally-referenced drawing.
?	Lists the names of externally-referenced drawings.

RELATED AUTOCAD COMMANDS

- **Insert**   Adds another drawing to the current drawing.
- **XBind**   Binds parts of the externally-referenced drawing to the current drawing.
- **XrefClip**   Clips an area of an externally-referenced drawing to attach to the current drawing.

RELATED SYSTEM VARIABLE

- **XRefCtl**   Controls whether XLG external reference log files are written:
  - 0   XLG files are not written.
  - 1   XLG files are written.

TIPS

- The **XRef** command lets you view other drawings at the same time as the currently-loaded drawing; however, you cannot edit the externally-referenced drawing.

- If you are working with AutoCAD on a network, no other user can access the externally referenced drawing while you are loading it; this is called "soft file locking."

- By using the **Reload** option of the **XRef** command, you can periodically update the externally-referenced drawings; since you can xref the same drawing many times, you can keep track of changes in the drawing.

XrefClip

Clips and inserts a portion of an externally-referenced drawing (*short for eXternal REFerence CLIP; an external command in XRefClip.Lsp*).

Command	Alias	Side Menu	Pull-down	Tablet
xrefclip	...	...	[File]	...
			[External Reference]	
			[Clip]	

```
Command: xrefclip
Xref name:
Clip onto what layer?
First corner of clip box: [pick]
Other corner: [pick]
Number of paper space units <1.0>:  [Enter]
Number of model space units <1.0>:  [Enter]
Insertion point for clip: [pick]
```

COMMAND OPTIONS
None

RELATED AUTOCAD COMMANDS
- **Insert**   Adds another drawing to the current drawing.
- **XBind**   Binds parts of the externally-referenced drawing to the current drawing.
- **Xref**   Displays an externally-referenced drawing in the current drawing.

RELATED SYSTEM VARIABLE
- **TileMode** Must be set to 0 for **XRefClip** to work.

TIPS
- **TileMode** must be set to 0 before starting the **XRefClip** command.

- During the **XRefClip** command, layers and viewports are turned off.

- The layer name must exist before you start the **XRefClip** command.

- The 'clip box' becomes a paper space viewport.

- You cannot have an irregularly-clipped xref.

'Zoom

Displays a drawing larger or smaller in the current viewport.

Command	Alias	Side Menu	Pull-down	Tablet
'zoom	z	[VIEW]	[View]	Q 7-9
		[ZOOM:]	[Zoom]	R 7-10

```
Command: zoom
All/Center/Dynamic/Extents/Left/Previous/Vmax/Window/
    <Scale(X/XP)>:
```

*The **Zoom Dynamic** screen:*

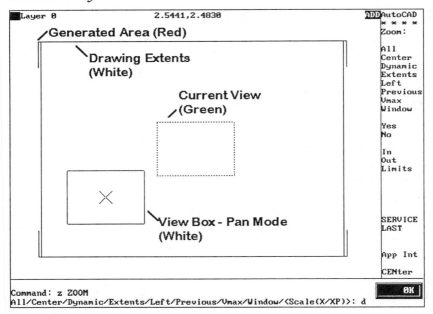

COMMAND OPTIONS

All   Displays the drawing limits or extents, whichever is greater.
Center   Zooms in about a center point:
  Center point   Indicates the center point of the new view.
  Magnification or Height
           Indicates a magnification value or height of view.

Dynamic   Brings up the dynamic zoom view.
Extents   Displays the current drawing extents.

438 ■ The Illustrated AutoCAD Quick Reference

Left Displays a view with a new lower-left corner:
Lower left corner point
Indicates the lower-left corner of the new view.
Magnification or Height
Indicates a magnification value or height of view.
Previous Displays the previous view generated by Pan, View, or Zoom.
Vmax Displays the current virtual screen limits (*short for Virtual MAXimum*).
Window Indicates the two corners of the new view.
<Scale(X/XP)> Displays a new view as a factor of the drawing limits:
X Displays a new view as a factor of the current view.
XP Displays a paper space view as a factor of model space.
<pick> Begin window option.

RELATED AUTOCAD COMMANDS

- **AV** Aerial View; available only when AutoCAD is configured with the 'Accelerated Display Driver.'
- **Limits** Specifies the limits of the drawing.
- **Pan** Moves the view to a different location.
- **RegenMin** Maximum zoom-in without a regen; only available when AutoCAD is configured with the 'Accelerated Display Driver.'
- **View** Saves views by name.

RELATED SYSTEM VARIABLES

- **ViewCtr** Coordinates of the current view's center point.
- **ViewSize** Height of the current view.
- **VsMax** Upper-right corner of the virtual screen.
- **VsMin** Lower-left corner of the virtual screen.

TIPS

- A scale factor of one displays the entire drawing as defined by the limits.

- A zoom factor of 2 enlarges objects (zooms in), while 0.5 makes objects smaller (zooms out).

3D

Draws 3D primitives with polymeshes (*an external command in 3D.Lsp*).

Command	Alias	Side Menu	Pull-down	Tablet
3d	...	[DRAW 2]	[Draw]	...
		[SURFACES]	[Surfaces]	
		[3d objects]	[3D Objects]	

Command: **3d**

Displays dialogue box.

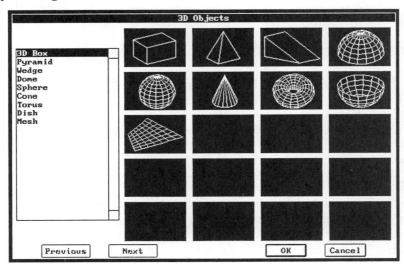

COMMAND OPTIONS

3D Box	Draws a 3D box or cube.
Pyramid	Draws pyramid shapes.
Wedge	Draws wedge shapes.
Dome	Draws a dome (top-half of a sphere).
Sphere	Draws a sphere.
Cone	Draws cone shapes.
Torus	Draw torus (3D donut) shapes.
Dish	Draws a dish (bottom-half of a sphere).
Mesh	Draws a 3D mesh.

RELATED AUTOCAD COMMANDS

- **Ai_Box**   Draws a 3D surface box or cube.
- **Ai_Cone**   Draws 3D surface cone shapes.
- **Ai_Dish**   Draws a 3D surface dish.
- **Ai_Dome**   Draws a 3D surface dome.
- **Ai_Mesh**   Draws a 3D mesh.
- **Ai_Pyramid** Draws a 3D surface pyramid.
- **Ai_Sphere** Draws a 3D surface sphere.
- **Ai_Torus** Draws a 3D surface torus.
- **Ai_Wedge** Draws a 3D surface wedge.
- **Box**   Draws a 3D solid box or cube.
- **Cone**   Draws a 3D solid cone.
- **Cylinder** Draws a 3D solid cylinder.
- **Sphere**   Draws a 3D solid sphere.
- **Torus**   Draws a 3D solid torus.
- **Wedge**   Draws a 3D solid wedge.

TIPS

- The **3D** command creates 3D objects made of 3D meshes and not 3D ACIS solids.

- See the **Ai_** command for more details on the objects created by the **3D** command.

3dArray

Creates 3D rectangular and polar arrays (*an external command in 3dAray.Lsp*).

Command	Alias	Side Menu	Pull-down	Tablet
3darray	. . .	[CONSTRCT]	[Construct]	. . .
		[3Darray:]	[3D Array]	

```
Command: 3darray
Select objects: [pick]
Select objects: [Enter]
Rectangular or Polar array (R/P):
```

Command prompts for a rectangular array:
```
Number of rows (---) <1>:
Number of columns (||||) <1>:
Number of levels (...) <1>:
Distance between rows (---) <1>:
Distance between columns (||||) <1>:
Distance between levels (...) <1>:
```

Command prompts for a polar array:
```
Number of items:
Angle to fill <360>:
Rotate objects as they are copied? <Y>:
Center point of array:
Second point on axis of rotation:
```

COMMAND OPTIONS
R	Creates rectangular 3D array.
P	Creates polar 3D array.
[Esc]	Interrupts drawing of array.

RELATED AUTOCAD COMMANDS
- **Array**   Creates rectangular or polar array in 2D space.
- **Copy**   Creates one or more copies of the selected object.
- **MInsert**   Creates a rectangular block array of blocks.

3dFace

Draws 3D faces with three or four corners.

Command	Alias	Side Menu	Pull-down	Tablet
3dface	. . .	[DRAW 2]	[Draw]	P 9
		[SURFACES]	[Surfaces]	
		[3Dface:]	[3D Face]	

```
Command: 3dface
First point: [pick]
Second point: [pick]
Third point: [pick]
Fourth point: [pick]
```

COMMAND OPTION

i   Prefix for corner coordinate to make edge invisible.

RELATED AUTOCAD COMMANDS

- **3D**   Draws 3D objects: box, cone, dome, dish, pyramid, sphere, torus, and wedge.
- **Edge**   Changes the visibility of the edges of 3D faces.
- **EdgeSurf** Draws 3D surfaces made of 3D meshes.
- **PEdit**   Edits 3D meshes.
- **PFace**   Draws generalized 3D meshes.

RELATED SYSTEM VARIABLE

- **SplFrame** Controls the visibility of edges.

TIPS

- A 3D face is the same as a 2D solid, except that each corner can have a different z-coordinate.

- Unlike the **Solid** command, corner coordinates are entered in natural order.

- The **i** (*short for invisible*) suffix must be entered before object snap modes, point filters, and corner coordinates.

- Invisible 3D faces (where all four edges are invisible) do not appear in wireframe views; however, they hide objects behind them in hidden-line mode and are rendered in shaded views.

- 3D faces cannot be extruded.

3dMesh

Draws open 3D rectangular meshes made of 3D faces.

Command	Alias	Side Menu	Pull-down	Tablet
3dmesh	. . .	[DRAW 2]	[Draw]	. . .
		[SURFACES]	[Surfaces]	
		[3Dmesh:]	[3D Mesh]	

```
Command: 3dmesh
Mesh |M size:
Mesh N size:
Vertex (0, 0):
Vertex (0, 1):
... etc.
```

COMMAND OPTIONS
None

RELATED AUTOCAD COMMANDS
- **3D**   Draws a variety of 3D objects.
- **Explode** Explodes a 3D mesh into individual 3D faces.
- **PEdit**   Edits a 3D mesh.
- **PFace**   Draws a generalized 3D face.
- **Xplode**   Explodes a group of 3D meshes.

RELATED SYSTEM VARIABLES
- **SurfU**   Surface density in m-direction.
- **SurfV**   Surface density in n-direction.

TIPS
- It is more convenient to use the **EdgeSurf, RevSurf, RuleSurf**, and **TabSurf** commands than the **3dMesh** command.

- The range of values for the m- and n-mesh size is 2 to 256.

3dPoly

Draws 3D polylines (*short for 3D POLYline*).

Command	Alias	Side Menu	Pull-down	Tablet
3dpoly	. . .	[DRAW 1]	[Draw]	P 10
		[3Dpoly:]	[Polylines >]	
		[3D Surfs]	[3D Polyline]	

```
Command: 3dpoly
From point: [pick]
Close/Undo/<Endpoint of line>: [pick]
```

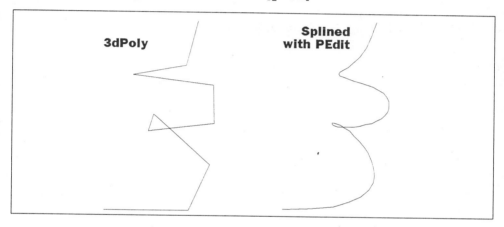

COMMAND OPTIONS

Close   Joins the last endpoint with the start point.

<Endpoint of line>
    Indicates the endpoint of the current segment.

Undo   Erases the last-drawn segment.

RELATED AUTOCAD COMMANDS

- **Explode** Reduces a 3D polyline into lines and arcs.
- **PEdit**   Edits 3D polylines.
- **PLine**   Draws 2D polylines.
- **Xplode** Explodes a group of 3D polylines.

RELATED SYSTEM VARIABLES

None

TIPS

■ Since 3D polylines are made of straight lines, use the **PEdit** command to spline the 3D polyline as a curve.

■ 3D polylines do not support linetypes and widths.

3dsIn

Imports a 3DS file created by 3D Studio (*an external command in Render.Arx*).

Command	Alias	Side Menu	Pull-down	Tablet
3dsin	...	[FILE]	[File]	...
		[IMPORT]	[Import]	
		[3DSin:]	[3D Studio]	

Command: **3dsin**

Displays dialogue box.

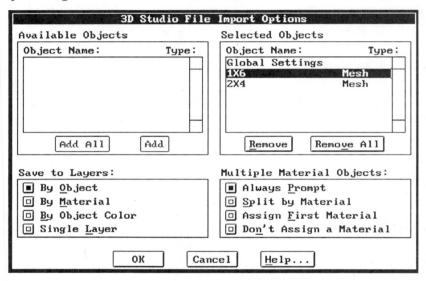

COMMAND OPTIONS

Available Objects
      Names and types of objects in 3D Studio drawing.
  Object Name Name of object.
  Type Type of object.
  Add Adds object to Selected Objects list.
  Add All Adds all objects to Selected Objects list.
  Remove Removes object from Selected Objects list.
  Remove All Removes all objects from Selected Objects list.
Save to Layers
      Allows you to control the assignment of 3D Studio objects to layers.
  By Object Places each object on its own layer.
  By Material Places objects on layers named after materials.

By Object Color Places objects on layers named "Color*nn*."

Single Layer Places all objects on layer "AvLayer."

Multiple Material Objects

Allows you to control how materials are assigned:

Always Prompt

Prompts you for each material.

Split by Material

Splits objects with more than one material into multiple objects, each with one material.

Assign First Material

Assigns first material to entire object.

Don't Assign to a Material

Loses all 3D Studio material definitions.

RELATED AUTOCAD COMMAND

■ **3dsOut** Exports drawing as a 3DS file.

RELATED FILES

■ ***.3DS** 3D studio files.

■ ***.TGA** Converted bitmap and animation files.

TIPS

■ Objects:

- ■ You are limited to selecting a maximum of 70 3D Studio objects.
- ■ Conflicting object names are truncated and given a sequence number.
- ■ The **By Object** option gives the AutoCAD layer the name of the object.
- ■ The **By Object Color** option places all objects on layer "ColorNone" when no colors are defined in 3DS file.
- ■ 3D Studio assigns materials to faces, elements, and objects; AutoCAD assigns materials by object, color, or layer.

■ Bitmap and animation conversion:

- ■ 3D Studio bitmaps are converted to TGA (Targa format) bitmaps.
- ■ Only the first frame of an animation file (CEL, CLI, FLC, and IFL) is converted to a Targa bitmap file.
- ■ Converted TGA files are saved to the 3DS file's subdirectory.

■ Light conversion:

- ■ 3D Studio ambient lights lose their color.
- ■ 3D Studio 'omni lights' become point lights in AutoCAD.
- ■ 3D Studio cameras become a named view in AutoCAD.

3dsOut

Exports the AutoCAD drawing as a 3DS file for 3D Studio (*an external command in Render.Arx*).

Command	Alias	Side Menu	Pull-down	Tablet
3dsout	. . .	[FILE]	[File]	. . .
		[EXPORT]	[Export]	
		[3DSout:]	[3D Studio]	

Command: **3dsout**

Displays dialogue box.

COMMAND OPTIONS

Layer   All objects on an AutoCAD layer become a single 3D Studio object.

ACI   All objects of an ACI color become a single 3D Studio object.

Object Type   All objects on an AutoCAD object type become a single 3D Studio object.

Override   Each AutoCAD block becomes a single 3D Studio object; overrides above three options.

Autosmoothing Creates a 3D Studio smoothing group.

Autowelding   Creates a 3D Studio welded vertex.

RELATED AUTOCAD COMMAND

■ **3dsIn**   Imports 3DS file to the drawing.

RELATED FILE

■ ***.3DS**   3D studio files.

TIPS

- Exported objects:
  - AutoCAD objects with 0 thickness are not exported, with the exception of circles, polygons, and polyface meshes.
  - Solids and 3D faces must have at least 3 vertices.
  - 3D solids and bodies are converted to meshes.
  - AutoSurf and AME objects must be converted to meshes with the **SolMesh** command in an earlier version of AutoCAD.
  - AutoCAD blocks are exploded unless **Override** is turned on.

- The weld threshold distance:
  - Minimum: 0.00 000 001
  - Default: 0.001
  - Maximum: 99,999,999

- Camera and light conversion:
  - AutoCAD's named views become 3D Studio cameras.
  - AutoCAD's point lights become 3D Studio 'omni lights.'

System Variables

AutoCAD stores information about the current state of itself, the drawing, and the operating system in *system variables*. The variables help programmers (who often work with menu macros and AutoLISP) determine the state of the AutoCAD system.

TIPS

■ You get a list of system variables at the Command: prompt with the **?** option of the **SetVar** command:

```
Command: setvar
Variable name or ?: ?
```

■ The **SetVar** command lets you can change the value of most variables.

■ *Italicized system variables* are not listed by the **SetVar ?** command nor in AutoCAD's *Command Reference*.

■ Some system variables have the same name as a command, such as **Area**; other variables do not work at the 'Command' prompt. These are prefixed by the ⌨ keyboard character.

■ **Default Value:** The table lists all known system variables, along with the default values as set in the Acad.Dwg prototype drawing.

■ **Ro:** Some system variables cannot be changed by the user or by programming; these are labeled "R/o" (short for "read only") in the table below.

■ **Loc:** System variables are located in a variety of places:
- ■ **Acad**   AutoCAD executable (hard-coded)
- ■ **Cfg**   Acad.Cfg or Acad.XmX files
- ■ **Dwg**   Current drawing
- ■ ...   Not saved

Variable	Default	Ro	Loc	Meaning
_PKSER	*117-999999*	*R/o*	*Acad*	*Software package serial number*
_SERVER	*0*	*R/o*	*Cfg*	*Network authorization code*

A

Variable	Default	Ro	Loc	Meaning
ACADPREFIX	"d:\ACAD13\"	R/o	...	Path spec'd by ACAD environment var.
ACADVER	"13"	R/o	...	AutoCAD version number
AFLAGS	0	...	...	Attribute display code:
				0 No mode specified
				1 Invisible
				2 Constant
				4 Verify
				8 Preset

Variable	Default	Ro	Loc	Meaning
ANGBASE	0	...	Dwg	Direction of zero degrees relative to UCS
ANGDIR	0	...	Dwg	Rotation of angles: 0 Clockwise 1 Counterclockwise
☞ APERTURE	10	...	Cfg	Object snap aperture in pixels: 1 Minimum size 10 Default size 50 Maximum size
☞ AREA	0.0000	R/o	...	Area measured by Area, List, or Dblist
ATTDIA	0	...	Dwg	Attribute entry interface: 0 Command-line prompts 1 Dialogue box
ATTMODE	1	...	Dwg	Display of attributes: 0 Off 1 Normal 2 On
ATTREQ	1	...	Dwg	Attribute values during insertion are: 0 Default values 1 Prompt for values
AUDITCTL	0	...	Cfg	Determines creation of ADT audit log file: 0 File not created 1 ADT file created
AUNITS	0	...	Dwg	Mode of angular units: 0 Decimal degrees 1 Degrees-minutes-seconds 2 Grads 3 Radians 4 Surveyor's units
AUPREC	0	...	Dwg	Decimals places displayed by angles
AUXSTAT	*0*	...	*Dwg*	*-32768 Minimum value* *32767 Maximum value*
AXISMODE	*0*	...	*Dwg*	*Obsolete system variable*
AXISUNIT	*0.0000*	...	*Dwg*	*Obsolete system variable*

B̄

Variable	Default	Ro	Loc	Meaning
BACKZ	0.0000	R/o	Dwg	Back clipping plane offset
☞ BLIPMODE	1	...	Dwg	Display of blip marks: 0 Off 1 On

C̄

Variable	Default	Ro	Loc	Meaning
CDATE	19950105.15560660	R/o	...	Current date and time in YyyyMmDd.HhMmSsDd format
CECOLOR	"BYLAYER"	...	Dwg	Current entity color
CELTSCALE	1.0000	...	Dwg	Global linetype scale
CELTYPE	"BYLAYER"	...	Dwg	Current layer color
CHAMFERA	0.0000	...	Dwg	First chamfer distance
CHAMFERB	0.0000	...	Dwg	Second chamfer distance
CHAMFERC	0.0000	...	Dwg	Chamfer length
CHAMFERD	0	...	Dwg	Chamfer angle
CHAMMODE	0	...	..	Chamfer input mode: 0 Chamfer by two lengths 1 Chamfer by length and angle
CIRCLERAD	0.0000	...	...	Most-recent circle radius: 0 No default
CLAYER	"0"	...	Dwg	Current layer name
CMDACTIVE	1	R/o	...	Type of current command: 1 Regular command 2 Transparent command 4 Script file 8 Dialogue box
CMDDIA	1	...	Cfg	Plot command interface: 0 Command line prompts 1 Dialogue box
CMDECHO	1	...	...	AutoLISP command display: 0 No command echoing 1 Command echoing
CMDNAMES	"SETVAR"	R/o	...	Current command
CMLJUST	0	...	Cfg	Multiline justification mode: 0 Top 1 Middle 2 Bottom
CMLSCALE	1.0000	...	Cfg	Scales width of multiline: -1 Flips offsets of multiline 0 Collapses to single line 1 Default 2 Doubles multiline width
CMLSTYLE	"STANDARD"	Cfg	...	Current multiline style name
COORDS	1	...	Dwg	Coordinate display style: 0 Updated by screen picks 1 Continuous display 2 Polar display upon request
CVPORT	2	...	Dwg	Current viewport number 2 Minimum (Default)

Variable	Default	Ro	Loc	Meaning

D̄

Variable	Default	Ro	Loc	Meaning
DATE	2448860.54043252	R/o	...	Current date and fraction in Julian format
DBGLISTALL	*0*	...	...	*Toggle*
DBMOD	0	R/o	...	Drawing modified in these areas:

    0 No modification made
    1 Entity database
    2 Symbol table
    4 Database variable
    8 Window
    16 View

Variable	Default	Ro	Loc	Meaning
DCTCUST	""	...	Cfg	Name of custom spelling dictionary
DCTMAIN	"enu"	...	Cfg	Code for spelling dictionary:

    ca   Catalan
    cs   Czech
    da   Danish
    de   German - sharp 's'
    ded German - double 's'
    ena English - Australian
    ens English - British: 'ise'
    enu English - American
    enz English - British: 'ize'
    es   Spanish - unaccented capitals
    esa Spanish - accented capitals
    fi   Finnish
    fr   French - unaccented capitals
    fra French - accented captials
    it   Italian
    nl   Dutch - primary
    nls Dutch - secondary
    no   Norwegian - Bokmal
    non Norwegian - Nynorsk
    pt   Portugese - Iberian
    ptb Portugese - Brazilian
    ru   Russian - infrequent 'io'
    rui Russian - frequent 'io'
    sv   Swedish

Variable	Default	Ro	Loc	Meaning
DELOBJ	1	...	Dwg	Toggle source objects deletion:

    0   Objects deleted
    1   Objects retained

Variable	Default	Ro	Loc	Meaning
DIASTAT	1	R/o	...	User exited dialogue box by clicking on:

    0   Cancel button
    1   OK button

Dimension Variables

Variable	Default	Ro	Loc	Meaning
DIMALT	0	...	Dwg	Alternate units selected
DIMALTD	2	...	Dwg	Alternate unit decimal places
DIMALTF	25.4000	...	Dwg	Alternate unit scale factor
DIMALTTD	2	...	Dwg	Tolerance alternate unit decimal places
DIMALTTZ	0	...	Dwg	Alternate tolerance units zeros:
				0 Zeros not suppressed
				1 Zeros suppressed
DIMALTU	2	...	Dwg	Alternate units:
				1 Scientific
				2 Decimal
				3 Engineering
				4 Architectural
				5 Fractional
DIMALTZ	0		Dwg	Zero suppression of alternate units:
				0 Zeros not suppressed
				1 Zeros suppressed
DIMAPOST	""	...	Dwg	Suffix for alternate text
DIMASO	1	...	Dwg	Create associative dimensions
DIMASZ	0.1800	...	Dwg	Arrow size
DIMAUNIT	0	...	Dwg	Angular dimension format:
				0 Decimal degrees
				1 Degrees.Minutes.Seconds
				2 Grad
				3 Radian
				4 Surveyor units
DIMBLK	""	R/o	Dwg	Arrow block name
DIMBLK1	""	R/o	Dwg	First arrow block name
DIMBLK2	""	R/o	Dwg	Second arrow block name
DIMCEN	0.0900	...	Dwg	Center mark size
DIMCLRD	0	...	Dwg	Dimension line color
DIMCLRE	0	...	Dwg	Extension line & leader color
DIMCLRT	0	...	Dwg	Dimension text color
DIMDEC	4	...	Dwg	Primary tolerance decimal places
DIMDLE	0.0000	...	Dwg	Dimension line extension
DIMDLI	0.3800	...	Dwg	Dimension line continuation increment
DIMEXE	0.1800	...	Dwg	Extension above dimension line
DIMEXO	0.0625	...	Dwg	Extension line origin offset
DIMFIT	3	...	Dwg	Placement of text and arrowheads:
				0 Between extension lines if possible
				1 Text has priority over arrowheads
				2 Whatever fits between ext lines
				3 Whatever fits
				4 Place text at end of leader line

Variable	Default	Ro	Loc	Meaning
DIMGAP	0.0900	...	Dwg	Gap from dimension line to text
DIMJUST	0	...	Dwg	Horizontal text positioning:
				0 Center justify
				1 Next to first extension line
				2 Next to second extension line
				3 Above first extension line
				4 Above second extension line
DIMLFAC	1.0000	...	Dwg	Linear unit scale factor
DIMLIM	0	...	Dwg	Generate dimension limits
DIMPOST	""	...	Dwg	Default suffix for dimension text
DIMRND	0.0000	...	Dwg	Rounding value
DIMSAH	0	...	Dwg	Separate arrow blocks
DIMSCALE	1.0000	...	Dwg	Overall scale factor
DIMSD1	Off	...	Dwg	Suppress first dimension line
DIMSD2	Off	...	Dwg	Suppress second dimension line
DIMSE1	0	...	Dwg	Suppress the first extension line
DIMSE2	0	...	Dwg	Suppress the second extension line
DIMSHO	1	...	Dwg	Update dimensions while dragging
DIMSOXD	0	...	Dwg	Suppress outside extension dimension
DIMSTYLE	"STANDARD"	R/o	Dwg	Current dimension style (read-only)
DIMTAD	0	...	Dwg	Place text above the dimension line
DIMTDEC	4	...	Dwg	Primary tolerance decimal places
DIMTFAC	1.0000	...	Dwg	Tolerance text height scaling factor
DIMTIH	1	...	Dwg	Text inside extensions is horizontal
DIMTIX	0	...	Dwg	Place text inside extensions
DIMTM	0.0000	...	Dwg	Minus tolerance
DIMTOFL	0	...	Dwg	Force line inside extension lines
DIMTOH	1	...	Dwg	Text outside extensions is horizontal
DIMTOL	0	...	Dwg	Generate dimension tolerances
DIMTOLJ	1	...	Dwg	Tolerance vertical justification:
				0 Bottom
				1 Middle
				2 Top
DIMTP	0.0000	...	Dwg	Plus tolerance
DIMTSZ	0.0000	...	Dwg	Tick size
DIMTVP	0.0000	...	Dwg	Text vertical position
DIMTXSTY	"STANDARD"	...	Dwg	Dimension text style
DIMTXT	0.1800	...	Dwg	Text height
DIMTZIN	0	...	Dwg	Tolerance zero suppression
DIMUNIT	2	...	Dwg	Dimension unit format
				1 Scientific
				2 Decimal
				3 Engineering
				4 Architectural
				5 Fractional

Variable	Default	Ro	Loc	Meaning
DIMUPT	Off	...	Dwg	User-positioned text: 0 Cursor positions dimension line 1 Cursor also positions text
DIMZIN	0	...	Dwg	Suppression of zero in feet-inches units: 0 Suppress 0 feet and 0 inches 1 Include 0 feet and 0 inches 2 Include 0 feet; suppress 0 inches 3 Suppress 0 feet; include 0 inches
DISPSILH	0	...	Dwg	Silhouette display of 3D solids: 0 Off 1 On
DISTANCE	0.0000	R/o	...	Distance measured by Dist command
DONUTID	0.5000	...	...	Inside radius of donut
DONUTOD	1.0000	...	...	Outside radius of donut
▤ DRAGMODE	2	...	Dwg	Drag mode: 0 No drag 1 On if requested 2 Automatic
DRAGP1	10	...	Cfg	Regen drag display
DRAGP2	25	...	Cfg	Fast drag display
DWGCODEPAGE	"dos850"	...	Dwg	Drawing code page
DWGNAME	"UNNAMED"	R/o	...	Current drawing filename
DWGPREFIX	"d:\"	R/o	...	Drawing's drive and subdirectory
DWGTITLED	0	R/o	...	Drawing has filename: 0 "Untitled.Dwg" 1 User-assigned name
DWGWRITE	1	...	...	Drawing read-write status: 0 Read-only 1 Read-write

E̅

Variable	Default	Ro	Loc	Meaning
EDGEMODE	0	...	...	Toggle edge mode for Trim & Extend: 0 No extension 1 Extends cutting edge
ELEVATION	0.0000	...	Dwg	Current elevation relative to current UCS
ENTMODS	*193*	*R/o*	...	
ERRNO	*0*	...	...	*Error number from AutoLISP,ADS,Arx*
EXPERT	0	...	...	Controls prompts: 0 Normal prompts 1 Suppress these messages: "About to regen, proceed?" "Really want to turn the current layer off?"

Variable	Default	Ro	Loc	Meaning
Expert (*continued*)				
				2 Also suppress: "Block already defined. Redefine it?" "A block with this name already exists. Overwrite it?"
				3 Also suppress messages related to the Linetype command
				4 Also suppress messages related to the UCS Save and VPorts Save commands
				5 Also suppress messages related to the DimStyle Save and DimOverride commands
EXPLMODE	1	...	Dwg	Toggle whether Explode and Xplode commands explode non-uniformly scaled blocks: 0 Does not explode 1 Does explode
EXTMAX	11.3706,10.0130,0,000	R/o	Dwg	Upper right coordinate of drawing extents
EXTMIN	1.0158,5.6333,0.000	R/o	Dwg	Lower left coordinate of drawing extents

F̄

Variable	Default	Ro	Loc	Meaning
FACETRES	0.5	...	Dwg	Adjusts smoothness of shaded and hidden-line objects: 0.01 Minimum value 0.05 Default value 10.0 Maximum value
FFLIMIT	0	...	Cfg	Maximum number of PostScript and TrueType fonts loaded into memory: 0 No limit 1 One font 100 Maximum value
FILEDIA	1	...	Cfg	User interface: 0 Command-line prompts 1 Dialogue boxes (when available)
FILLETRAD	0.0000	...	Dwg	Current fillet radius
FILLMODE	1	...	Dwg	Fill of solid objects: 0 Off 1 On
FLATLAND	*0*	*R/o*	*...*	*Obsolete system variable*
FONTALT	"txt"	...	Cfg	Name for substituted font
FONTMAP	""	...	Cfg	Name of font mapping file
FORCE_PAGING	*0*	*...*	*...*	*0 Minimum (Default)* *1,410,065,408 Maximum*
FRONTZ	0.0000	R/o	Dwg	Front clipping plane offset

Variable	Default	Ro	Loc	Meaning
G				
GLOBCHECK	*0*	...	...	*Reports statistics on dialogue boxes:*
				0 Turn off
				1 Warns if larger than 640x400
				2 Also reports size in pixels
				3 Additional info
GRIDMODE	0	...	Dwg	Display of grid:
				0 Off
				1 On
GRIDUNIT	0.0000,0.0000	...	Dwg	X,y-spacing of grid
GRIPBLOCK	0	...	...	Display of grips in blocks:
				0 At insertion point
				1 At all entities within block
GRIPCOLOR	5	...	Cfg	Color of unselected grips
				1 Minimum color number
				5 Default color: blue
				255 Maximum color number
GRIPHOT	1	...	Cfg	Color of selected grips
				1 Default: red
				255 Maximum color number
GRIPS	1	...	Cfg	Display of grips:
				0 Off
				1 On
GRIPSIZE	3	...	Cfg	Size of grip box, in pixels
				1 Minimum size
				3 Default size
				255 Maximum size
H				
🖫 HANDLES	1	R/o	...	Obsolete system variable
HIGHLIGHT	1	...	...	Object selection highlighting:
				0 Disabled
				1 Enabled
HPANG	0	...	...	Current hatch pattern angle
HPBOUND	1	...	Dwg	Object created by BHatch and Boundary
				commands:
				0 Polyline
				1 Region
HPDOUBLE	0	...	...	Double hatching:
				0 Disabled
				1 Enabled
HPNAME	"ANSI31"	...	...	Current hatch pattern name
				"" No default
				. Set no default

Variable	Default	Ro	Loc	Meaning
HPSCALE	1.0000	...	...	Current hatch pattern scale factor
HPSPACE	1.0000	...	...	Current spacing of user-defined hatching

I

Variable	Default	Ro	Loc	Meaning
INSBASE	0.0000,0.0000,0.0000 ...		Dwg	Insertion base point relative to current UCS
INSNAME	""	...	...	Current block name
				. Set to no default
				"" No default
ISOLINES	4	...	Dwg	Isolines on 3D solids:
				0 Minimum
				4 Default
				16 Good-looking
				2,047 Maximum

L

Variable	Default	Ro	Loc	Meaning
LASTANGLE	0	R/o	...	Ending angle of last-drawn arc
LASTPOINT	0.0000,0.0000,0.0000	...	Dwg	Last-entered point
☞ *LAZYLOAD*	*0*	...	...	*Toggle 0 or 1*
LENSLENGTH	50.0000	R/o	Dwg	Perspective view lens length, in mm
LIMCHECK	0	...	Dwg	Drawing limits checking:
				0 Disabled
				1 Enabled
LIMMAX	12.0000,9.0000	...	Dwg	Upper right drawing limits
LIMMIN	0.0000,0.0000	...	Dwg	Lower left drawing limits
LOCALE	"en"	R/o		ISO language code
LOGINNAME	"??"	R/o	Dwg	User's login name
☞ LTSCALE	1.0000	...	Dwg	Current linetype scale factor
LUNITS	2	...	...	Linear units mode:
				1 Scientific
				2 Decimal
				3 Engineering
				4 Architectural
				5 Fractional
LUPREC	4	...	Dwg	Decimal places of linear units

M

Variable	Default	Ro	Loc	Meaning
MACROTRACE	*0*	...	...	*Diesel debug mode:*
				0 Off
				1 On
MAXACTVP	16	...	...	Maximum viewports to regenerate:
				0 Minimum
				16 Default
				32767 Maximum

Variable	Default	Ro	Loc	Meaning
MAXSORT	200	...	Cfg	Maximum filenames to sort alphabetically:
				0 Minimum
				16 Default
				32767 Maximum
MAXOBJMEM	*2,147,483,647*	*...*	*...*	*Maximum number of objects in memory*
MENUCTL	1	...	...	Submenu display:
				0 Only with menu picks
				1 Also with keyboard entry
MENUECHO	0		...	Menu and prompt echoing:
				0 All prompts displayed
				1 Suppress menu echoing
				2 Suppress system prompts
				4 Disable ^P toggle
				8 Display all input-output strings
MENUNAME	"acad"	R/o	...	Current menu filename
MIRRTEXT	1	...	Dwg	Text handling during Mirror command:
				0 Mirror text
				1 Retain text orientation
MODEMACRO	""	...	...	Invoke Diesel programming language
MTEXTED	""	...	Cfg	External mtext editor

N

Variable	Default	Ro	Loc	Meaning
NODENAME	*"AC$"*	*R/o*	*Cfg*	*Name of network node (1 to 3 chars)*

O

Variable	Default	Ro	Loc	Meaning
OFFSETDIST	-1.0000	...	...	Current offset distance;
				through mode, if negative
ORTHOMODE	0	...	Dwg	Orthographic mode:
				0 Off
				1 On
OSMODE	0	...	Dwg	Current object snap mode:
				0 NONe
				1 ENDpoint
				2 MIDpoint
				4 CENter
				8 NODe
				16 QUAdrant
				32 INTersection
				64 INSertion
				128 PERpendicular
				256 TANgent
				512 NEARest
				1024 QUIck
				2048 APPint

P

Variable	Default	Ro	Loc	Meaning
PDMODE	0	...	Dwg	Point display mode:
				0 Dot
				1 No display
				2 +-symbol
				3 x-symbol
				4 Short line
				32 Circle
				64 Square
PDSIZE	0.0000	...	Dwg	Point display size, in pixels
				-1 Absolute size
				0 5% of drawing area height
				+1 Percentage of viewport size
PELLIPSE	0	...	Dwg	Toggle Ellipse creation:
				0 True ellipse
				1 Polyline
PERIMETER	0.0000	R/o	...	Perimeter calculated by Area command
PFACEVMAX	4	R/o	...	Maximum vertices per 3D face
				2,803,348,672 Maximum
PHANDLE	*0*	...	...	
PICKADD	1	...	Cfg	Effect of [Shift] key on selection set:
				0 Adds to selection set
				1 Removes from selection set
PICKAUTO	1	...	Cfg	Selection set mode:
				0 Single pick mode
				1 Automatic windowing and crossing
PICKBOX	3	...	Cfg	Object selection pickbox size, in pixels
PICKDRAG	0	...	Cfg	Selection window mode:
				0 Pick two corners
				1 Pick 1 corner; drag to 2nd corner
PICKFIRST	1	...	Cfg	Command-selection mode:
				0 Enter command first
				1 Select objects first
PICKSTYLE	1	...	Dwg	Included groups and associative hatches in selection:
				0 Neither included
				1 Include groups
				2 Include associative hatches
				3 Include both
PLATFORM	"386 DOS Extender"	R/o	Acad	AutoCAD platform name:
				"386 DOS Extender"
PLINEGEN	0	...	Dwg	Polyline linetype generation:
				0 From vertex to vertex
				1 From end to end

Variable	Default	Ro	Loc	Meaning
PLINEWID	0.0000	...	Dwg	Current polyline width
PLOTID	""	...	Cfg	Current plotter
PLOTROTMODE	1	...	Dwg	Orientation of plots: 0 Lowerleft = 0 1 Lowerleft plotter area = lowerleft of media
PLOTTER	1	...	Cfg	Current plotter configuration number: 0 No plotter configured 29 Maximum configurations
POLYSIDES	4	...	...	Current number of polygon sides: 3 Minimum sides 4 Default 1024 Maximum sides
POPUPS	1	R/o	...	Display driver support of AUI: 0 Not available 1 Available
PROJMODE	1	...	Cfg	Projection mode for Trim & Extend: 0 No projection 1 Project to x,y-plane of current UCS 2 Project to view plane
PSLTSCALE	1	...	Dwg	Paper space linetype scaling: 0 Use model space scale factor 1 Use viewport scale factor
PSPROLOG	""	...	Cfg	PostScript prologue filename
PSQUALITY	75	...	Dwg	Resolution of PostScript display, in pixels: -n Display as outlines; no fill 0 No display +n Display filled

Q

Variable	Default	Ro	Loc	Meaning
QAFLAGS	*1*	...	...	*Quality assurance flags*
QTEXTMODE	0	...	Dwg	Quick text mode: 0 Off 1 On

R

Variable	Default	Ro	Loc	Meaning
RASTERPREVIEW	0	...	Dwg	Preview image: 0 BMP format 1 BMP and WMF formats 2 WMF format 3 None saved.
REGENMODE	1	...	Dwg	Regeneration mode: 0 Regen with each new view 1 Regen only when required

Variable	Default	Ro	Loc	Meaning
RE-INIT		...	...	Reinitialize I/O devices:
				1 Digitizer port
				2 Plotter port
				4 Digitizer
				8 Plotter
				16 Reload PGP file
RIASPECT	1.0000	...	...	Raster image aspect ratio
RIBACKG	0	...	...	Raster image background color
				0 Black (*Default*)
				7 White
				255 Maximum value
RIEDGE	0	...	...	Raster image edge detection mode:
				0 Off
				1 On
				255 Maximum value
RIGAMUT	256	...	...	Raster image gamut of colors
				8 Minimum value
				256 Maximum (*Default*)
RIGREY	0	...	...	Raster image gray scale conversion:
				0 Off
				1 On
RITHRESH	0	...	...	Raster image brightness threshold
				0 Off
				255 Maximum threshold value

S̄

Variable	Default	Ro	Loc	Meaning
SAVEFILE	"AUTO.SV$"	R/o	Cfg	Automatic save filename
SAVEIMAGES	0	...	...	ARx-related system variable
SAVENAME	""	R/o	...	Drawing save-as filename
SAVETIME	120	...	Cfg	Automatic save interval, in minutes
				0 Disable auto save
				120 Default
SCREENBOXES	26	R/o	Cfg	Maximum number of menu items
				0 Screen menu turned off
SCREENMODE	0	R/o	Cfg	State of AutoCAD display screen:
				0 Text screen
				1 Graphics screen
				2 Dual-screen display
SCREENSIZE	575.0000,423.0000	R/o	...	Current viewport size, in pixels
SHADEDGE	3	...	Dwg	Shade style:
				0 Shade faces (256-color shading)
				1 Shade faces; edges background color
				2 Simulate hidden-line removal
				3 16-color shading

Variable	Default	Ro	Loc	Meaning
SHADEDIF	70	...	Dwg	Percent of diffuse to ambient light
				0 Minimum
				70 Default
				100 Maximum
SHPNAME	""	...	...	Current shape name
				. Set to no default
				"" No default
SKETCHINC	0.1000	...	Dwg	Sketch command's recording increment
SKPOLY	0	...	Dwg	Sketch line mode:
				0 Record as lines
				1 Record as polylines
SNAPANG	0	...	Dwg	Current rotation angle for snap and grid
SNAPBASE	0.0000,0.0000	...	Dwg	Current origin for snap and grid
SNAPISOPAIR	0	...	Dwg	Current isometric drawing plane:
				0 Left isoplane
				1 Top isoplane
				2 Right isoplane
SNAPMODE	0	...	Dwg	Snap mode:
				0 Off
				1 On
SNAPSTYL	0	...	Dwg	Snap style:
				0 Normal
				1 Isometric
SNAPUNIT	1.0000,1.0000	...	Dwg	X,y-spacing for snap
SORTENTS	96	...	Cfg	Entity display sort order:
				0 Off
				1 Object selection
				2 Object snap
				4 Redraw
				8 Slide generation
				16 Regeneration
				32 Plots
				64 PostScript output
SPLFRAME	0	...	Dwg	Polyline and mesh display:
				0 Polyline control frame not displayed; display polygon fit mesh; 3D faces invisible edges not displayed
				1 Polyline control frame displayed; display polygon defining mesh; 3D faces invisible edges displayed
SPLINESEGS	8	...	Dwg	Number of line segments that define a splined polyline

Variable	Default	Ro	Loc	Meaning
SPLINETYPE	6	...	Dwg	Spline curve type: 5 Quadratic bezier spline 6 Cubic bezier spline
SURFTAB1	6	...	Dwg	Density of surfaces and meshes: 2 Minimum 6 Default 32766 Maximum
SURFTAB2	6	...	Dwg	Density of surfaces and meshes 2 Minimum 6 Default 32766 Maximum
SURFTYPE	6	...	Dwg	Pedit surface smoothing: 5 Quadratic bezier spline 6 Cubic bezier spline 8 Bezier surface
SURFU	6	...	Dwg	Surface density in m-direction 2 Minimum 6 Default 200 Maximum
SURFV	6	...	Dwg	Surface density in n-direction 2 Minimum 6 Default 200 Maximum
SYSCODEPAGE	"dos850"	R/o	Dwg	System code page

T̄

Variable	Default	Ro	Loc	Meaning
TABMODE	0	...	...	Tablet mode: 0 Off 1 On
TARGET	0.0000,0.0000,0.0000	R/o	Dwg	Target in current viewport
TDCREATE	2448860.54014699	R/o	Dwg	Time and date drawing created
TDINDWG	0.00040625	R/o	Dwg	Duration drawing loaded
TDUPDATE	2448860.54014699	R/o	Dwg	Time and date of last update
TDUSRTIMER	0.00040694	R/o	Dwg	Time elapsed by user-timer
TEMPPREFIX	""	R/o	...	Path for temporary files
TEXTEVAL	0	...	...	Interpretation of text input: 0 Literal text 1 Read '(' and '!' as AutoLISP code
TEXTFILL	0	...	Dwg	Toggle fill of PostScript & TrueType fonts: 0 Outline text 1 Filled text

Variable	Default	Ro	Loc	Meaning
TEXTQLTY	50	...	Dwg	Resolution of PostScript & TrueType fonts: 0 Minimum resolution 50 Default 100 Maximum resolution
TEXTSIZE	0.2000	...	Dwg	Current height of text
TEXTSTYLE	"STANDARD"	...	Dwg	Current name of text style
THICKNESS	0.0000	...	Dwg	Current entity thickness
TILEMODE	1	...	Dwg	Viewport mode: 0 Display tiled viewports 1 Display overlapping viewports
TOOLTIPS	1	...	Cfg	Display tooltips (works in Windows only): 0 Off 1 On
TRACEWID	0.0500	...	Dwg	Current width of traces
TREEDEPTH	3020	...	Dwg	Maximum branch depth in xxyy format: xx Model-space nodes yy Paper-space nodes $+n$ 3D drawing $-n$ 2D drawing
TREEMAX	10000000	...	Cfg	Limits memory consumption during drawing regeneration
TRIMMODE	1			Trim toggle for Chamfer & Fillet: 0 Leave selected edges in place 1 Trim selected edges

Ū

Variable	Default	Ro	Loc	Meaning
UCSFOLLOW	0	...	Dwg	New UCS views: 0 No change 1 Automatic display of plan view
📷 UCSICON	1	...	Dwg	Display of UCS icon: 0 Off 1 On 2 Display at UCS origin, if possible
UCSNAME	""	R/o	Dwg	Name of current UCS view "" Current UCS is unnamed
UCSORG	0.0000,0.0000,0.0000	R/o	Dwg	Origin of current UCS relative to WCS
UCSXDIR	1.0000,0.0000,0.0000	R/o	Dwg	X-dir of current UCS relative to WCS
UCSYDIR	0.0000,1.0000,0.0000	R/o	Dwg	Y-dir of current UCS relative to WCS
UNDOCTL	5	R/o	...	State of undo: 0 Undo disabled 1 Undo enabled 2 Undo limited to one command 4 Auto-group mode 8 Group currently active

Variable	Default	Ro	Loc	Meaning
UNDOMARKS	0	R/o	...	Current number of undo marks
UNITMODE	0	...	Dwg	Units display: 0 As set by Units command 1 As entered by user
USERI1–I5	*0*	...	...	*Five user-definable integer variables*
USERR1–R5	*0.0000*	...	...	*Five user-definable real variables*
USERS1–S5	*" "*	...	...	*Five user-definable string variables*

$\overline{\textbf{V}}$

Variable	Default	Ro	Loc	Meaning
VIEWCTR	6.2433,4.5000,0.0000	R/o	Dwg	X,y-coordinate of center of current view
VIEWDIR	0.0000,0.0000,1.0000	R/o	Dwg	Current view direction relative to UCS
VIEWMODE	0	R/o	Dwg	Current view mode: 0 Normal view 1 Perspective mode on 2 Front clipping on 4 Back clipping on 8 UCS-follow on 16 Front clip not at eye
VIEWSIZE	9.0000	R/o	Dwg	Height of current view
VIEWTWIST	0	R/o	Dwg	Twist angle of current view
VISRETAIN	0	...	Dwg	Determination of xref drawing's layers: 0 Current drawing 1 Xref drawing
VSMAX	37.4600,27.00,0.00	R/o	Dwg	Upper right corner of virtual screen
VSMIN	-24.9734,-18.00,0.00	R/o	Dwg	Lower left corner of virtual screen

$\overline{\textbf{W}}$

Variable	Default	Ro	Loc	Meaning
WORLDUCS	1	R/o	...	Matching of WCS with UCS: 0 Current UCS is not WCS 1 UCS is WCS
WORLDVIEW	1	...	Dwg	Display during DView & VPoint commands: 0 Display UCS 1 Display WCS

$\overline{\textbf{X}}$

Variable	Default	Ro	Loc	Meaning
XREFCTL	0	...	Cfg	Determines creation of XLG xref log files: 0 File not written 1 XLG file written

Obsolete Commands

The following commands have been removed from AutoCAD DOS over the years:

Command	Introduced	Removed	Replacement	Reaction
3dLine	R9	R11	Line	"Line"
AmeLite	R11	R12	Region	"Unknown command"
AscText	R11	R13	MText	"Unknown command"
Ase...	R12	R12	ASE...	"Unknown command"
(Most R12 ASE commands were combined into fewer ASE commands.)				
Axis	v1.4	R12	*none*	"Discontinued command."
DL, DLine	R11	R13	MLine	"Unknown command"
EndRep	v1.0	v2.5	MInsert	"Discontinued command."
EndSv	v2.0	v2.5	End	"End"
Filmroll	v2.6	R13	*none*	"Unknown command"
Flatland	R10	R11	*none*	"Cannot set Flatland to that value."
IgesIn, IgesOut	v2.5	R13	*none*	"Discontinued command"
PrPlot	v2.1	R12	Plot	"Discontinued command."
QPlot	v1.1	v2.0	SaveImg	*no reaction*
Repeat	v1.0	v2.5	MInsert	"Discontinued command."
Snapshot	v2.0	v2.1	SaveImg	"Unknown command."
Sol...	R11, R12	R13	*ACIS-based solid modelling commands.*	
(AME commands lost their SOL-prefix.)				

TIPS

■ In addition to the commands listed above, the following features (found in Release 12) were dropped from Release 13:

- **SolChP**, the ability to edit primitives in a solid model.
- **SolMat**, to assign a material property to a solid model, including density.
- Export of AutoShade's RND (*ReNDer*) and import of AutoShade's FLM (*FiLmRoll*) file formats.
- The "Release 11" hidden-line removal algorithm.
- Freeplot, starting AutoCAD with -p.
- **AcsText** command, for ASCII text file import.
- Some device drivers, including a basic VGA display driver.
- Handles toggle is now always turned on.

Obsolete Commands

The following commands have been removed from AutoCAD DOS over the years:

Command	Introduced	Removed	Replacement	Reaction
3dLine	R9	R11	Line	"Line"
AmeLite	R11	R12	Region	"Unknown command"
AscText	R11	R13	MText	"Unknown command"
Ase...	R12	R12	ASE...	"Unknown command"
(Most R12 ASE commands were combined into fewer ASE commands.)				
Axis	v1.4	R12	*none*	"Discontinued command."
DL, DLine	R11	R13	MLine	"Unknown command"
EndRep	v1.0	v2.5	MInsert	"Discontinued command."
EndSv	v2.0	v2.5	End	"End"
Filmroll	v2.6	R13	*none*	"Unknown command"
Flatland	R10	R11	*none*	"Cannot set Flatland to that value."
IgesIn,IgesOut	v2.5	R13	*none*	"Discontinued command"
PrPlot	v2.1	R12	Plot	"Discontinued command."
QPlot	v1.1	v2.0	SaveImg	*no reaction*
Repeat	v1.0	v2.5	MInsert	"Discontinued command."
Snapshot	v2.0	v2.1	SaveImg	"Unknown command."
Sol...	R11, R12	R13	*(AME commands lost their SOL-prefix.)*	

TIPS

■ Support for the RND (*short for render*) file format, used by AutoCAD and AutoShade, was dropped in Release 13.

■ The "Release 11" hidden-line removal algorithm was dropped in Release 13.

Topical Index

A

AutoCAD SQL Extension Commands:

AseAdmin	17
AseExport	20
AseLinks	21
AseRows	22
AseSelect	24
AseSqlEd	26

Assist Menu:

Area	13
DbList	70
DdSelect	110
Dist	140
Filter	176
Grid	181
Group	183
Id	199
List	222
MassProp	229
Multiple	255
Ortho	267
OSnap	268
Redo	314
Select	362
Snap	373
TreeStat	409
U	413
Undo	418
VlConv	424

C

Color Numbers, Names, and Abbreviations	60

Construct Menu:

Array	14
AttDef	28
Block	44
Boundary	46
Chamfer	53

Construct Menu (*continued*)

Copy 66
DdAttDef 71
Fillet 174
Intersect 204
Mirror 239
Mirror3d 240
Offset 263
Region 321
Rotate3d 342
Subtract 393
Union 419
3dArray 442

D

Data Menu:

Color or Colour 60
DdColor 77
DdEModes 79
DdLModes 90
DdLtype 92
DdRename 106
DdRModes 107
DdUnits 116
DimStyle 137
Layer 206
Limits 215
Linetype 218
MlStyle 245
MtProp 254
Purge 303
Redefine 313
Rename 324
Status 382
Style 388
Time 403
Undefine 417
Units 420
VpLayer 425

Definitions:

Light: Lighting Terms 214
MassProp: Mass Property Terms 230

RevSurf: Revolved Surfacing Terms 336
RMat: Rendering Material Terms 339
Stats: Rendering Statistics Terms 381
Status: Drawing Status Terms 383
StlOut: Stereolithography Terms 385
Tablet: Tablet Configuration Terms 396
Tolerance: Tolerance Dimensioning Terms 406
TreeStat: Tree-Node Statistics Terms 410
Ucs: User Coordinate System Terms 415

Dimension Commands:
DDim 84
Dim 123
Dim1 125
DimAligned 126
DimAngular 127
DimBaseline 128
DimCenter 129
DimContinue 130
DimDiameter 131
DimEdit 132
DimLinear 133
DimOrdinate 134
DimOverride 135
DimRadius 136
DimStyle 137
DimTEdit 138
Leader 207
Tolerance 404
Variables 455

Draw Menu:
Ai_Box, *etc.* 4
AmeConvert 8
Arc 11
BHatch 40
Box 48
Circle 58
Cone 61
Cylinder 68
DdInsert 89
Divide 141
Donut *or* Doughnut 147
DText 149

Draw Menu (*continued*)

Edge 156
EdgeSurf 157
Ellipse 160
Extrude 168
Hatch 185
Insert 200
Interfer 202
Leader 207
Line 217
Measure 234
MInsert 237
MLine 243
MText 252
PFace 280
PLine 282
Point 290
Polygon 291
PsFill 295
Ray 308
Rectang 312
Revolve 333
RevSurf 335
RuleSurf 346
Section 360
Shape 366
Sketch 370
Slice 372
Solid 374
Sphere 377
Spline 378
TabSurf 397
Text 399
Tolerance 404
Torus 407
Trace 408
Wedge 431
XLine 434
3D 440
3dFace 443
3dMesh 444
3dPoly 445

F̄

File Menu:

AcisIn	2
AcisOut	3
AttExt	33
Audit	37
DdAttExt	74
DxbIn	153
DxfIn	154
DxfOut	155
End	162
Files	170
GiffIn	178
HpMPLot	195
Load	223
MakePreview	227
New	261
Open	265
PcxIn	273
Plot	284
PsDrag	294
PsIn	298
PsOut	300
QSave	304
Quit	307
Recover	311
RenderUnload	328
Replay	330
Save	348
SaveAs	349
SaveAsR12	350
StlOut	384
TiffIn	402
WBlock	430
XBind	433
XRef	436
XRefClip	437
3dsIn	446
3dsOut	448
Font library: PostScript, Shx, and TrueType	389

H

Hatch Pattern Library 186

Help Menu:
   About 1
   DlxHelp 144
   Help or ? 191
   WhatsNew 432

L

Linetype Library 219

M

Modify Menu:
   Align 7
   AttEdit 31
   AttRedef 36
   Break 50
   Change 55
   ChProp 57
   DdAttE 73
   DdChProp 75
   DdEdit 78
   DdModify 93
   Erase 163
   Explode 164
   Extend 166
   HatchEdit 189
   Lengthen 208
   MlEdit 241
   Move 249
   Oops 264
   PEdit 275
   Rotate 341
   Scale 355
   SplinEdit 379
   Stretch 386
   Trim 411
   Xplode 435

O

Object Snap Modes 270
Obsolete Commands 469

Options Menu:
    Aperture 9
    AttDisp 30
    Base 39
    BlipMode 43
    Config 64
    DdGrips 82
    DDim 84
    DdOsnap 104
    DdPType 105
    DdRModes 107
    DlgColor 142
    Dragmode 148
    Elev 159
    Fill 172
    Isoplane 205
    LogFileOff 224
    LogFileOn 225
    LtScale 226
    Preferences 293
    QText 305
    RConfig 309
    RegenAuto 320
    SetVar 363
    Tablet 394
    UcsIcon 416
    ViewRes 423

P

PostScript Fill Library 295

Q

Quick Start Tutorials:
    AttExt: Extracting Attributes from the Drawing 34
    HpMPlot: Using HpMPlot.. 196
    Linetype: Creating a Custom Linetype 221
    Load: Using Shapes in Your Drawing 223
    MvSetup: Adding a Border and Views 260

Quick Start Tutorials (*continued*)

PSpace: Enabling Paper Space 302
RConfig: Setting Up Render for the First Time 310
Render: Your First Rendering 327
Script: Writing a Script File 358
Shell: Adding a Command to Acad.Pgp 367

R̄

Render Commands:

Light 210
MatLib 232
RConfig 309
Render 325
RenderUnload 328
RendScr 329
Replay 330
RMat 337
RPref 345
SaveImg 353
Scene 356
ShowMat 369
Stats 381
VlConv 424
3dsIn 446
3dsOut 448

S̄

Sketch Button Definitions 371

Solid Modelling (ACIS) Commands:

AcisIn 2
AcisOut 3
AmeConvert 8
Box 48
Cone 62
Cylinder 68
Extrude 168
Interfere 202
Intersect 204
MassProp 229
Region 321
Revolve 333

Section 360

Slice 372

Sphere 377

StlOut 384

Subtract 393

Torus 407

Union 419

Wedge 431

System Variables 451

T

Tablet Drawing 395

Tools Menu:

AppLoad 10

AseAdmin 17

AseExport 20

AseLinks 21

AseRows 22

AseSelect 24

AseSqlEd 26

Arx 16

Av 38

Cal 51

Compile 61

Delay 122

Hide 193

Light 210

MatLib 232

Menu 235

MSlide 250

Reinit 323

RendScr 329

Render 325

Resume 332

RMat 337

RPref 343

Tools Menu (*continues*)

RScript 345
SaveImg 353
Scene 356
Script 358
Shade 364
Shell 367
ShowMat 369
Spell 375
Stats 381
VSlide 429

$\overline{\text{V}}$

View Menu:

DdUcs 113
DdUcsP 115
DView 151
DdVpoint 120
GraphScr 180
MSpace 251
MView 256
MvSetup 258
Pan 271
Plan 281
PSpace 301
Redraw 315
RedrawAll 317
Regen 318
RegenAll 319
TextScr 401
Ucs 414
View 422
VPoint 426
VPorts or Viewports 427
Zoom 438

-Notes-

-Notes-

-Notes-

-Notes-

-Notes-

-Notes-

-Notes-

-Notes-

-Notes-

-Notes-

-Notes-

-Notes-

-Notes-

Dear Reader,

I would like to take this opportunity to extend to you an invitation to subscribe to the *CAD++ Newsletter*. *CAD++* is an exciting new concept that delivers:

- CAD industry news, and interviews with CAD vendor representatives.
- Analysis (and predictions) of CAD industry trends.
- CAD software programming tips.
- Issues in CAD data exchange.
- Tips on starting and running your own CAD business.

Every month, subscribers in 14 countries and at seven of the top CAD companies read articles by Cliff Jennings (Fitting Solutions), Scott Taylor (Tailor Made Software), Jake Richter (Panacea), Dietmar Rudolph (CR/LF GmbH), and other leaders of the CAD industry.

I look forward to having you join our readership!

Ralph Grabowski
Author, *The Illustrated AutoCAD Quick Reference*
Editor, *CAD++ Newsletter*

Special Subscription Offer

Save 20% Today!

This discount is available to readers of *The Illustrated AutoCAD Quick Reference*:

- ☐ $240.00 Corporations (*more than 20 employees*) and libraries.
  The corporate rate is higher because the pass-along readership rate is higher. Think of this as a site licence.
- ☐ $ 48.00 Individual subscribers (*includes the 20% discount*).
- ☐ $ 5.00 Back issues, each (*many are still available*).
- ☐ $ 18.00 Additional postage for addresses outside of North America.

Payment Instructions

Please make out checks, money orders, and purchase orders to <u>XYZ Publishing, Ltd.</u>. No Visa, Master Card, or AmEx credit card orders, please! Mail your order to:

XYZ Publishing, PO Box 3053, Sumas WA 98295-3053, USA

Corporations can fax their order (*with purchase order number*) to +1 (604) 859-9597, 24 hours a day, 7 days a week.

International Orders

Canadians addresses remit in Canadian funds; please add 7% GST (*R138245949*). Outside North America: please remit in US funds drawn on a bank with an American address. Most international banks have a US branch (or have an arrangement with an American bank) that allows you to have the check drawn on the US bank address.

COORDINATE 🖳 MODIFERS

COORDINATE INPUT

Default directions
  x-positive: Right.
  y-positive: Up.
  z-positive: Right-hand rule.

x,y	2D cartesian coordinates:	
	`From point: 2,3.1`	
x,y,z	3D cartesian coordinates:	
	`From point: 2,3,4`	
d<a	2D polar coordinates:	
	`From point: 2<45`	
@d<a	Relative coordinates:	
	`From point: @12<34`	
d<a,z	3D cylindical coordinates:	
	`From point: 5<45,5`	
@d<a,z	Relative cylindical coordinates:	
	`From point: @5<45,5`	
d<a<a	3D spherical coordinates:	
	`From point: 5<45<30`	

DISTANCE MODIFIERS

,	Coordinate separator:
	`From point: 2,3`
'	Feet (*Required*).
"	Inches (*Optional*):
	`From point: 2'3",5'4`
— and /	Fractional inches:
	`From point: 2'3-3/4`
@	Relative distance.
*	Force use of WCS coordinates:
	`From line: *3,4,2`
@*	Force relative WCS coordinates:
	`From line: @*3<45`

POINT FILTERS

.x	pick x, enter y,z.
.y	pick y, enter x,z.
.z	pick z, enter x,y.
.xy	pick xy, enter z.
.xz	pick xz, enter y.
.yz	pick yz, enter x.

ANGLE MODIFIERS

Angle defaults
  0-degrees: East (3 o'clock).
  Positive direction: counter clockwise.

'	Minutes.
"	Seconds.
.	Decimal of a degree or seconds.
d	Degrees (*Default*).
r	Radian.
g	Grad.
<	Angle.
<<	Force 0 degrees=east and decimal degrees.
<<<	Force 0 = east but use current degree format.
+	Counter clockwise.
—	Clockwise.

SURVEYOR'S UNITS

E	East	0 degrees (*Default*).
N	North	90 degrees.
W	West	180 degrees.
S	South	270 degrees.

FILTER MODES

Logical operators:

*	Equal to any value (*Default*).
=	Equal.
!=	Not equal.
<	Less than.
>	Greater than.
<=	Less than or equal.
>=	Greater than or equal.

Grouping operators:

**BEGIN	Begin group.
AND	intersection.
OR	union.
NOT	exclude.
XOR	eXclusive or.
**END	End of group.